The Fifth Massachusetts
Colored Cavalry
in the Civil War

D1547614

The Fifth Massachusetts Colored Cavalry in the Civil War

Steven M. LaBarre

McFarland & Company, Inc., Publishers
Jefferson, North Carolina

Names: LaBarre, Steven M., 1976–
Title: The Fifth Massachusetts Colored Cavalry in the Civil War /
    Steven M. LaBarre.
Description: Jefferson, North Carolina : McFarland & Company, Inc.,
    Publishers, 2016. | Includes bibliographical references and index.
Identifiers: LCCN 2016026054 | ISBN 9781476663845 (softcover :
    acid free paper) ∞
Subjects: LCSH: United States. Army. Massachusetts Cavalry
    Regiment, 5th (1864–1865) | United States—History—Civil War,
    1861–1865—Regimental histories. | Massachusetts—History—
    Civil War, 1861–1865—Regimental histories. | United States—
    History—Civil War, 1861–1865—Participation, African American. |
    African American soldiers—History—19th century.
Classification: LCC E513.6 5th .L33 2016 | DDC 973.7/415—dc23
LC record available at https://lccn.loc.gov/2016026054

BRITISH LIBRARY CATALOGUING DATA ARE AVAILABLE

ISBN 978-1-4766-6384-5 (softcover : acid free paper)
ISBN 978-1-4766-2342-9 (ebook)

Front cover image of Charles Douglass in full cavalry uniform
(Howard University Archives)

Printed in the United States of America

McFarland & Company, Inc., Publishers
  Box 611, Jefferson, North Carolina 28640
    www.mcfarlandpub.com

In memory of my grandmother,
Alice J. Smith McGuire (1915–2011),
who lit the match that sparked my interest,
and my father,
James R. LaBarre (1951–2011),
who kept the flame burning

Table of Contents

Acknowledgments

Throughout the years of researching and writing this book there have been several individuals and repositories deserving special recognition. First and foremost, I would like to thank my grandmother, Alice McGuire, for her love and support of me and everything I have strived to become in life. Without her love and devotion this project would not have been a success. When I was very young she introduced to me a passion for American history through family genealogy and preserving and collecting antiques. Her thoughtfulness in passing along a piece of family history allowed for the completion of this book and fueled an ongoing quest to know more about our family history.

Likewise, my parents, James and Michelle, have always encouraged my love of and devotion to keeping history alive. They have provided more to me then words can ever express and continually given of themselves. I would especially like to acknowledge my father for his encouragement. He was always there to lift my spirits when the research and writing seemed to become overwhelming and frustrations began to set in. His willingness to make a multitude of long-distance phone calls to numerous archives, libraries, museums, and historical sites helped immensely.

I also owe a debt of gratitude to my mother for being a sounding board for ideas and listening to me thinking out loud. She sat for hours listening and providing important revision ideas to make this book what it is. Although her name is not connected to this work she deserves much praise. She has been there since the beginning of my research and when it was in its infancy as a college honors thesis.

Furthermore, my brother Jason has been a tremendous supporter. He was a listening ear and an advocate, always cheering me on with encouraging words and expressing interest in my progress.

Many blessings and love to my wife, Becky, who learned of my desire to write and publish this book when we first met. She helped immensely in proofreading and providing feedback and suggestions. She listened to my ramblings on little known historical facts related to my research. Becky additionally gave her time in producing the map along with assisting in correlating and producing captions. She is my rock and my pillar and, above all, my true love.

There are other individuals who have helped make this book a reality through their support in various ways. Thanks to Leroy Martin, Jr., who I first met when he spoke on the African American role during the Civil War. He has since become a friend and has always been there to hear about my research progress. Much gratitude is given towards Michael A. Black, a longtime friend and author who gave insight and suggestions to editorial revisions. Much appreciation goes towards the late historian, author, and friend Brian Pohanka, who encouraged me at a young age to "always keep studying the war." He will be missed but always remembered. Friend and researcher Vonnie Zullo of The Horse Soldier, who provided legwork into many Civil War soldiers' military and pension records at the National Archives; she is a true professional.

A very special thank you is extended to Robert Irving, Chicago, former English professor at Georgetown University and now docent to Glessner House and Clarke House museums Chicago. Bob's forty plus years of association and dedication to the Chicago Architecture Foundation have provided me many hours of enjoyment listening and talking about architecture, Chicago history and the historical past with him. Bob was gracious enough to take time out of his own schedule to lend insightful and constructive criticism and editing suggestions.

For his work as an advisor to this book in its honors thesis form, a special thanks is extended to Dr. William W. Dean, professor and chair of History at Olivet Nazarene University. Likewise, I would also like to thank educator and friend Dr. James Vandermulen for his support and encouragement.

Many thanks go to the Kankakee Illinois and South Suburban Illinois Civil War roundtables. Their respectful crowds allowed me to present my research findings and supported my endeavor. I would like to especially acknowledge Larry Gibbs, Art Schumacher, David Corbett, Bill Menig, and Dennis Tenk.

Furthermore, much appreciation and thanks is extended to author and historian Bruce Allardice. Our friendship has extended over these many years with shared membership to Chicagoland Civil War roundtables. I have always enjoyed sitting in on Bruce's lectures whether related to the American Civil War or the history of baseball. As past president of The Chicago Civil War Roundtable and author of several publications, his vast knowledge and contributions to the study of the Civil War have contributed significantly to this publication. In reading this manuscript, Bruce's willingness to lend thoughtful comment and revision suggestions has assisted me beyond measure; I owe him a debt of gratitude.

There have been a number of research facilities, museums and national parks that have provided a helping hand in the completion of this book over the years. The staff at the Ellsworth County, Kansas, Historical Society; Lee County, Iowa, Historical Society; Linn County, Iowa, Genealogical Society; Blairsville, Pennsylvania, Historical Society; Massachusetts State Historical Society; Massachusetts State Library; Point Lookout, Maryland, State Park; St. Mary's County, Maryland, Historical Society; Adams County, Pennsylvania, Historical Society; Gettysburg, Pennsylvania, Public Library; Petersburg National Military Park; Army War College Photographic Archives, Carlisle, Pennsylvania; Newberry and Harold Washington Libraries, Chicago; and the National Archives Administration in Washington, D.C.; St. Louis; and Chicago.

Although too numerous to fit on paper, there have been multitudes of individuals who have offered support in my quest throughout the years to publish this history. Although specifically not mentioned they have all provided encouragement and I am very grateful.

"The Colored Soldiers"

If the muse were mine to tempt it
And my feeble voice were strong,
If my tongue were trained to measures,
I would sing a stirring song.
I would sing a song heroic
Of those noble sons of Ham,
Of the gallant colored soldiers
Who fought for Uncle Sam!

In the early days you scorned them,
And with many a flip and flout
Said "These battles are the white man's,
And the whites will fight them out."
Up the hills you fought and faltered,
In the vales you strove and bled,
While your ears still heard the thunder
Of the foes' advancing tread.

Then distress fell on the nation,
And the flag was drooping low;
Should the dust pollute your banner?
No! the nation shouted, No!
So when War, in savage triumph,
Spread abroad his funeral pall—
Then you called the colored soldiers,
And they answered to your call.

And like hounds unleashed and eager
For the life blood of the prey,
Spring they forth and bore them bravely
In the thickest of the fray.
And where'er the fight was hottest,
Where the bullets fastest fell,

There they pressed unblanched and fearless
At the very mouth of hell.

Ah, they rallied to the standard
To uphold it by their might;
None were stronger in the labors,
None were braver in the fight.
From the blazing breach of Wagner
To the plains of Olustee,
They were foremost in the fight
Of the battles of the free.

And at Pillow! God have mercy
On the deeds committed there,
And the souls of those poor victims
Sent to Thee without a prayer.
Let the fulness of Thy pity
O'er the hot wrought spirits sway
Of the gallant colored soldiers
Who fell fighting on that day!

Yes, the Blacks enjoy their freedom,
And they won it dearly, too;
For the life blood of their thousands
Did the southern fields bedew.
In the darkness of their bondage,
In the depths of slavery's night,
Their muskets flashed the dawning,
And they fought their way to light.

They were comrades then and brothers.
Are they more or less to-day?
They were good to stop a bullet
And to front the fearful fray.
They were citizens and soldiers,
When rebellion raised its head;
And the traits that made them worthy,—
Ah! Those virtues are not dead.

They have shared your nightly vigils,
They have shared your daily toil;
And their blood with yours commingling
Has enriched the Southern soil.
They have slept and marched and suffered
'Neath the same dark skies as you,
They have met as fierce a foeman,
And have been as brave and true.

And their deeds shall find a record
In the registry of Fame;

For their blood has cleansed completely
Every blot of Slavery's shame.
So all honor and all glory
To those noble sons of Ham—
The gallant colored soldiers
Who fought for Uncle Sam!

Paul Laurence Dunbar
1st Published 1898
Son of Joshua Dunbar,
Fifth Massachusetts Cavalry[1]

Preface

I sat in the darkened room, watching the scenes flicker across the cloth projection screen. Nestled between my parents and older brother Jason, I listened intently to the narrator recounting the life of Abraham Lincoln at his family home located at the intersection of Eighth and Jackson streets in Springfield, Illinois. Mesmerized, I soaked up the continuous series of facts espoused by the less-than-accurately-attired actor portraying a fictitious photographer who had been acquainted with our sixteenth president. "He didn't like being called Ham," the narrator explained. "*Abraham* is much more distinguished. If you must shorten it, then Abe would do." As a four-year-old, this curious tidbit stuck with me as the film concluded. *Don't ever call him Ham*, I thought.

I climbed back into my stroller and we exited from the visitors' center out into the bright sunlight. After a short walk, we arrived at the front door. A tidy brass plate read *A. Lincoln*. We were here! At *his* house. I left the stroller and took my mother's hand. "Welcome to the Lincoln Home." A young guide, dressed in park ranger drab, greeted us at the entrance. A string of rules quickly spewed from his mouth. "No gum. No flash photography. Stay on the path. Please don't touch the wallpaper." He completed the necessary instructions and finally allowed us to enter.

The clash of period pattern and color swirled around me. That carpet! I had never seen anything like it. Horse hair on the chairs? Wow. The ranger walked us through the first floor rooms. "Mr. Lincoln accepted the presidential nomination in this room in 1860." Next we approached the staircase leading to the second floor. "And when you touch this railing," the ranger said dramatically, "your hand will rest upon the very spot where Mr. Lincoln placed his own before retiring

1

for the night." We continued, room by room, each more intriguing than the previous one. "This stove remained in place when the Lincolns moved to Washington City," the ranger continued. "Mrs. Lincoln was sad to leave it behind." Before I knew it, we had completed the tour.

"Could we do that again?" I asked my father eagerly. "Sure," he said. "We can tour the home, again!" However, I didn't just want to re-tour the house. I wanted to *relive* the whole experience from viewing the film-strip, to touring the house, to walking the same streets in the neighborhood that Lincoln once did. I wanted to experience history. To be absorbed in it. To be a part of it. To make new discoveries about the past as I had done that day when I was just a young boy of four years. I would never be the same.

That strong fascination and love of American history stayed with me as I grew up just south of Chicago. My parents, who enjoyed incorporating historical sites and themes into our family vacations, encouraged Jason and me to experience history firsthand as we traveled. We ventured west and toured places like Deadwood, South Dakota, home of the Number 10 Saloon. This was where Wild Bill Hickock was gunned down holding aces and eights, the Dead Man's Hand. When we visited Mount Rushmore, my father held me up in his arms so I could gain a better look over the crowds of people. Just gazing at the faces of four of the most important presidents of our nation, immortalized in stone, was something that I have never forgotten.

When I was in high school, I began traveling east to Gettysburg, Pennsylvania, each year for vacation, to research and use that location as a base camp to explore other historical destinations throughout Pennsylvania, Maryland, and Virginia. This fascination with American history, and especially American military history, has led me to dub myself an American history junkie.

As a historian and collector of military antiques, I am especially drawn to anything Civil War related. One of my favorite pieces is a Union cavalry jacket I received at my college graduation. Really, my now sizable collection began with an interest in Joseph Brunson, a private in the Union Army. It started out as a simple junior high school class assignment. Mr. Shultz, my eighth grade history teacher, asked us to bring to class an item from our family history to share, and I jumped at the opportunity to present something special.

After school that day I called my maternal grandmother, Alice McGuire.

"Grandma," I said excitedly. "I need something to show my history class. It has to be a hundred years or older. Do you have anything I could take?"

"Well." She paused for a moment as she thought. "Come on over and we'll see what we can find."

My mom and I drove over to my grandparents' house. We followed my grandmother upstairs to seek out that family artifact.

It wasn't often that the grandkids were allowed to go into Grandma and Grandpa's bedroom. Really, there wasn't much to look at or even do in there. In great anticipation, I watched as Grandma Alice rummaged about in her dresser. Opening up the bottom of her antique bureau drawer she pulled out a small green metal document box. We all sat down on the bed as she began to open the box and lay out the contents in front of us.

My grandmother revealed that I had a relative who served during the Civil War.

"These things," she explained, "were entrusted to me by Aunt Sade before she passed away."

Grandma unfolded several documents, including pension papers and a Massachusetts Service Certificate for a Civil War soldier named Joseph Brunson. These documents sparked my imagination. I wanted to envision who Joseph Brunson was and what his life may have been like. My grandmother knew very little about the soldier other than Joseph was her Aunt Sade's husband. The Massachusetts Service Certificate read in a flowery hand:

> The name of Joseph Brunson of Boston, aged 21, occupation farmer, is borne upon the Muster-out Roll of Co. "E. 5" Regt. Mass. Volunteer Cavalry [under] Col. Chamberlain; enlisted on the 5th day of Feb'y 1864, for 3-years. Mustered out on the 31st day of October 1865. Mustered out, absent sick. Signed by the Adjutant General Commonwealth of Massachusetts.

This small amount of information was enough to begin my detective work. I began tracking down clues about my ancestor and in doing so I began to reveal the history of the 5th Massachusetts Volunteer Cavalry. The first stop on my quest for knowledge was to obtain Brunson's military records from the National Archives in Washington, D.C., using the data from the pension paper. A few months later a large manila envelope was delivered from the archives bearing the news that not only was the 5th Massachusetts Volunteers a cavalry unit, but it was designated the 5th Massachusetts *Colored* Cavalry. Furthermore, Joseph Brunson was listed as a private in the unit; an African American from Indiana County, Pennsylvania.

What made this revelation all the more intriguing was that my grandmother had never mentioned that we had family roots tied to an African American. In fact, I remember plainly the day I informed her of what I had obtained from the archives.

When I mentioned that the 5th Massachusetts Cavalry was an African American unit she wasn't necessarily surprised or taken aback. I would have to say she was more intrigued that it happened to be an African American unit, something that wasn't expected to be found in the research. My mother's family was of Irish and German decent. My mom is a fair-skinned strawberry blonde who had passed her features and coloring on to me. I had definitely taken on the McGuire build and have the ruddy-hued hair to match my Irish roots.

When I told my grandmother that Brunson was a volunteer enlisted private in the unit and was an African American she exclaimed, "Why, good Lord, I had no idea! Mom and Aunt Sade never mentioned anything about him being black." Pausing for a moment she added, "I wonder why they kept it a secret and never mentioned this to me."

Growing up, I had seen images of both Aunt Sade and Lucy, my grandmother's adopted mother. They looked of darker complexion, but not as dark as to make one feel that they were of African American decent. My mom was born in Cedar Rapids, Iowa, but when my grandfather took employment in California they relocated when she was just a toddler. Lucy would pass away shortly before my mother was born. My mother's brother, on the other hand, was born during World War II and was assisted in being raised by Lucy while my grandfather was overseas in France. He recalls that as a little boy, he would exclaim to Lucy that she had a keen resemblance to "the lady on the pancake mix." Lucy was heavy-set, had a darker complexion, and wore her hair up in a scarf while doing chores around the house. Of course he didn't understand what he was saying, being only a few years old. Lucy would gently quiet him down and scold him, saying, "Now you mustn't say things like that." My uncle has also mentioned that the African American neighbors down the street from Grandma Lucy and Aunt Sade would come visiting often. The women seemed to have known them all their lives. There was the warmth of love in their laughter and conversation; a familiarity beyond residential proximity. What my uncle didn't realize, and that the family never spoke of, was that those neighbors were Aunt Sade's older brother and his children.

With the paper trail and clues revealing the true heritage of my ancestor, I had to find out more about Brunson. I needed to know how he made it through the war and into my family tree. Now my journey started full speed ahead in discovering the story behind this particular man and the Civil War unit in which he served. The result of that research has become the basis of this book.

In recent years, accounts of individual soldiers have become more widely circulated and movies produced in Hollywood have opened our hearts and our eyes to the units that contributed the most to the great conflict and the personal experiences of those that served. We can draw upon two motion pictures, *Gettysburg* and *Glory*, which exemplify this very idea. The 1993 release of *Gettysburg* was based on the Pulitzer Prize winning novel *The Killer Angels* by Michael Shaara. The movie inspired a renewed fascination with the battle of Gettysburg and the Civil War as a whole. In relating the history of the battle, the movie wove the story of the heroic 20th Maine Infantry and its commander, Colonel Joshua Lawrence Chamberlain, who together fought to save the Union's left flank on Little Round Top. Likewise, the 1989 movie *Glory* recognized the gallant 54th Massachusetts Volunteer Infantry and paved a new wave of interest in the historical impact of the African American role during the Civil War and what he experienced when given the opportunity to fight for freedom.

Unfortunately, Hollywood's portrayal of a select few regiments seems to exclude other well-deserving units from public consciousness. The average movie-goer might assume the 20th Maine was the only regiment that defended Little Round Top on July 2, 1863, when the Maine unit was only one of many that fought gallantly in the heat of that day. The fact is, following the release of *Glory*, many people view the 54th Massachusetts as the *only* African American unit to serve in the war. They are utterly unaware that there were numerous African American units that answered the call to arms and were just as worthy of praise. Historian Gary W. Gallagher makes mention of this in his book *Causes Won, Lost and Forgotten: How Hollywood and Popular Art Shape what We Know about the Civil War* (2008), stating "films undeniably teach Americans about the past—to a lamentable degree in the minds of many academic historians." He emphasizes, "More people have formed perceptions about the Civil War from watching *Gone with the Wind* than from reading all the books written by historians since Selznick's blockbuster debuted in 1939."[1]

There is no doubt that both these units' histories should be told; they are two splendid stories, deserving of chronicling on film. However, I believe every unit that served—whether a nine-month or a three-year unit, a unit that saw heavy combat or one that may not have seen any substantial action, a white unit or a colored unit—has something to contribute to the study of this great epic in our American history.

I would be remiss if I did not make mention of the 2012 Steven Spielberg motion picture *Lincoln* as it specifically makes mention of the 5th Massachusetts Cavalry. Just as the films *Glory* and *Gettysburg* provided the viewing audience with a better understanding of the events which transpired in relation to their respective narratives, so has Spielberg's *Lincoln*. The film is set during the first four months of 1865 with a primary focus on President Lincoln's effort to bring about the passing of the Thirteenth Amendment to the Constitution and the political wrangling which ensued to pass the bill on the floor of the United States House of Representatives. Since the film's release it has garnered extreme praise for its cinematography and historically accurate depiction of the events which transpired during the last months and days of the American Civil War. Indeed, it has become a blockbuster film which was nominated for seven Golden Globe awards and twelve Academy Awards, with Daniel Day-Lewis winning for Best Actor.

However, although it has received countless accolades, many historians have found fault with the film. The debate over whether or not the film *Lincoln* or, for that matter, any historically based film (like *Glory* and *Gettysburg*) provides the audience with an accurate historical representation of the events depicted is one which continues to be contested. If by not fulfilling that purpose, does the lack of historical authenticity provide a disservice to the general movie going audience and in a larger sense to our ancestors? What does this say about the telling of the role and events our ancestors participated in?

Early in the movie, with rain falling, President Lincoln is seen speaking with two African American soldiers: Harold Green, an infantryman, and Ira Clark, a cavalryman. The soldiers talk about the battle of Jenkins Ferry which took place April 29 and 30, 1864. The cavalryman, when asked by Lincoln what their names are, states, "I'm Corporal Ira Clark, sir. Fifth Massachusetts Cavalry. We're waiting over there. We're leaving our horses behind, and shipping out with the 24th Infantry for the assault next week on Wilmington." This is a prime example of where the movie script does not match up to the historical record.

As will be told in this book, the history of the 5th Massachusetts Cavalry does not coincide with Clark's assertion. The regiment at no time was ordered to Wilmington, North Carolina, for the assault which took place from February 11th through the 22nd of 1865.

In actuality, the regiment was stationed at Point Lookout, Maryland, guarding Confederate prisoners of war. We do not know why writer Tony Kushner or Spielberg elected to include the 5th Massachusetts Cavalry as the unit designation for the character Ira Clark, but they did. How does this inaccuracy in the film impact our understanding of the soldiers who served with the 5th Massachusetts Cavalry, and what does it say in terms of honoring their legacy? Their story should be told. A voice should be given to the common soldier, especially the black man, who proudly served his country for the cause of freedom then quietly returned to civilian life in a world forever changed. But shouldn't we draw from the actual historical record which is by far more intriguing than any movie script?

This book is not a narrative of the overall history of the United States Colored Soldiers who served from 1861 to 1865. That aspect has been examined by historians such as Dudley Taylor Cornish in *The Sable Arm: Black Troops in the Union Army, 1861–1865* (1987); Benjamin Quarles' *The Negro in the Civil War* (1969); William A. Gladstone's *United States Colored Troops 1863–1867* (1990); Edwin S. Redkey's *A Grand Army of Black Men: Letters from African-American Soldiers in the Union Army, 1861–1865* (1992); Noah Andre Trudeau's *Like Men of War: Black Troops in the Civil War 1862–1865* (1998), and many others. I do not profess to be a historian of the U.S.C.T.; in my opinion the above authors and historians have truly mastered the subject.

However, the most insightful way a researcher or historian can relate the events of a historical time period is to delve into or explore the ordinary folk of that era. Using this approach in my research, I have examined firsthand accounts in personal diaries, pension affidavits from the Veterans Administration, and official battle reports and correspondences from the *Compilation of the Official Records of the Union and Confederate Armies* that acknowledged many fundamental facts. By using genealogical research methods I discovered many of the personal aspects of the lives of the soldiers serving with the 5th Massachusetts Cavalry. These sources were public records such as obituaries and marriage and death records. Newspaper articles from the time revealed the flavor of the era and added essential facts to the narrative. Traveling to historical sites, museums, national parks, historical societies, and cemeteries helped me in completing the overall history.

In order to preserve the sentiments of the period, I have kept the inaccuracies in spelling and sensitive wording within personal affidavits and records intact. Although touchy for our "politically correct" modern sensibilities, my feeling is that to change the phrasing would dishonor and judge the historical context of the middle to late Nineteenth and early Twentieth century eras. For this reason alone, the phrasing and spelling are as is, for no one could reveal the story better than the Americans who lived the part.

Although the years 1861 to 1865 are a very tragic time period in our country's history, there has still always been an overall fascination with the Civil War. Most of the studies about the war relate primarily to the battles themselves. Just in recent years has there been a new awakening into the role African Americans contributed. Gary W. Gallagher states in his work *The Union War* (2011), "Beginning in the 1970s, historians embarked on a massive reevaluation of emancipation and black military participation as elements of the Union war effort."[2]

Why have I been determined to research, write, and publish this history? In his book *Half Slave and Half Free: The Roots of the Civil War* (1992), Bruce Levine contends, "We need far more information about the origins and daily life of free blacks in the North."[3] From the beginning, it was a personal quest for genealogical research, later developing into a more detailed regimental history, one that has not previously been published in depth. In compiling research for this book I found very few *published* works relating to the history of the 5th Massachusetts Cavalry. John D. Warner, Jr., for instance, wrote an unpublished dissertation in 1997 entitled *Crossed Sabres: A History of the Fifth Massachusetts Cavalry, An African-American Regiment in the Civil War*. Furthermore, Nick Salvatore, *We All Got History: The Memory Books of Amos Weber* (1996); *Proud Shoes: The Story of An American Family* (1956) by Pauli Murray; *Massachusetts Soldiers, Sailors and Marines in the Civil War* (1932), along with P. C. Headly, *Massachusetts in the Rebellion* (1866), for example, all provide a glimpse into the unit's history. However, the 5th Massachusetts' history was neither a subject nor the central theme which was extensively discussed in these writings; Salvatore comes the closest by devoting an entire chapter to the history of the 5th Massachusetts Cavalry.

This is a glimpse into one specific unit that made up a part of the greater whole of the regiments of color that fought during the Civil War. The question then must be what role and contribution did the 5th Massachusetts Cavalry regiment have in this great American epic?

Through an in-depth study of the full scope of the unit's service, from mustering in at Camp Meigs, Readville, Massachusetts, to deployment in the opening campaigns of Petersburg, Virginia, to their triumphant entry into Richmond after the fall of the Confederate capital, along with an exploration into many of the men's post-war lives and contributions, the reader will be provided with an intimate glimpse into the experiences shared by a generation caught up in the struggle for freedom and equality. In so doing, the following pages set forth to fill a void within the contemporary historical research and study of the nineteenth century African American experience.

Introduction

When considering the American Civil War we most often look toward the battles themselves to gain a better grasp of the overall struggle that took place over four long years. As historians and readers alike we revel in maneuvers and strategy, the moving of troops as mass war machines across the field of battle. Sometimes we overlook the soldiers themselves, neglecting to recognize them as individuals with real lives. Sometimes heroic, sometimes mundane, the experiences of the fighting men who made up the regiments of great armies, both North and South, are pushed aside for the grand sum of their parts.

The members of the 5th Massachusetts Volunteer Cavalry, as a regiment, served through one of the United States' extremely influential periods of history. The era was one of profound emotional feeling in almost a romantic sense. It is this factor that compels many to keep alive the history of that time. The father of Civil War historians, Bruce Catton, once summed up this overall essence in the following terms:

> We are people to whom the past is forever speaking. We listen to it because we cannot help ourselves, for the past speaks to us with many voices. Far out of that dark nowhere which is the time before we were born, men who were flesh of our flesh and bone went through fire and storm to break a path to the future. We are part of the future they died for; they are part of the past that brought the future. What they did—the lives they lived, the sacrifices they made, the stories they told and the songs they sang and, finally, the deaths they died—make up a part of our own experience. We cannot cut ourselves off from it. It is as real to us as something that happened last week. It is a basic part of our heritage as Americans.[1]

To understand the service of the soldiers who made up the 5th Massachusetts Cavalry we must first understand the times in which they lived. From 1861 to 1865 our great American nation was in a state of disastrous upheaval. The Civil War is a central event in America's history and also played an intricate part in the shaping of the soldiers' lives. As with the nation itself, the experiences of the regiment's enlistees reflected both the favorable and the harmful ramifications of the war.

On October 16, 1859, John Brown, the fanatical abolitionist, seized the United States Arsenal at Harper's Ferry, located at the meeting point of the Potomac and Shenandoah rivers in what was then Virginia.[2] Prior to seizing the arsenal, Brown had made a reputation for himself in May 1856. Brown, along with his band of antislavery settlers, attacked and killed several individuals with pro-slavery sentiments, an incident that would come to be called the Pottawatomie Creek Massacre. During this period this region of the United States would rightfully become known as "Bleeding Kansas." Brown perceived the raid on Harper's Ferry as a first step in an attempt to arm and free slaves. Ironically, the first civilian killed by Brown's raiders was a free black man, Heyward Shepherd. Still, abolitionists called Brown a martyr. Meanwhile, in the South, the incident was regarded as an indication of a Northern campaign to release the slaves from bondage.

In March 1861, Abraham Lincoln occupied the office of president of the United States of America. The doctrine of states' rights, the legality of secession, and the institution of black slavery had been divisive issues for decades. Subsequently, Lincoln's election brought forth threats of secession by Southern states. Officially seceding from the Union on December 20, 1860, South Carolina declared, "We, the people of the State of South Carolina in convention assembled, do declare and ordain ... that the Union now subsisting between South Carolina and other States, under name of the 'United States of America,' is hereby dissolved."[3] Mississippi adopted a similar ordinance on January 9, 1861, followed by Florida on January 10th, Alabama on January 11th, Georgia on January 19th, Louisiana on January 26th, and Texas on February 1st. Southern diarist Mary Chestnut wrote, "We are divorced, North and South because we have hated each other so."[4]

On April 15, 1861, after the firing on Fort Sumter, in Charleston Harbor, South Carolina, President Lincoln issued his first proclamation. He called for seventy-five thousand militiamen for three months' service, that being his estimate of the strength needed to defeat the rebellion. As a result of this call to arms, Virginia, Arkansas, North Carolina, and Tennessee also seceded from the Union. Now, not only was the nation divided, but also households throughout the country. It was believed that the war would not last long, hence the three month call; however it continued for four long years. Months earlier, on Christmas

Eve 1860, the superintendent of the Louisiana State Seminary of Learning and Military Academy and future major general during the Civil War, William Tecumseh Sherman, made mention of his prediction for the future of the Southern Confederacy to Professor David F. Boyd: "*You*, [emphasis added] you the people of the South, believe there can be such a thing as peaceable secession. You don't know what you are doing.... This country will be drenched in blood. God only knows how it will end." Sherman concluded, "At first you will make headway, but as your limited resources begin to fail, and shut out from the markets of Europe by blockade as you will be, your cause will begin to wane.... If your people will but stop and think, they must see that in the end you will surely fail."[5]

One of the hardest fought engagements of the war—one that turned the tide of the cause—was the battle of Antietam, at Sharpsburg, Maryland, on September 17, 1862. Here Robert E. Lee and the Army of Northern Virginia were forced to withdraw back into Virginia, subsequently handing the Federal Army of the Potomac a marginal victory. This triumph was one of the catalysts which resulted in President Lincoln issuing a proclamation declaring "all slaves in states or parts of states still in rebellion by January 1, 1863, should thereafter be free." Joseph Medill's *Chicago Tribune* avowed on September 23, 1862, "President Lincoln has set his hand and affixed the great seal of the nation to the grandest proclamation ever issued by man."[6]

An interesting facet of Lincoln's Emancipation Proclamation was that theoretically it freed no one. By issuing the proclamation Lincoln did not free any slaves in areas of the country controlled by the federal government (Northern states). He freed slaves in areas of rebellion and under Confederate control (Southern states), precisely where his word had no effect. The border states of Maryland, Delaware, West Virginia, Kentucky, Missouri, and parts of Tennessee, Louisiana, and Virginia, which had both Union and Confederate sympathizers, were not included in this proclamation. However, the act of emancipation brought a new dimension to the Union's fight, presenting the quality of a moral crusade for the eradication of slavery.[7] Lincoln stated , "I never, in my life, felt more certain that I was doing right than I do in signing this paper." He further declared, "If my name ever goes into history it will be for this act, and my whole soul is in it." In a larger sense, the proclamation was a direct stepping stone toward setting the groundwork for the total abolition of slavery throughout all of the country, both North and South, in 1865 through the 13th Amendment. Now, however, during the height of the American Civil War, President Lincoln affirmed through the proclamation that "such persons of suitable condition, will be received into the armed service of the United States to garrison forts, positions, stations and other places, and to man vessels of all sorts in said service."[8] Thus, African Americans were not only inspired by their potential as future citizens in this country, they now were given the opportunity to enter center stage upon this great national calamity and fight for their own freedom.

By 1865 the closing of the war was in sight. On April 3rd, Union troops had captured and marched into the Confederate capital of Richmond, Virginia. Six days later Confederate general Robert E. Lee surrendered his forces to General Ulysses S. Grant's army at Appomattox Court House, Virginia. Based on William F. Fox's *Regimental Losses in the American Civil War 1861–1865*, the total deaths in the Civil War, either in action or from disease, amounted to over 620,000, approximately 2 percent of the population. This was more American casualties than in all other wars combined in which American military personnel served.[9] There have been recent studies and assertions claiming the number of casualties to be 750,000 to 850,000. Binghamton University professor Dr. J. David Hacker contends that the casualties are as high as 750,000, a 20 percent increase from Fox's estimate.[10] Nicholas Marshall challenges these assertions in his March 2014 article, "The Great Exaggeration: Death and the Civil War." In relation to the analogy made by many individuals in terms of comparing the statistics of total deaths during the Civil War to our modern population statistics, which equates to approximately 7 million deaths, Marshall makes clear that "simple statistics while informative on one level, serves to obfuscate the historical experience. Put another way, the modern analogy does not help situate us in the minds of those who lived through the Civil War."[11]

Since the first shots of the Civil War rang out, anti-slavery advocates had spoken out for the African Americans who wanted to enlist in the struggle. At the outset of hostilities, many blacks had offered their services to fight for the Union. They were at first turned away because of varied reasons ranging from outright racial prejudice to the common belief that the war would be short. The *Chicago Tribune* asserted to readers that "blacks are loyal and want to help us. But mean, blind, suicidal prejudice refuses them the privilege."[12] On the other end of the spectrum, the *New York Tribune* on May 1, 1863, addressed the concerns that many Northerners sensed regarding the arming of the black man: "Loyal Whites have generally become willing that they [blacks] should fight, but the great majority have no faith that they will really do so. Many hope they will prove cowards and sneaks ... others greatly fear it."[13] Bostonian anti-slavery leader and orator Wendell Phillips avowed to an applauding crowd of the Sixteenth Ward Republican Association in New York, "Will the slave fight? Well, if any man asks you, tell him no. Will he work? If any man asks you, tell him no. But if he asks you whether the negro will fight, tell him, yes."[14] Speaking July 6, 1863, in Philadelphia at a recruitment meeting for the raising of black troops, Frederick Douglass stepped forward and affirmed, "Once let the black man get upon his person the brass letters U.S., let him get an eagle on his button, and a musket on his shoulder, and bullets in his pocket; and there is no power on earth, or under the earth, which can deny that he has earned the right to citizenship in the United States."[15]

History has shown that African Americans have willingly and faithfully fought in the United States' military conflicts prior to the American Civil War. It should be noted that before and during the American Revolution, for instance, numerous African Americans served among local militia companies fighting at Lexington, Concord and Bunker Hill. It is estimated that overall approximately 5,000 served throughout the conflict most primarily in response to General George Washington lifting the restrictions on blacks serving in the Continental Army. Nevertheless, after the colonies won independence from Britain, the United States Congress established in 1792 militia acts prohibiting enlistments of blacks into the United States Army, a policy which held firm until the summer of 1862. On the other hand, the United States Navy, from its earliest establishment by the Continental Congress and after its official authorization by the Navy Department in April 1798, openly permitted enlistments of African Americans to sea service. This authorization continued throughout the hostilities of the American Civil War.[16]

The first official authorization to use black men in the army was the Second Confiscation and Militia Act of July 17, 1862. Section 12 of the act authorized the president to "receive into service of the United States, for the purpose of constructing entrenchments or performing camp duty, or any labor, or any military or naval service for which they were found to be competent, persons of African descent, and provided that such persons should be enrolled and organized, under such regulations not inconsistent with the constitution and laws as the President might prescribe."[17]

Section 15 of the Act provided "that persons of African descent [of any rank] who under this law shall be employed, shall receive $10 a month, and one ration, $3 of which monthly pay may be in clothes." White privates received $13 per month plus $3.50 in clothing allowance.[18] In May 1863, with the forming of the Bureau of Colored Troops, Secretary of War Edwin M. Stanton was unsuccessful in pushing for a congressional ruling on the discrepancy of the colored soldier's pay. Protests and refusal to accept monthly pay erupted throughout the ranks of the colored units. The debate over rectifying the pay and bounty discrepancy would not end until June 15, 1864, at which time Congress granted equal pay to the black soldier.[19]

General Ulysses S. Grant voiced his opinion of the arming of the black man. Writing August 23, 1863, to President Lincoln, Grant declared, "I have given the subject of arming the negro my hearty support. This, with the emancipation of the negro is the heaviest blow yet given to the Confederacy.... By arming the negro we have added a powerful ally. They will make good soldiers."[20] Black men constituted less than 1 percent of the North's population; however, by the cessation of military hostilities they would make up one-tenth of the Union Army.[21] Although these were regiments formed exclusively of colored men, they were commanded almost entirely by white officers. Along with reasons stemming from racial discrimination in allowing blacks to serve as officers, many blacks, it was believed, did not have the proper education to serve as officers. Many lacked the skills needed in writing and ciphering the myriad amounts of military orders and paperwork, let alone having the ability to read and learn the military manuals of the day. Although many African Americans felt disheartened by the notion that they would be denied opportunities to achieve higher rank among the field officers and staff, it is, however, estimated that over 100 black men faithfully served and achieved the status of commissioned officers within regiments of color during the American Civil War.[22]

According to the annals of the United States Colored Soldiers, five African American regiments had been formed and shouldered arms prior to Lincoln's signing the Emancipation Proclamation. These regiments consisted of the 1st South Carolina Infantry Regiment (African Descent), the 1st, 2nd, and 3rd Louisiana Native Guards and the 1st Kansas Colored Infantry, all Federal units later to be reauthorized as the 33rd, 73rd, 74th, 75th, and 79th (new) USCT regiments.

Secretary of War Stanton provided a directive to authorize Brigadier

General Rufus Saxton, then military governor of the Department of the South, to raise 5,000 black soldiers under his command. Through his diligence the raising of a black regiment comprising former slaves from South Carolina and Florida would come to fruition and be named the 1st South Carolina Infantry Regiment (African Descent). The devout pre-war abolitionist Thomas Wentworth Higginson would be

General Ulysses S. Grant, City Point, Virginia, August 1864. Grant wrote President Lincoln, "I have given the subject of arming the negro my hearty support. This, with the emancipation of the negro is the heaviest blow yet given to the Confederacy.... By arming the negro we have added a powerful ally. They will make good soldiers" (Library of Congress Prints and Photographs Division Washington, D.C. LC-DIG-ppmsca-35236).

appointed to lead this first federally recognized regiment of African Americans as its colonel.[23]

When New Orleans fell in April 1862, Benjamin Butler took to commanding the occupation forces. On August 22nd, Butler issued General Order No. 63, calling upon the free colored population then acting as free colored militiamen in Louisiana to enlist into the Federal ranks. Butler's order skirted around the issue of arming slaves into Federal service without prior government approval by declaring that the order was specifically directed at the already established free African American militia known as the Native Guards. Governor Thomas Moore, in charge of the Louisiana state militia, had already sworn in the organization in 1861. Within a month of opening the doors to enlistment into the Federal ranks, Butler was able to establish and muster fully into service the 1st Louisiana Native Guards on September 27, 1862, followed in October by the 2nd Louisiana Native Guards and in November the 3rd Louisiana Native Guards.[24]

On the 4th day of August 1862, without Federal authorization from the War Department, the 1st Kansas Colored Infantry, by order of James Henry Lane (recruiting commissioner for that portion of Kansas lying north of the Kansas River) was formally recruited. Captain James M. Williams, formally of the 5th Kansas Cavalry, was given the authority to commence the work of recruiting, procuring supplies and officers to formally muster the regiment into Federal service between January 13 and May 2, 1863. Noteworthy of their service to the Union cause was the fact that not only was it the first African American regiment recruited in the North, even before its formal mustering and being officially recognized by the United States government, but it would, on October 29, 1862, be the first black unit to take an active role alongside white regiments in combat at Island Mound, Missouri. It would go on to serve courageously at the future battles of Honey Springs, Indian Territory and Poison Spring, Arkansas.[25]

One of the many forgotten histories with reference to the contributions of black men, not only assisting to defend their communities but the country, was witnessed in September 1862. Major General Lew Wallace, having previously commanded a military division under General Grant during the spring battle of Shiloh, Tennessee, and in the post-war authoring the historically acclaimed book *Ben Hur: A Tale of the Christ* (1880), was now in command of the defense of Cincinnati, Ohio, within the larger Department of the Ohio. In early July, Confederate colonel John Hunt Morgan had wreaked havoc upon Union Major

General Don Carlos Buell's army throughout Kentucky. Along with this, Confederate general Braxton Bragg, with the combined force of Major General Edmund Kirby Smith, had proceeded to march their armies into Kentucky during the fall campaigns of 1862. As a result, the city of Cincinnati was put on heightened alert and fortified the outer defenses of the city from any potential attack.

On September 2nd, Cincinnati mayor George Hatch proclaimed, "In accordance with a resolution passed by the City Council of Cincinnati on the 1st instant, I hereby request that all business, of every kind or character, be suspended at ten o'clock of this day, and that all persons, employers and employees, assemble in their respective wards, at the usual places of voting, and then and there organize themselves in such a manner as may be thought best for the defense of the city. Every man, of every age, be he citizen or alien, who lives under the protection of our laws, is expected to take part in the organization."[26]

Cincinnati's black citizens eagerly answered the proclamation's call, but their willingness to come to the assistance of the city was dealt with by many in a less than respectful fashion. In writing to Ohio governor John Brough in 1864, William M. Dickson stated, "It was well understood that this order was not intended to, and did not, include colored citizens. Numbers of these, however, offered themselves for any service in which they might be useful." Dickson further recalled that, "on the morning of the 3rd of September, 1862, the police, acting in concert, and in obedience to some common order, in a rude and violent manner, arrested the colored men wherever found—in the streets, at their places of business, in their homes—and hurried them to a mule-pen on Plum Street, and thence across the river to the fortifications, giving them no explanation of this conduct, and no opportunity to prepare for camp-life."[27] General Wallace had caught wind of this treatment and immediately provided orders for the protection of the black citizens related to their assistance as laborers on the city fortifications. Wallace ordered that, "William M. Dickson is hereby assigned to the command of the negro forces from Cincinnati, working on the fortifications near Newport and Covington, and will be obeyed accordingly."[28]

Author Peter H. Clark, in writing the history of the Black Brigade entitled *Black Brigade of Cincinnati: Being a Report of Its Labors and a Muster-Roll of Its Members* (1864) declared, "The Black Brigade was the first organization of the colored people of the North actually employed for military purposes."[29] Although the Black Brigade of Cincinnati, as it has come to be known, did not take up military arms to defend the city and was not recognized by the state or federal government for its service, it did contribute to and make a lasting mark on the history of the black soldier during the Civil War. Men like Cincinnati resident Powhatan Beaty, having served in the Cincinnati Black Brigades' Third Regiment, Company Number One, would later go on to serve as first sergeant of Company G, 5th United States Colored Infantry. Beaty received the Medal of Honor while in company with his regiment at the battle of New Market Heights, or Chapin's Farm, on September 29, 1864. His citation reads, "[Beaty] took command of his company, all the officers having been killed or wounded, and gallantly led it."[30]

Two states raised colored regiments that maintained their state designations; Connecticut and Massachusetts. These regiments were the 29th Connecticut Infantry, 54th Massachusetts and 55th Massachusetts Infantries and the 5th Massachusetts Cavalry. By the end of the war, some 180,000 enlisted men served in the U.S. Army as members of the U.S. Colored Troops. Another 10,000 to 20,000 black men served in the U.S. Navy. Of that number some 30,000 made the ultimate sacrifice by losing their lives during the war. Altogether 166 all-black regiments were formed during the conflict (145 infantry, 7 cavalry, 12 heavy artillery, 1 light artillery and 1 engineer unit). The largest number of black soldiers came from Louisiana (24,052) followed by Kentucky (23,703) and Tennessee (20,133). Pennsylvania contributed more black soldiers than any other Northern state (8,612). Black soldiers participated in 449 battles, 39 of which were major engagements.[31] Of the 1,523 Medals of Honor awarded to Civil War soldiers a total of twenty-five were bestowed upon African Americans for their service during the conflict; seventeen were for service in the Army, the most recent being posthumously awarded in 2001, along with eight for service in the United States Navy.[32]

Arriving on the desk of Governor John Andrew of Massachusetts was an order dated Washington City, January 26, 1863. It was received from the secretary of war, granting the governor authority to raise Massachusetts regiments of colored men. The directive was as follows:

> War Department, Adjutant-General's Office,
> Washington, D. C., Jan 27, 1863.
>
> Capt. J. B. Collins, *United States Army, Mustering and Disbursing Officer, Boston, Mass.*
>
> *Sir*,—The following has been received from the Secretary of War, and is respectfully communicated for your information and guidance:

War Department, Washington City, Jan. 26, 1863.

Ordered, That Gov. Andrew, of Massachusetts, is authorized, until further orders, to raise such number of volunteers, companies of artillery, for duty in the forts of Massachusetts and elsewhere, and such corps of infantry for the volunteer military service, as he may find convenient; such volunteers to be enlisted for three years, or until sooner discharged, and may include persons of African descent, organized into special corps. He will make the usual needful requisitions on the appropriate staff bureaus and officers for the proper transportation, organization, supplies, subsistence, arms, and equipments of such volunteers.

Edwin M. Stanton, *Secretary of War.*[33]

With the authorization by Governor John Andrew, three regiments from Massachusetts were formed and designated as all-black units. These were the 54th and 55th Massachusetts Infantries and the 5th Massachusetts Cavalry (Colored). Although the most common enlistment of blacks was in the United States Colored Troops (U.S.C.T.), these three units retained their state designation of Massachusetts. This established the units as state volunteer regiments rather than Federal units. Concurrently, the 5th Massachusetts Cavalry (Colored) was the only African American regiment of cavalry raised in the Northern states during the Civil War.

On May 22, 1863, by authority of the United States War Department, General Orders, No. 143, was issued establishing the Bureau of Colored Troops: "A Bureau is established in the Adjutant General's Office for the record of all matters relating to the organization of Colored Troops."[34] Section IV expressly indicated that "no persons shall be allowed to recruit for colored troops except specially authorized by the War Department; and no such authority will be given to persons who have not been examined and passed by a board; nor will such authority be given any one person to raise more than one regiment."[35] Furthermore, by the establishment of the bureau, Section VI stipulated that "colored troops may be accepted by companies, to be afterward consolidated in battalions and regiments by the Adjutant General. The regiments will be numbered seriatim, in the order in which they are raised, the numbers to be determined by the Adjutant General. They will be designated: '—Regiment of U.S. Colored Troops.'"[36] By establishing the Bureau of Colored Troops the United States War Department closely regulated the recruiting and formation of black regiments by individual state governments, ultimately placing them under Federal control. Following this change in policy, Massachusetts governor John Andrew was still permitted to recruit colored soldiers. However, these units would no longer be given state designations, now being recognized as United States Colored Troops.

Having successfully raised two previous regiments of color, the 54th and 55th Massachusetts Infantries, Governor Andrew proposed to Edwin Stanton in September 1863 a "Massachusetts cavalry regiment of colored men." He informed Stanton that he had recently stopped the recruitment of blacks, "because the order of the War Department [General Order 143] seemed to afford an opportunity for colored men in other free states to volunteer for the defence of their country."[37] Additionally, Andrew stipulated that "nor had I the right by our laws to pay bounties to these men unless they came here and enlisted here, in our regiments and were entitled to be credited as our soldiers."[38]

In a letter dated September 10, Governor Andrew received wholehearted support from Secretary Stanton in favor of the measure to raise a regiment of cavalry. Support through a letter was not what Governor Andrew wanted or needed, so he waited for official War Department orders to cross his desk so he could proceed in the recruiting and eventual commissioning of the 5th Massachusetts Cavalry for service under Massachusetts state designation. All the while, Andrew pressed for John Murray Forbes, who was then working in Washington, D.C., to urge Secretary Stanton to move on the matter and issue orders in raising a colored regiment of cavalry. Andrew advised Forbes, "Try him [Stanton] and see if he does not think it worthwhile to have this experiment tried of Colored Cavalry enough to accept four companies to be mustered in at the minimum one by one."[39]

Consequently, Major Charles W. Foster, assistant adjutant general of the United States Colored Bureau, directed on November 23rd that Governor Andrew should henceforth proceed in the establishment of a colored cavalry regiment: "Sir: I am instructed by the Secretary of War to inform you that you are hereby authorized to raise a battalion or a regiment of cavalry to be composed of colored men and to be mustered into service of the United States for three years or during the war."[40] Foster's directive continues,

> To these troops no bounties will be paid. They will receive $10 per month and one ration per day, $3 of which monthly pay may be in clothing.
>
> The organization of the battalion or regiment must conform in all respects with the requirements of General Orders No. 110, current series, War Department, a copy of which is herewith.
>
> The respective companies of the battalion or regiment may be mustered into service as soon as the minimum number of enlisted men in each case are ready for muster.

The prescribed number of commissioned officers will be appointed on your recommendation by the President of the United States, and the officers so appointed
will be regularly mustered into service in accordance with the requirements of the
Revised Mustering Regulations.

In cases where persons in service are recommended for appointment, the full
name, rank, company, and regiment to which they are attached should be stated.

The necessary supplies will be furnished by the respective departments upon
requisitions approved by you.

The preliminary examination of candidates for appointment is waved in this
case, for the reason that the exigencies of the public service will not permit of a
board convened for the examination of cavalry officers.[41]

Two days after receiving Major Foster's orders, Governor Andrew
corresponded with Stanton to air his concerns in relation to the laws
regulating the state quotas, bounty, and pay of enlisted men, along with
the commissioning of officers of the cavalry regiment. Governor
Andrew informed Stanton, "Colored cavalry must be counted to our
quota under present call, and officers must be commissioned by me
and regiment organized as was the Fifty-fourth Regiment, to enable
me to pay the large State bounty to the regiment as Massachusetts Volunteers. This is of absolute importance." Furthermore, Andrew stipulated that Major Foster had sent him orders "in effect to raise U.S.
colored troops." Governor Andrew voiced that he "can only pay Massachusetts Volunteers. The question of U.S. pay does not trouble,
because our volunteers have their choice of $325 bounty, or $50 bounty
and $20 per month from the State. Please give me similar order to for-
mer one."[42] It seems that Governor Andrew's concerns were addressed
by Stanton as he now received on December 2, 1863, the following
communique from Major Foster:

Sir: In consequence of your dispatch to the effect that the laws of Massachusetts
will not permit the payment of bounties to volunteers unless their officers are commissioned by the Governor of the State, I am directed by the Secretary of War to
say that so much of Department letter of the 23d ultimo as states that the officers
of the colored cavalry regiment which you were therein authorized to raise would
be appointed by the President is annulled, and the officers of said regiment may be
appointed by you. Said appointments and muster into service to be in accordance
with the Revised Mustering Regulations."[43]

Governor Andrew now had been granted full authority by the War
Department to proceed in instituting a colored cavalry regiment with
the state designation of Massachusetts. Years after the Civil War, in
1884, Oliver Wendell Holmes, Jr., addressed a Memorial Day audience
before the John Sedgwick Post No. 4, Grand Army of the Republic, in
Keene, New Hampshire, stating: "Throughout our great good fortune,

in our youth our hearts were touched by fire."[44] With that same fire in the hearts of the enlisted recruits, burning the fuel to be part of something momentous and profoundly effective in shaping the outcome of their whole lives, they began arriving in Boston in the late months of 1863 and into the early months of 1864, volunteering to serve in the 5th Massachusetts Cavalry.

1

Do You Think
I'll Make a Soldier?

"Therefore put on the full armor of God, so that when the day of evil comes, you may be able to stand your ground, and after you have done everything, to stand."

—Ephesians 6:13

The opening line of an African American plantation spiritual asks: "Do you think I'll make a soldier?"

> Do you think I'll make a soldier, soldier?
> Do you think I'll make a soldier, soldier?
> Do you think I'll make a soldier, soldier?
> In the year of jubilee.
>
> CHORUS
> Rise and shine and give God the glory, glory;
> Rise and shine and give God the glory, glory;
> Rise and shine and give God the glory, glory;
> In the year of jubilee.
>
> Think I saw the mighty army, army.
> CHORUS—Rise and shine, etc.
>
> We are climbing Jacob's ladder, ladder.
> CHORUS—Rise and shine, etc.
>
> See the mighty Savior coming, coming.
> CHORUS—Rise and shine, etc.
>
> We are listed in the army, army.
> CHORUS—Rise and shine, etc.
>
> Fighting for our Master Jesus, Jesus.
> CHORUS—Rise and shine, etc.
>
> In the battle he will lead us, lead us.
> CHORUS—Rise and shine, etc.[1]

The Bible refers to the believer as a Christian soldier, instructing the faithful to "endure hardship with us like a good soldier of Jesus Christ. No one serving as a soldier gets involved in civilian affairs—he wants to please his commanding officer"—2 Timothy 2:3–4.[2] Ephesians 6:13 says, "Therefore put on the full armor of God, so that when the day of evil comes, you may be able to stand your ground, and after you have done everything, to stand."[3] Taking these and other military metaphors to heart, the old plantation melody proved powerfully inspirational for the enslaved. Encouraged by the promise that, upon Christ's second coming, they would at last cast off their shackles and fall into rank as soldiers in his mighty army, they endured. With that sentiment, the recruits of the 5th Massachusetts Cavalry began their training, seeking to make good soldiers and to fight for their own freedoms.

The 5th Regiment Massachusetts Volunteer Cavalry was organized at Camp Meigs, Readville, Massachusetts, during the autumn and winter of 1863 and into the spring of 1864 to serve three years. Camp Meigs, named in honor of Quartermaster General Montgomery Meigs, was established in September 1862 and located on the outskirts and within only a few miles of the city of Boston. Centrally located along the Neponset River and within a short distance of the Boston and Providence Railroad line, it afforded ease of access to incoming raw recruits flooding into camp to enlist.[4]

The 139 acres encompassing the camp in 1863 provided a terrain for training with its flat, open expanse and afforded itself to drilling large men in company and regimental formations. Unfortunately, this flat expanse of land tended to become rather muddy, especially with the coming of the winter months as the 5th Cavalry began its training. The layout of the enlisted men's quarters consisted of parallel lines of bunks inside "great wooden barn-like structures" as one Massachusetts soldier recalled.[5] The field, staff and company officers established their sleeping quarters separate from the enlisted recruits in smaller wooden buildings. Along with these barracks the camp was equipped with all the amenities and infrastructure to support the training of regiments; these included a commissary, cook houses, a sutler (a civilian merchant selling provisions and camp necessities), a chapel, an armory, laundry facilities, and a hospital that in June 1864 consisted of 71 support buildings named Readville General Hospital. Camp Meigs was also supported with a complement of storehouses, horse stables, and guardhouses.[6]

Company A was mustered in January 9, 1864, but the last company,

M, was not mustered until May 5th of that year.[7] The commissioned officers of the regiment were exclusively white men. As with many African American units in the Civil War, the majority of the officers who would command these units held previous enlistments of field and staff positions with white regiments. Many of these men took promotions into colored units for the expressed purpose of obtaining higher rank. This rank would include benefits of higher pay and the social status that came from holding high ranking office. Massachusetts governor John Andrew said that he would draw officers from those men already serving with Massachusetts regiments, so that "brave, devoted and noble fellows, like those who were selected for the 54th and 55th (infantry) volunteers" would command the cavalry regiment.[8]

The officers that made up the 5th Massachusetts Cavalry came from many distinct and varied backgrounds. Listed in *Massachusetts Soldiers, Sailors and Marines in the Civil War* (1932), the civilian occupations of the field and staff command included police officers, lawyers, clergymen, bookkeepers, painters, carpenters, students, and shoemakers. There was even one distinct occupation simply entitled "Gentlemen," that being the regiment's colonel, Henry Sturgis Russell.

Henry Sturgis Russell, an 1860 Harvard graduate, previously served with excellence as an officer with the 2nd Regiment Massachusetts Volunteer Infantry. Massachusetts governor John Andrew expressed that he would draw from those men already serving with Massachusetts regiments as he stated, so that "brave, devoted and noble fellows, like those who were selected for the 54th and 55th [infantry] volunteers" would command the cavalry regiment (author's collection).

Born the 21st of June 1838 at Savin Hill, Dorchester, Massachusetts, he was a first cousin to Col. Robert Gould Shaw, commander of the gallant 54th Massachusetts Infantry, who was killed leading his regiment upon the fortress of Fort Wagner, South Carolina. Russell, an 1860 Harvard graduate, previously served with excellence as an officer with the 2nd Regiment Massachusetts Volunteer Infantry, having been captured at Cedar Mountain, Virginia, on August 9, 1862, and exchanged from Libby Prison.[9]

Speaking at the Harvard Commemoration Day ceremony July 21, 1865, honoring alumni of Harvard College who had sacrificed the last full measure during the Civil War, Governor John Andrew recalled the devotion Henry Russell had showed his comrade and fellow Harvard alum Major James Savage, Jr. (Harvard class of 1854). Andrew stated, "I know of no incident of more perfect, of more heroic gentility, bespeaking a noble nature, than the act performed by one captain of the Second Massachusetts ... who, standing by the side of Lieutenant-Colonel Savage [promoted September 1862], who was fatally wounded, not believed by the enemy to be worth the saving, refused to surrender until he had wrung from the enemy the pledge that they would, in capturing him, save also his comrade and bear him back to the nearest hospital; declaring that, if they did not, he, single-handed and alone, would fight it out, and sell his life at the dearest cost."[10] Major James Savage, Jr., having been promoted to lieutenant colonel on September 17, 1862, was captured on the field of Cedar Mountain and sent to Charlottesville, Virginia, where he lingered in a hospital and succumbed to his wounds on October 22, 1862. Henry Sturgis Russell wrote from behind the walls of Libby Prison, "I was taken while tying a handkerchief round Jim Savage's leg. Write to his father that he was wounded in the arm and leg, and taken. I have not seen him since I left Culpeper [Virginia], as he was not well enough to march."[11]

Russell remained in Libby Prison until November 15, 1862, at which time he was paroled and exchanged. Upon returning to military service he was commissioned lieutenant colonel of the 2nd Regiment Massachusetts Volunteer Cavalry. In May 1863, Colonel Russell married Mary Hathaway Forbes, daughter of John Murray Forbes. Her father was the very person Governor John Andrew had asked to assist him in persuading Secretary of War Stanton to give authorization in raising and forming the 5th Massachusetts Cavalry. Now with the forming of the cavalry regiment in December 1863, Governor Andrew began the process of reviewing the pool of potential candidates to fill the position of colonel. Seeking to fill the position with someone of noble character, capable military experience, along with having a devoted and proven track record in training and leading men on the field of battle, Governor Andrew placed his faith and support behind Henry Sturgis Russell to lead this regiment of colored cavalry.

The American Unitarian Association in writing after the war the biographical sketches of men who stood up to their puritan descent chronicled Henry Sturgis Russell and declared, "He was loath to leave his comrades of the Second Cavalry; the advancement in rank was inconsiderable; the command of colored troops was then little desired. The inducement, however, was characteristic."[12] Harry, as he was affectionately called by family along with close friends and acquaintances, stated simply upon taking the commission at the head of the newly raised 5th Massachusetts Colored Cavalry, "Bob [Robert Gould Shaw] would have liked to have me do it!"[13] Having grown up and raised in a decidedly abolitionist home, it was noted of Harry Russell that he "shared his father's views, insisting always that the war was for the Union, but welcoming the disappearance of slavery as a happy result."[14]

Although the main residences of officers were listed within the state of Massachusetts, a few came from such far reaching locations as San Francisco, California. When news reached California regarding the surrender of Fort Sumter in Charleston Harbor, South Carolina, the citizens of the state took an active role in expressing their loyalties. Whether they were the predominant Secessionist views of the southern half of the state or the upper northern tier's Unionist sentiments, California found itself wrapped around the political and social debate taking place back east and ultimately found itself amid the military struggle. In August 1861, California governor John Downey issued orders calling for the recruitment of California troops to support the Union cause. Many of these early recruits would serve in outposts along the western territories guarding against raids on stagecoach routes and disputes with Native American tribes.

As the Civil War escalated into 1862, California provided a contingent of loyal citizens to the Union Army for the eastern theater of war. Many of these enlistees would serve in Massachusetts regiments. James Sewell Reed received a dispatch from Governor John Andrew of Massachusetts authorizing Reed to raise a cavalry company of 100 men to fill Massachusetts state military quotas. These first 100 men would ultimately be sent to Massachusetts and would formally serve as the California Hundred Company A, 2nd Massachusetts Cavalry.

An additional 400 residents of California would be recruited and form companies E, F, L, & M of the 2nd Massachusetts Cavalry, respectively being termed the California Battalion.[15]

These Californians, many of whom were transplanted natives of Massachusetts, having served with the 2nd Massachusetts Cavalry, would in due course go on to take commissions in the newly formed 5th Massachusetts Colored Cavalry. For instance, Zabdiel Boylston Adams, who previously held a captaincy with Company L of the 2nd Massachusetts Cavalry, was one of several men Henry Sturgis Russell recommended to fill the officer ranks of the 5th Massachusetts Cavalry. Adams would be commissioned January 22, 1864, and a few weeks later on February 6th officially mustered as a major, taking command of the second battalion. Additionally, Captain Horace B. Welch would be commissioned captain of Company C on January 18, 1864, along with John Anderson, first lieutenant, Company C. Formerly an officer in Company F of the 2nd Massachusetts Cavalry, George F. Wilson was commissioned March 2, 1864, as a second lieutenant in Company I of the 5th Massachusetts Cavalry. Lastly, San Francisco resident, Corporal Robert M. Parker, of Company A 2nd Massachusetts Cavalry, was commissioned April 29, 1864, as second lieutenant within Company M of the 5th Massachusetts Cavalry.[16]

Second Lieutenant Rienzi Loud was born

Captain Horace B. Welch was one of many transplanted natives of Massachusetts living in California who, having served with the 2nd Massachusetts Cavalry, would take a commission with the 5th Massachusetts Colored Cavalry (author's collection).

in Rockland, Massachusetts; he relocated to Michigan prior to the outbreak of the Civil War. Loud was employed as a teacher in the town of Dowagiac, Michigan, and had attended Tuft's College in Medford, Massachusetts, prior to enlisting into Company A, 1st Michigan Cavalry, a regiment which subsequently was associated with General George Armstrong Custer's famed Michigan Cavalry Brigade. Having served in the 1st Michigan Cavalry with the rank of quartermaster sergeant, Loud, in January 1864, formally accepted promotion and a commission as an officer in Company G of the 5th Massachusetts Cavalry.[17]

Coming from a rather common background, Daniel Henry Chamberlain rose to take his place within the history of the 5th Massachusetts Cavalry. Chamberlain was the ninth child of Eli and Achsah (Forbes) Chamberlain. Born June 23, 1835, Chamberlain worked his family farm as a boy in West Brookfield, Massachusetts. Attending several secondary schools throughout his youth he ultimately entered Yale in 1858 and graduated four years later.[18] In the fall of 1862, Chamberlain was attending Harvard Law School and by November 1863 he would withdraw to take a commission on January 25, 1864, as a second lieutenant with the regiment. Rising quickly in rank he was commissioned March 15, 1864, as first lieutenant and adjutant within the field and staff.[19]

Another alum attending Harvard was George Albert Fisher, class of 1865. He left his studies to enlist in the 5th Massachusetts Cavalry on December 29, 1863, having been commissioned a second lieutenant in Company E. During Fisher's service he carried an inscribed William H. Horstmann & Sons of Philadelphia manufactured officers presentation sword. The March 1864 edition of the *Harvard Magazine* acknowledged that he was "presented with a sword and equipment prior to his departure to accept a commission as Second Lieutenant in the 5th Massachusetts Cavalry." The inscription read, "George A. Fisher/from his/Classmates/Harvard College/Jan. 11, 1864."[20]

The Civil War has always been considered a family war. The notion of brother against brother can be recorded in many family histories. However, in the instance of the 5th Massachusetts Cavalry's officer corps brother against brother was reversed and took its shape as comrades in arms. This is recorded in the telling of brothers Henry Pickering Bowditch and Charles Pickering Bowditch.

Henry and Charles were the sons of Jonathan Ingersoll Bowditch and Lucy Orne Nichols, and the grandsons of Nathaniel Bowditch. Their father was a Boston merchant and an author of works on nautical navigation. Nathaniel Bowditch, their grandfather, an astronomer and mathematician, was most famous for his work *The New American Practical Navigator*, which was one of the foremost leading works on navigation written by an American of his time.[21]

Henry Pickering Bowditch was born April 4, 1840, in Boston. He entered Harvard in 1857 with an aptitude for medicine. Upon graduating in 1861 he entered Lawrence Scientific School (today Cambridge University) where he studied chemistry and natural history, but his studies were interrupted by the outbreak of the war. In November 1861 he was commissioned second lieutenant in Company G, 2nd Battalion, 1st Massachusetts Cavalry. While serving with the 1st Massachusetts he was wounded in the right forearm leading a charge at New Hope Church on November 27, 1863.[22] According to author Allen Johnson, *Dictionary of American Biography* (1929), Bowditch's colleague Major Henry Lee Higginson described him "as handsome, refined, homegrown, 'with a fondness of keeping face clean and clothing neat when those attributes were a rarity.'" Johnson continues, he was "reserved and unbending in manner, of unequivocal loyalty and courage, yet with no particular liking for army life."[23] With the forming of the 5th Massachusetts Cavalry Bowditch took a commission as major

Major Henry P. Bowditch. With the forming of the 5th Massachusetts Cavalry, Bowditch took a commission as major in the regiment. He was mustered into service with the unit on May 5, 1864 (author's collection).

in the regiment. He was mustered into service with the unit on May 5, 1864.[24]

Henry's younger brother, Charles Pickering Bowditch, was born September 30, 1842. Like his older brother, with an analytical mind, he received his degree from Harvard College in 1863. He entered the war with the 55th Massachusetts Infantry and rose through the ranks serving as second lieutenant, first lieutenant and captain. While stationed at Folly Island, South Carolina, Charles wrote to his father on December 15, 1863, asking, "Don't you think it would be a good idea for me to try and get into the negro Cavalry Regiment which Governor

Andrew has received permission to raise in Massachusetts? I should then get a horse and the objection which occurred to you when I thought of a Captaincy in the 1st Mass. Cavalry, that it would look like deserting the cause of the blacks, would be entirely obviated." Charles noted in writing to his father that, "I have just seen Major [James] Sturgis who tells me that the new regiment of cavalry is to be commanded by Henry Sturgis Russell," further adding that Russell's appointment as colonel in his estimation was "rather a come around, since he did not use to be quite right on the negro question."[25]

Captain Charles P. Bowditch entered the war with the 55th Massachusetts Infantry and rose through the ranks, serving as second lieutenant, first lieutenant and captain. Charles would take command of Company F on February 23, 1864 (author's collection).

Charles sought out a commission as a captain with the 5th Massachusetts Cavalry, hoping that he would "have a commission in the Cavalry with Henry" who had recently been commissioned a major in the newly formed cavalry regiment.[26] Charles would take command of Company F on February 23, 1864.[27] In regard to his leadership qualities he had been noted as having "a striking appearance with a commanding figure. He had a very strong personality, trying to carry out the letter of the law and expecting others to do so. He was forceful yet full of modesty, always with opinions but willing to reason, wrathful before underhandedness but just to all."[28]

Clearly, since the officers were from such distinct and varied backgrounds, likewise the contingent of enlisted men in the unit represented even more of a diverse conglomeration. Like the branches on a tree, recruiting agents extended out beyond Massachusetts reaching throughout the heart of the North and recruiting into the South. Announcements appeared in Boston and throughout Massachusetts along with national papers such as the *New York Tribune* immediately following Governor Andrew's notice from Secretary of War Stanton to "recruit a regiment of colored cavalry" as the *Milwaukee Daily Sentinel* on Saturday, December 5, 1863, announced.[29] Many of these newspapers published and circulated in full Governor Andrew's recent General Order No. 44 in which Andrew announced "pursuant to authority received from the United States Department of War, a Regiment of Cavalry Volunteers, to be composed of men of color, enlisted for three years, unless sooner discharged, is now in the process of recruitment in the Commonwealth." Andrew further made known that this regiment was to be recognized as the "Fifth Massachusetts Cavalry Volunteers" along with the fact that "Lieut. Col. Henry S. Russell, of the Second Massachusetts Cavalry Volunteers, is designated its Colonel."[30]

Andrew's General Order No. 44, made it clearly known that any potential recruits reading the orders set forth or considering the possible opportunity in joining the regiment would understand that the "United States [government] pays no bounty to the recruits for this Regiment under existing regulations, nor wages exceeding $10 per month, including $3 per month for clothing." However, Governor Andrew assured new recruits that the Commonwealth of Massachusetts "offers precisely the same bounty offered to all other Volunteers, viz:—$325 bounty, paid in Massachusetts after the Volunteer is mustered into his Regiment; or, if he shall so elect, then $50 bounty payable as aforesaid, and $20 monthly bounty or pay, in addition to the pay now or hereafter received by him from the United States."[31]

If anyone had any doubts as to how the regiment of cavalry was to be formed and structured, Governor Andrew laid out in detail through General Order No. 44 the established military organization of a volunteer cavalry regiment and its respective contingent of companies, along with number of officers and compliment of enlisted men to successfully provide a regiment for active service in the field. This also would make available an understanding of the amount of recruiting it would entail to effectively establish the regiment. The least approximate number of men to field a cavalry regiment was slightly over 1,000 strong, this being considered the ideal by the military regulations. However, as history has shown, often recruitment of regiments frequently fell short of the ideal amount prescribed in the regulations. In any event, Governor Andrew set forth that twelve companies or troops, as they were termed in the cavalry branch, were to be established, these companies being designated "A" through "M" excluding "J."

Andrew made clear that the field and staff would consist of "1 Colonel, 1 Lieutenant Colonel, 3 Majors, 1 Surgeon, 2 Assistant Surgeons, 1 Regimental Adjutant, (an extra Lieutenant), 1 Regimental Quartermaster, (an extra Lieutenant), 1 Regimental Commissary, (an extra Lieutenant), 1 Chaplain, 1 Veterinary Surgeon, 1 Sergeant Major, 1 Quarter Master Sergeant, 1 Commissary Sergeant, 2 Hospital Stewards, 1 Saddler Sergeant, 1 Chief Trumpeter." Along with these staff positions, Andrew outlined that for each company or troop, a compliment of "1 Captain, 1 First Lieutenant, 1 Second Lieutenant, 1 First Sergeant, 1 Quartermaster Sergeant, 1 Commissary Sergeant, 5 Sergeants, 8 corporals, 2 Trumpeters, 2 Farriers or Blacksmiths, 1 Saddler, 1 Wagoner" would be assigned. Furthermore, each company would muster between "60 privates minimum, 78 Privates maximum." In drumming up support in the recruitment of enlisted men for the regiment along with providing a rallying call to all able-bodied men of color, Andrew placed a final exclamation point to his general order. The adjutant general of Massachusetts, in expressing and publishing Andrew's thoughts, declared:

> The Governor regards in great satisfaction the progress since the inauguration of the 54th Massachusetts Infantry Volunteers. And he confidently contemplates the accession from this Commonwealth to the National Army, of a Cavalry Regiment of Colored Americans, which will illustrate their capacity for that dashing and brilliant arm of the military service. In this hour of hope for our common country and for themselves; at a time when they hold the destiny of their race in their own grasp; and when its certain emancipation from prejudice, as well as slavery, is in the hands of those now invited to unite in the final blow which will annihilate the rebel power, let no brave and strong man hesitate. One can not exaggerate the call

sounding in the ears of all men, in whose veins flows the blood of Africa, and whose color has been the badge of slavery. It offers the opportunity of years, crowded into an hour. It bids them come and be numbered with the peoples of every race, who, by their own arms, have vindicated their right to all the blessings, and all the powers of Liberty.[32]

Having been duly chosen by Governor Andrew to command the regiment, Henry Russell, prior to arriving at Camp Meigs, had established his offices at 21 School Street in the heart of Boston, then being the location of the American Institute of Instruction. Governor Andrew had expressly stated in his general order that "communications concerning the regiment may be made to Col. Henry S. Russell No. 21 School St., Boston."[33] This still set forth a sea of potential inquiring recruits' correspondences being placed upon the desk of Governor Andrew for his consideration concerning not only providing their military service within this newly forming regiment, but also being considered for authorization as formal recruiting agents.[34]

The notable African American Chicago merchant and clothing tailor John Jones, who in 1816 was born free to a black mother and white father in North Carolina, had made his way west to Memphis, Tennessee, and by 1845 had ventured north through

Colonel Henry Sturgis Russell, Harry, as he was affectionately named by family along with close friends and acquaintances, stated simply upon taking the commission at the head of the newly raised 5th Massachusetts Colored Cavalry, "Bob [Colonel Robert Gould Shaw, 54th Mass. Inf.] would have liked to have me do it!" (author's collection).

Alton, Illinois, and settled in Chicago, Illinois. Along with his wife, Mary, he established his residence and business at 119 Dearborn Street in the heart of the booming and up and coming metropolis. Jones was a steadfast abolitionist who was known on occasion to have opened his home to men like John Brown, Frederick Douglass and Allen Pinkerton. Along with his staunch abolitionist sentiments, Jones assisted in harboring fugitive slaves at his home along with being a successful lobbyist for legislative action in abolishing the so-called Illinois Black Codes, laws instituted in restricting full civil rights to black Illinois residents. In December 1863, Jones wrote Governor Andrew, "I would respectfully solicit permission to open correspondence with your authorities with a view to securing a contract for raising men in the West." Jones further maintained that "in connection with some able and influential colored men I am perfecting arrangements for recruiting our people which will doubtless be more successful than any yet adopted." Jones further reminded Andrew that he had assisted in recruiting men for the 54th and 55th Massachusetts Infantry regiments.[35]

Historian John D. Warner states in *Crossed Sabres* (1997) that there is no evidence that Andrew ever employed the recruiting services of John Jones.[36] Governor Andrew's refusal in authorizing Jones as a recruiter most likely was a direct result of the negative outcry it had on other states' recruiting efforts to obtain their own local African American population to serve and fill their state quotas. Along with this, there were potential violations of individual state recruitment laws.[37] The *Chicago Tribune* declared on December 23, 1863, in an article headlined "Illinois Colored Regiment," "We are informed that recruiting agents are still in this city picking up colored men for Rhode Island, Connecticut, and Michigan regiments, and that from six to fourteen men are recruited daily and shipped East on the night trains. Now, this is clearly in violation of the Governor's proclamation, forbidding the recruiting of men in Illinois for the States, which applies to blacks just the same as whites. Every man thus inveigled out of the State is counted as part of the quota of the State to which he is sent, and Illinois must make good the loss by taking some other man. This thing should be peremptorily stopped; the Provost Marshal should take steps to arrest and imprison those foreign agents." The *Chicago Tribune* opined, "After lying in the saw-dust a few nights and paying a bill of costs, perhaps their zeal to fill the quota of other States at the expense of Illinois, would cool off enough to induce them to keep within the

limits of the law, and to mind their own business."[38] Although not officially a recruiting agent of the 5th Massachusetts Cavalry, one must
assume that John Jones had rendered substantial influence throughout
Chicago and the states of the old Northwest Territories in directing
and assisting free blacks and fugitive slaves to venture east into Massachusetts to enlist in the cavalry regiment.

Furthermore, Governor Andrew at the outset of recruiting men
for the 54th Massachusetts Infantry in 1863 established a Black Committee to help in the recruitment and to provide financial assistance
in the organization of the unit. Andrew hand-selected a list of some of
the most ardent abolitionists and wealthiest entrepreneurs and busi-
nessmen, both black and white, within the state to actively assist in
allowing this regiment of color to succeed. Recalling the establishment
of the Black Committee, Captain Luis Emilio of the 54th Massachusetts
Infantry stated, "About February 15th [1863], Governor Andrew
appointed a committee to superintend the raising of recruits for the
colored regiment, consisting of George L. Stearns, Amos A. Lawrence,
John M. Forbes, William I. Bowditch, Le Baron Russell, and Richard P.
Hallowell, of Boston; Mayor Howland and James B. Congdon, of New
Bedford; William P. Phillips, of Salem; Francis G. Shaw, of New York."
Several of these committee members were of direct family relation to
many of the officers who would lead the 5th Massachusetts Cavalry.
Emilio further stresses that the committee was increased through
membership "to one hundred" and that it at that point became "known
as the 'Black Committee.'" Thus, as Emilio so aptly stated, "It was mainly
instrumental in procuring the men of the Fifty-Fourth and Fifty-Fifth
Massachusetts Infantry, the Fifth Massachusetts Cavalry, besides 3,967
other colored men credited to the state."[39]

Former slave and outspoken abolitionist Harriet Ann Jacobs, who
is most remembered for her 1861 autobiographical account *Incidents
in the Life of a Slave Girl*, speaks directly to this recruitment of men
into the ranks of the 5th Massachusetts Cavalry. Working outside
Washington, D.C., in Alexandria, Virginia, Harriet, along with her
daughter, Louisa Matilda Jacobs, was influential in establishing schools,
hospitals, and churches for the improvement of free people of color
and black refugees. Writing to fellow abolitionist Lydia Maria Francis
Child, who in 1861 wrote the preface and edited Harriets' autobiography, *Harriet*, on March 26, 1864, stated:

> We went to the wharf last Tuesday, to welcome the emigrants returned from Hayti
> [sic]. It was a bitter cold day, the snow was falling, and they were barefooted and

bareheaded, with scarcely rags enough to cover them. They were put in wagons and carried to Green Heights. We did what we could for them. I went to see them next day, and found that three had died during the night. I was grieved for their hard lot; but I comforted myself with the idea that this would put an end to colonization projects. They are eight miles from here, but I shall go to see them again tomorrow. I hope to obtain among them some recruits for the [5th] Massachusetts Cavalry. I am trying to help Mr. [George T.] Downing and Mr. [Charles L.] Remond; not for money, but because I want to do all I can to strengthen the hands of those who are battling for Freedom.[40]

Again, the *Massachusetts Soldiers, Sailors and Marines in the Civil War* acquaints us with a list of these diverse mixtures of enlisted men. Company A" listed Private Henry L. Brison, who was a seaman from Le Havre, France. He died at the age of twenty, just two months after he enlisted at Readville, Massachusetts. Farther down the roll is a nineteen-year-old Southern grocer, Private Henry N. Guice, who hailed from the interesting sounding locale of Waterproof, Louisiana. Also registered were Private Charles Waters, from Chicago, whose skill as a blacksmith would surely be needed in the horse cavalry. Company B logs Private Amos Cormac, who hailed from Gettysburg, Pennsylvania (contemplate the devastation he must have seen in his own community if he was in residence in July 1863). In May 1864, he enlisted with the regiment at the age of eighteen. Also noted is the name of William Williamson, a laborer, whose residence is stated as Halifax, Nova Scotia. Monroe Perez, a private in Company H, registered himself as a peddler from New York City.[41]

There were numerous sailors or seamen as they were referred to, that listed their residence from many far-off ports. Private John Frank of Company A and Private George Albert of Company C both came from the exotic Sandwich Islands (Hawaii). Private Charles Stuart, twenty-nine years old from Valparaiso, Chile, deserted June 15, 1865, at Norfolk, Virginia (one might wonder if he had hopped a ship at Norfolk to return to Chile.) Private John Doughty, twenty-seven, claimed to be from Mexico. Listed from the West Indies were Private Joseph Sullivan from Company "D," who was a seaman, and Private James Bash of Company F, who stated he was a cook.[42]

Then there was Private George Whitsel, a twenty-five-year-old teacher from Bellevue, Ohio, who was promoted to the position of hospital steward in September 1864. When he was mustered out on October 31, 1865, he held this non-commissioned officer rank. The medical position of a hospital steward bears evidence that Whitsel was an educated man.[43]

Included in Company F's ranks was Robert George Fitzgerald. Born October 24, 1840, in Newcastle County, Delaware, to Thomas Fitzgerald, a manumitted slave whose ethnicity was both of Irish and African extraction along with his wife, Sarah (Burton) Fitzgerald, Sarah being of Caucasian descent. At a young age the family would relocate to Chester County, Pennsylvania, where Robert's brothers, Richard and William, worked in their father's brickyard and Robert grew up attending the local Quaker School. In 1859, he would enroll in Ashmun Institute, later to be named Lincoln University, in Oxford, Pennsylvania. A noted classmate of Robert's was future Medal of Honor winner and veteran of the 4th Regiment United States Colored Infantry, Christian Abraham Fleetwood.[44]

At the outbreak of the Civil War, the Fitzgerald brothers, along with their father, sought to serve in any way they could, whether civilian or militarily, in preserving the Union and fighting for their right to freedom. They would be hired on as civilian contractors and teamsters working for the Philadelphia Quartermaster Department and ultimately serving throughout the Army of the Potomac's Virginia theater of war. As the war progressed throughout 1863 and into January 1864, Robert would serve a stint in the Union Navy aboard the U.S.S. *North Carolina* and U.S.S. *William G. Anderson*. While on the *Anderson*, Robert suffered a bout of blindness called amaurosis and was transferred to the supply ship U.S.S. *Circasian* to be sent to Boston, where he was admitted into Chelsea Naval Hospital. It was here that Robert Fitzgerald heard of the raising and recruiting of the 5th Massachusetts Cavalry. At twenty-three years of age he would leave the service of the United States Navy and on January 15, 1864, enlist into the newly formed Massachusetts cavalry regiment.[45]

Notwithstanding, Company I held one of the more noteworthy African American soldiers of the period. Private Charles R. Douglass was a nineteen-year-old printer from West Roxbury, Massachusetts. The son of prominent abolitionist Frederick Douglass, Charles had been transferred to the 5th Massachusetts Cavalry from the 54th Massachusetts Infantry where he had been continuously ill with lung complaints for most of his service. Massachusetts governor John A. Andrew intervened through Secretary of War Edwin M. Stanton to have Douglass transferred to the 5th Cavalry. Writing on March 14, 1864, Governor Andrew begged to request that:

> Private Charles F. Douglass of Company F, 54th Reg't Mass. Vol. Infty may be discharged from the service in order to enable him to reenlist and receive a First

Sergeant's warrant in the 5th Massachusetts Vol. Cavalry now raising here. C. F. Douglass is a son of Frederick Douglass. He, with a brother, enlisted in The 54th Mass. Infty, when that reg't was commenced early in 1863. Just before the reg't marched Charles was taken ill with lung complaints, and was in hospital here for several months. Since his recovery he has remained here on recruiting service, and has rendered valuable assistance in recruiting the 5th Mass. Cavalry.

By reason of his having been prevented by sickness from ever taking field with the 54th, and by reason of the influential position of his father among the colored people of the U.S. and the important aid and influence he has exerted in promoting colored military organizations, I present this application as entitled to special favor and I hope you may grant it.

Private Charles R. Douglass, son of abolitionist Frederick Douglass, had formerly served with the 54th Massachusetts Infantry prior to being transferred to the 5th. Douglass was granted the rank of 1st sergeant by special order of Secretary of War Edwin M. Stanton (James M. Gregory, *Frederick Douglass the Orator* [Springfield, MA: Wiley & Co., 1893]).

I request his discharge from the 54th Infty so that he may reenlist into the 5th cavalry, as avoiding the objections incident to requests for transfers.[46]

With Stanton's approval, Douglass was thus promoted to the rank of sergeant.[47]

Private Joseph Brunson of Company E was a free, educated Pennsylvanian from Indiana County who entered his occupation as farmer.[48] This occupation, being the most commonly quoted no matter what affiliation (White, African American, Federal or Confederate), was by much estimation the all-encompassing way of life in the 1860s. Prewar and wartime America was predominately a rural country. The Industrial Revolution had not come to fruition causing the great urbanization as in the post-war second industrial revolution society.[49] As previously stated, President Abraham Lincoln called for volunteers to defend the Union. Hundreds of men and boys from Indiana County joined regiments which would see combat on major battlefields in both Eastern and Western theaters. Brunson recalled his experience in enlisting into the military:

> ... after the death of my parents, I was taken to raise, by my Grandparents, George and Ellen Brunson, in Blairsville Pa. My Grandmother died in Blairsville Pa, in the spring of the year that I enlisted in the Fall, and my Grandfather died while I was in the service.
> ... before, and at the time of my enlistment, I made my Grandfather's home, my home ... at the time of my enlistment, there was a recruiting office in Blairsville, and a list of names of citizens of Blairsville, was being prepared, subject to draft, among which was my name, and I said to my Grandfather, that I was going to enlist, as I might be drafted anyhow, and he replied, that I was of age, and could do as I pleased, and that same evening, in company with about fifteen colored boys, I went up to Boston, where all of the company that I was with did enlist. So that, acting upon my Grandfather's word as authority, I enlisted as of the age of twenty-one...[50]

Two soldiers, Lewis and John Brunson, were most likely traveling in company with Joseph Brunson and the "fifteen colored boys." The *Massachusetts Soldiers, Sailors, and Marines in the Civil War* (1932), provides a regimental roster of the 5th Massachusetts Cavalry wherein it lists Lewis Brunson in Company E age 21, and Company I lists John Brunson, age 22. Although the regimental roster lists both as residing in Boston, their service records divulge that both Lewis and John Brunson hailed from Blairsville, Indiana County, Pennsylvania.[51]

Recruitment of enlisted men along with the commissioning of officers into the regiment continued in earnest as 1864 dawned. Men continued to steadily stream into Camp Meigs filling the needed quotas to effectively muster into service the first battalion of the regiment, comprising companies A, B, C and D.[52] In the early weeks of February, Colonel Russell was still receiving requests to fill his regiment with commissioned officers. A letter dated February 3rd from Concord, Massachusetts, arrived addressed to Russell from the noted Transcendentalist Ralph Waldo Emerson who was writing personally to Colonel Russell regarding the continued efforts to fill the regiment's compliment of officer commissions. Emerson in writing stated, "I beg leave to present to you the claims of Mr. Edward Bartlett of this town for such appointment." Emerson, being a close friend and acquaintance of Russell's father-in-law, John Murray Forbes, sought to assist the young Edward "Ned" Jarvis Bartlett in securing a commission. Emerson continues, "Mr. B. is son of our Dr. Josiah Bartlett; he was a private in Company F of the 44th Massachusetts, during its whole term of service.

Afterwards, he joined Major Geo. L. Stearns, & assisted him in his recruiting of negro soldiers in Tennessee."[53]

Edward Bartlett had enlisted in August 1862 with the 44th Massachusetts Militia. Throughout his nine month service he would see combat action in North Carolina. With the expiration of his term of service, in June 1863, he worked as a civilian recruiter in Philadelphia and by September of that year had secured a position in Nashville, Tennessee, under the guidance of George L. Stearns. Stearns had been given a commission as assistant adjutant general to recruit throughout the nation for the enlistment of colored soldiers into the newly forming Massachusetts infantry regiments by Governor John Andrew. Emerson in writing to Colonel Russell regarding Bartlett as a potential officer indicated, "The resignation of Major Stearns, who highly valued his [Bartlett's] service, & had charged him not to seek any other employment, leaves him now at liberty to re-enter the Army." Emerson closed by informing Russell that the young Bartlett "is known to me from his childhood for an excellent boy, & a favorite with his mates," adding that "he is an intelligent, well-educated, active young man, with hardy habits, & of great endurance. I have confidence that he will approve himself faithful to every duty."[54]

Edward Bartlett, although having backing by Emerson, did not receive the commission he was seeking in early 1864. Although he had previous military experience, it is probable that his commission was turned down due to the fact that he had no prior involvement as an officer or in the capacity of training and leading cavalry troops. Henry Russell having recently been forwarded a recommendation by Governor Andrew for another possible recruited officer, informed Governor Andrew by letter on the 17th of February that "when I tell you that I already have seventeen officers designate, not familiar with the cavalry arm, I hope you will allow me to fill the few remaining vacancies by deserving men from the cavalry regiments now in the field."[55] Edward Bartlett would go on to serve out nearly the rest of the year working for the United States Sanitary Commission in Washington, D.C.[56]

Throughout the early months of 1864, the unit's training was similar to any other Civil War cavalry regiment. They were made skilled in the art of combat through hours and hours of drill and inspection. They learned to ride and maneuver their horses in squads and in regimental formations using the latest cavalry tactics of the day, primarily Philip St. George Cooke's 1862 single rank cavalry tactics. A manual of instruction which stressed the single rank of maneuvering in column of fours, Cooke's tactics replaced the previous pre-war double rank structure. Also, the men trained in firing and cleaning their weapons properly and, above all, learned to be competent and well-disciplined military fighting men. As the companies began to fill their allotted quota of men, Company A received three months more training than the last company, M. Writing to the *Anglo-African* on April 24, Private Amos Webber shared his impression of life at Camp Meigs. He explained that the enlistee's overall health was "pretty good" and the "officers are much respected" among the men.[57] Captain Charles Bowditch, having taken command of Company F, noted his thoughts of the enlisted men and officers: "We went into camp at Readville, the same camp which we had occupied in the latter part of our stay there in the 55th [Massachusetts Infantry].... The men were by no means equal in character to those of the 54th and 55th, and the officers were not the same class in many cases as those of my old regiment."[58]

During hours away from drilling, members of the regiment sought out opportunities for relaxation as noted in the *Springfield Weekly Republican*: "The members of the 5th Massachusetts Cavalry (colored) encamped at Readville, have organized a debating club, and are discussing the important questions of the day with signal ability."[59] Camp Readville, with its close proximity to its numerous inhabitants of the greater Boston area, played host to many dignitaries and local citizens. On May 1, 1864, the regiment had the extreme pleasure of hearing an address from Massachusetts governor John Andrew. Andrew spoke on the facts relating to the bounty and monthly pay of colored soldiers, an issue that struck a very close chord in the hearts of the colored troops.

Previously, in 1863, the 54th Massachusetts along with men of the 55th Massachusetts Infantry had refused government pay until the discrepancy could be rectified. Historian Donald Yacovone, in addressing the struggle over equal payment and the refusal among colored troops writes in "The Fifty-Fourth Massachusetts Regiment, the Pay Crisis, and 'Lincoln Despotism,'" that colored soldiers were in essence fighting a two front war, one against the Confederacy for their freedom, but also against their own Federal government's refusal to provide equal rights in the form of equal pay. Yacovone not only cuts to the heart of what so many of the black soldiers believed and felt, but also succinctly states the sentiments expressed by the men in the 5th Massachusetts Cavalry: "Unequal pay struck at the heart of black motivation to serve, undermined their claims to equality, threatened the safety and lives of the soldiers' families, and imperiled black hopes for the postwar world."[60]

If the Federal government would not step up to the plate and remedy the issue, then Governor Andrew would work to implement legislation in the Commonwealth of Massachusetts to provide for a provision that would satisfy the concerns being waged by the men. Andrew proposed and successfully passed on November 16, 1863, "An Act to make up the Deficiencies in the Monthly Pay of the Fifty-fourth and Fifty-fifth Regiments." Section 1 of the act declared:

> There shall be paid, out of the Treasury of the Commonwealth, to the non-commissioned officers musicians and privates of the Fifty Fourth and Fifty Fifth Regiments of Massachusetts Volunteer Infantry, to those who have been honorably discharged from the service, and to the legal representatives of those who have died in the service, such sums of money, as, added to the amounts paid them by the United States, shall render their monthly pay and allowance from the time of their being mustered into service of the United States equal to that of the other non-commissioned officers, musicians and privates in the volunteer or regular military service of the United States."[61]

However, this was only a bandage placed upon a larger wound, a wound to the soldiers' pride and self-respect. One soldier in the 54th Massachusetts Infantry, when hearing of Governor Andrew's intention, wrote, "Imagine our surprise and disappointment on the receipt by the last mail ... to find him [Gov. Andrew] making a proposition to them to pay this regiment the difference between what the United States Government offers us and what they are legally bound to pay us, which, in effect, advertises us to the world as holding out for money and not from principle—that we sink our manhood in consideration of a few more dollars." He added, "What false friend has been misrepresenting us to the Governor, to make him think that our necessities outweigh our self-respect?"[62]

For the men of the 5th Massachusetts Cavalry, besides the matter of equal pay, there was also the matter of keeping one's word when it came to the payment of bounties. Previously, on January 14, 1864, eleven troopers within companies A, B and C took it upon themselves to boldly skirt around their chain of command and sign a petition related to the failure in receiving bounties paid to them as promised upon enlistment and directed their appeal straight to the desk of Governor Andrew. Upon opening the petition Governor Andrew read, "Your Honor, we the colored soldiers, composing the Fifth Massachusetts Cavalry do appeal unto you for information respecting our bounty money. We were informed by our Recruiting Officer that we were to receive our bounty as soon as we were mustered into U.S. Service, but we have found matters to be the contrary." The eleven men further expounded upon the reasons for pressing the terms laid out in receiving their bounty: "The reason why we want to know this, is because we want some time to dispose of it. We have families that are in utter need of it. We would like to know, if our families, residing out of the state, can receive the state aid of Massachusetts, by sending their affidavit."[63]

It seems that Governor Andrew deferred the communique back to Colonel Russell who most likely sent it to Colonel J.F.B. Marshall, paymaster of state bounties, for his review and decision. Upon reviewing the complaints filed by the men of the regiment Colonel Marshall instructed Colonel Russell that by authority of the Commonwealth of Massachusetts and the laws governing the payment of bounties he was revoking the request because "we [Paymaster's Department] do not feel disposed to relax any of our rules in their case, but rather to subject their orders to a closer scrutiny."[64] In other words, because there was no way to substantiate the claims provided by the enlisted recruits regarding whether or not recruiting agents promised payment in full at time of enlistment, the paymaster department was not inclined to further pursue the matter. Colonel Marshall further instructed Russell that he was informing the men of the regiment who had signed the petition that they "shall require either the endorsement of the city or town authorities or that of yourself, as Colonel of the regiment, before we can receive such orders."[65] Rather than dragging out the debate any further, as there was no way the enlisted men could at this point take leave from Camp Meigs to garner the needed endorsements, Colonel Russell took it upon himself to advance out of his own monthly pay the money requested by the men; Russell was reimbursed by the paymaster.[66]

Again in March the regiment was faced with further issues regarding the bounty pay. This time, however, it came in the form of Massachusetts adjutant general William Schouler writing to Governor Andrew that in a very short time two battalions of the 5th Massachusetts Cavalry would be fully mustered and ready for service. Furthermore, he had received a letter from L. H. Giles, a recruiter in Philadelphia who had recruited men for the regiment, enquiring as to when the men would be receiving their bounty pay. It seems that several family members of the enlisted men had confronted Giles regarding the payment as they were destitute and could not apply for Massachusetts state aid. Schouler recommended to Governor Andrew that the "pay rolls of the two battalions be made up, and the men paid."[67]

Colonel Russell feared that if the bounties were paid outright at time of enlistment rather than waiting after mustering the men into service, there was a chance that the men would take the money and run, increasing the chance of desertions and a failure to secure the needed quotas to form the regiment. Furthermore, Governor Andrew was receiving frequent letters from other recruiters besides L. H. Giles, such as Lewis Hayden. A former slave, agent on the Underground Railroad, abolitionist lecturer, and ardent supporter of Andrew, Hayden had been recruiting previously for the 54th and 55th Massachusetts regiments. Having recruited several men for the 5th Massachusetts Cavalry, Hayden informed the governor that he believed he was being dishonest and not totally forthright in what he was instructing the men upon signing the enlistment rolls. Having Massachusetts renege on furnishing the $325 bounties upon enlistment was deemed by many as blatantly disloyal and cut to the heart of the inequality faced by the colored soldiers. By not paying the bounty up front, it provided for a significant impact upon the recruiting and willingness of men to seek enlistment in Massachusetts.[68]

In the end, Governor Andrew held firm in keeping with the statutes stipulated under the November 18, 1863, "Act to provide for the Payment of Bounties to Volunteers and for other Purposes." The act provided that "the governor shall offer a bounty of three hundred and twenty-five dollars to each volunteer, who should enlist for three years or the war, and should duly be mustered into the service of the United States and credited to the quota of the Commonwealth." It further stipulated under section 3 that any volunteer could elect to decline the $325 dollar bounty for the receiving of "a bounty of fifty dollars, and twenty dollars monthly, so long as he shall remain in said service."[69] Undoubtedly, the unsettled issues stemming from unequal pay and bounties were on the minds of every soldier who assembled on May 1st to hear Andrew's thoughts. Private Robert Fitzgerald of Company F wrote in his diary that day regarding Andrew's oration, "I feel perfectly satisfied now. The regiment gave him nine rousing cheers as he walked down the line." Fitzgerald further related that he felt Governor Andrew was a "true patriotic man."[70]

Governor Andrew that day was not only addressing the men's concerns regarding soldier pay, but also had arrived to formally inspect the entire regiment. In less than a year Andrew was again, for the third time, addressing and ceremonially sending off to war a regiment of color. In a matter of days the men of the 5th Massachusetts Colored Cavalry would embark on their journey to prove to themselves and to the nation whether or not they would "make a soldier."

2

A Precarious Predicament

"When leaving Readville I was surprised to see a great many white people weeping as the train moved south and I have formed a firm conclusion that the people are our only true friends."
—Private Robert Fitzgerald

Many of the men who had grown accustomed to the pleasures of the city of Boston regretted the need to leave. Still others longed for a change of place and yearned to be at the front where they could prove their love of liberty and ability as fighting men. While the 5th Massachusetts Cavalry organized and trained throughout the early months of 1864, donations of food, clothing and money were received to aid the colored soldiers of Massachusetts. J. H. Stephenson, treasurer for the Sanitary Commission, provided an acknowledgment to the citizens of Massachusetts:

I have received, in aid of the Massachusetts Colored Volunteers, not heretofore acknowledged, the Following sums, viz:—

Miss Abby Francis, $20; Geo. C. Davis, 5; Mary G. Chapman, 5; A Friend, 4; W. W. Churchill, 25; Sam'l May, Jr., 5; Union League, Ward 11, 38.50; Mrs. Tebbets, 2; Allen Lane & Co., 20; J. A. Ordway, 5; Albert Davis, 5; D. B. Jewtt, 5; A Friend, 25; Pierce, Bros. & Co. 5; A Friend, 2; E. Allen & Co., 5; F. K. & Co. $10; Cash $5; Mrs. Sarah R. Russell, 50; cash, 5.

Also, from ladies of Newton, 66 pr. socks; J. J. May, 2 gross combs; Mrs. Theodore Parker, 25 books, 7 pr. socks; Mrs. P. T. Jackson, 5 doz. socks; Mrs. Waterston, 10 pr. socks; from Soldiers' Relief Society of Vine Street Church, Roxbury, a generous supply of socks; a Friend, 1 doz. socks; Mrs. E. D. Cheney, 12 pr. socks; a Friend, 1 doz. socks.

The committee have frequent calls from the brave soldiers of the 54th and 55th, and from their suffering families, and from the recruits of the 5th Mass. Cavalry, while their funds are nearly exhausted.[1]

An appeal to the public was announced in the May 13th issue of the *Liberator*:

It being a well-known fact that the brave men composing the 54th and 55th Regiments Mass. Vols. have, since they have been in their country's service, received no pay, and also that hundreds of them have fallen in defence of the American flag, leaving her in our midst their poor, suffering and destitute wives and children, the Colored Ladies of Massachusetts, knowing the urgent necessity there is, just at this time, of doing something for these suffering ones, are preparing to hold a Fair in this city at as early a day as possible, this being, in their judgment, the most practical method of accomplishing their object. Donations, either of goods or money, will be most thankfully received by the President, Madam Caryeaux Bannister, 31 Winter street, and the Treasurer, Rev. Mrs. Grimes, 28 Grove street. As we have just sent into the field another brave regiment, the 5th Cavalry, and their families are left with us, while their husbands, brothers and fathers have gone to uphold the honor of our flag, there will be a demand for all our friends may assist us in raising.[2]

With the culmination of many months of training, the first week of May brought orders for the regiment to proceed to Washington, D.C., and report to General Silas Casey. "The 5th Regiment of Massachusetts Colored Cavalry, mounted, armed, equipped, and ready for service, is organized, and embraces one thousand one hundred black men," wrote the abolitionist newspaper *Liberator* on Friday, May 13, 1864, adding:

The first battalion of this regiment reached New York Friday from Boston, and after remaining here a few hours, took its departure for Washington. More than two-thirds of those men were originally slaves, who escaped from slavery either before or since the outbreak of the Rebellion. They are skillful horsemen. Some of them acquired their skill in the management of horses while serving their master in the rebel service. Major H. [Horace] N. Weld, an officer of five years' experience in the Regular Army, and who participated in the Mexican war, has command of the 1st Battalion, comprising four of the twelve companies. The commanders of the companies are as follows: Company A, Capt A. R. [Albert] Howe; Company B, Cyrus Emery; Company C, Horace Welch; Company D, C. C. [Charles] Parson[s]. Most of the line officers are white men and have seen service. Col. H. S. [Henry Sturgis] Russell is commander of the regiment.[3]

The regimental officers who would lead these stalwart young fighting soldiers off to war were as follows:

Colonel Henry S. Russell, Boston
Major Horace N. Weld, Belmont
Major Zabdiel B. Adams, California
Major Henry P. Bowditch, Boston
Adjutant Daniel H. Chamberlain, Cambridge
1st Lieut. and Quartermaster Windsor Hatch, 2nd, Boston
Surgeon Harlow Gamwell, Huntington
Asst. Surgeon Frederick G. Parker, East Corinth, Maine

Company A
Captain Albert R. Howe, Boston
First Lieutenant James S. Newell, Boston
First Lieutenant Andrew F. Chapman
Second Lieutenant Robert M. Higginson, Boston
Second Lieutenant Henry R. Hinckley, Northampton

Company B
Captain Cyrus C. Emery, Roxbury
First Lieutenant Charles E. Allan, Louisville, Kentucky

Company C
Captain Horace B. Welch, San Francisco, California
First Lieutenant John Anderson, San Francisco, California
Second Lieutenant George B. Farnsworth, Roxbury

Company D
Captain Charles C. Parsons, Cambridge
First Lieutenant Jacob B. Cook, Charlestown

Company E
Captain James L. Wheat, Roxbury
Second Lieutenant George A. Fisher, Cambridge

Company F
Captain Charles P. Bowditch, Boston
First Lieutenant Abner R. Mallory, Roxbury
Second Lieutenant Curtis H. Whittemore, Boston

Company G
Captain Hiram E. W. Clark, New Salem
First Lieutenant Edgar M. Blanch, Pennsylvania
Second Lieutenant Rienzi Loud, Michigan

Company H
Captain Peter J. Rooney, Boston
First Lieutenant J. Davenport Fisher, Boston
Second Lieutenant John G. S. White, Boston
Second Lieutenant George A. Rogers, Roxbury

Company I
Captain Erick Wulff, Boston
First Lieutenant Patrick T. Jackson, Boston
Second Lieutenant George F. Wilson, San Francisco, California

Company K
    Captain Francis L. Higginson, Boston
    First Lieutenant George D. Odell, Sanbornton, New Hampshire
    Second Lieutenant Abram O. Swain, Boston

Company L
    First Lieutenant Francis L. Gilman, New Bedford
    First Lieutenant Edward H. Adams, Boston
    Second Lieutenant Curt Gurdsdorff, San Francisco, California

Company M
    Captain Cornelius Kaler, Bradford
    Second Lieutenant Robert M. Parker, San Francisco, California[4]

With this, the 1st Battalion consisting of 13 commissioned officers and 266 men under the command of Major Horace N. Weld, comprising companies A, B, C, and D having been mustered into service in January, moved to Washington, D. C., on May 5–8th. Next the battalion moved to Camp Stoneman, Giesboro Point, Maryland, on May 8–12th. It then dismounted and was relocated to Camp Casey, near Fort Albany, May 12th. The 2nd Battalion under Major Zabdiel B. Adams, composed of 13 commissioned officers and 308 men, comprising companies E, F, G and H having been mustered into service throughout February and March, moved to Washington May 6–8th and then on to Camp Casey May 9th. Likewise, the 3rd Battalion, 11 commissioned officers and 319 men, under Major Henry P. Bowditch, comprising companies I, K, L and M having been mustered into service in May, moved to Washington May 8–10th and to Camp Casey May 11, 1864.[5]

Camp Casey lay two miles from Long Bridge on the Virginia side of the Potomac River, near Fort Albany. The encampment was named in honor of Major General Silas M. Casey, who is best known for his three volume publication *System of Infantry Tactics* along with *Infantry Tactics for Colored Troops*, published in 1862 and 1863 respectively. Fort Albany, like all of the earthen fortifications around the Union capital, was for the purpose of defending Washington, D.C., and its vital supply routes from an attack.[6] On May 6th, Private Robert Fitzgerald expressed his remorse about parting ways with the friends he and the unit had made in Boston, "When leaving Readville I was surprised to see a great many white people weeping as the train moved south and I have formed a firm conclusion that the people are our only true friends."[7] Captain Charles Bowditch wrote his mother, "After our departure from Readville everything went along quietly till we got to New London [Connecticut], where we had to wait from six till two in the morning before we started. Then at New York they were entirely unaware of our coming, and we had to wait awhile there, so that we did not get to Philadelphia till six or seven Saturday night, and by a series of delays we arrived at Washington on Sunday morning."[8]

As the regiment proceeded to make its travel towards the seat of the Virginia theater of operations, it found respite in its journey at a two story brick building on Otsego Street in the heart of Philadelphia. Established within fifty yards of the rail lines along the terminus for arriving and departing Union soldiers, the Cooper Shop Volunteer Saloon beckoned its weary travelers with savory delights of "hams, corned beef, Bologna sausage, bread made of the finest wheat, butter of the best quality, cheese, pepper-sauce, beets, pickles, dried beef, coffee and tea, and vegetables."[9] Here between May 7th and 9th both the enlisted men and officers of the 5th Massachusetts Cavalry partook of the Cooper Shop. Captain Charles Bowditch recalled, "In Philadelphia we went to the Soldiers' Rest and got a jolly good supper and wash and in the morning we had breakfast in Baltimore. While we remained in Washington we were also fed at a Soldiers' Rest. They are great institutions, very refreshing indeed."[10]

Briefly stopping in Baltimore on their way to Washington the regiment found relaxation at the Union Relief and Soldiers' Rest Rooms. The establishment was located near Camden Hospital and the B & O Railroad terminus near the intersection of Eutaw and Conway streets (today being the current vicinity of the Baltimore Orioles' Camden Yards). Here was witnessed an incident involving Captain Erick Wulff of Company I along with several soldiers under his command, resulting in the fatal shooting of Private Albert White. Erick Wulff was a native of Sweden; he was born in 1837 and lived in Plymouth, Massachusetts. Just like many of the officers commissioned into the regiment, Wulff had previous military service during the war. That service, however, was by all accounts lackluster as indicated in his military service records along with personal letters written by men who served alongside him. One may even conclude that Captain Wulff had a knack for shirking his duties and working the system to his advantage.[11]

Enlisting as a private in Company I, 20th Massachusetts Infantry, Wulff only served from August 13th until October 15, 1862, when he was discharged from the regiment. Henry Livermore Abbott, commanding officer of Company I of the 20th Massachusetts, sent word

Philadelphia Refreshment Saloon volunteer recognition certificate awarded to Miss Susanne Filer on September 15, 1862. Captain Charles Bowditch recalled, "In Philadelphia we went to the Soldiers' Rest and got a jolly good supper and wash and in the morning we had breakfast in Baltimore. While we remained in Washington we were also fed at a Soldiers' Rest. They are great institutions, very refreshing indeed" (author's collection).

to his mother in December 1862 regarding Wulff, writing, "My Dear Mamma, I forgot ... in each of my last letters to tell you about Wolf, & so I write this in order that you people at home may no longer remain in ignorance of the fellow's character." Providing his mother with a comparison to another private in the company, Private Francis V. Balch, who by his estimation was a model soldier, Abbott continued, "He can't plead ignorance of what a private's life is, especially if, as he claims, he was an officer before, because I warned him before he enlisted & told him he'd better not do it." Abbott further explains, "He is a mere flighty, flashy, foreigner, all in a blaze one moment & then dying out. Instead of buckling manfully to his work, Alley [2nd Lieut. Leander Alley], after long indulgence, was obliged to reprimand him for having the dirtiest gun in the company, & he was actually caught hiring another man to do his police work, a court-martial offense. Instead of, Balch, taking his private's position fairly, he [Wulff] was always trying to intrude himself on officers, & giving the men an idea that although nominally a private, he was, in fact, altogether differently situated from them."[12]

Wulff, having by October 1862 secured a discharge from the War Department, left Henry Abbott in a feeling of astonishment and outright disgust, exclaiming to his mother, "What do you think of a man who comes clear over here from Sweden to fight his way up from the ranks, win military glory, & battle for the right, &c &c, takes $150 bounty (Balch didn't) & then, after two months' duty, or shirking of duty, gets his discharge because he happens to be a gentleman? He can't suppose the town of Plymouth meant to pay him $150 or $200 for two months' service." Abbott's blood must have been up, as he concluded, "And now by the merest favoritism of the Washington government, he has fairly got his discharge, instead of being contented with getting out of the scrape & pocketing the $150 bounty & the money that several officers were fools enough to lend him, he actually has the cheek to send for his final statement order that he may get his pay."[13]

Now back in civilian life, Erick Wulff, with the forming of the 54th Massachusetts Infantry through Special Order #108 of the state of Massachusetts, obtained a commission as 2nd lieutenant in February 1863, whereupon he was promoted to 1st lieutenant one month later. On May 27, 1863, the 54th Massachusetts was preparing to embark on its journey to begin its service in South Carolina. Wulff was, by Colonel Shaw's request, left to remain in Massachusetts detached to staff duty at Camp Meigs. He was instructed to specifically report for orders for the "purpose of arresting deserters from his [Shaw's] regiment." Thus, from June 1863 until the forming of the 5th Massachusetts Cavalry in late December, Erick Wulff was assigned to the staff of Brig. General R. A. Pierce, assistant quartermaster general of Massachusetts and commandant of Camp Meigs.[14]

On January 12, 1864, General Pierce informed Colonel Hallowell of the 54th Massachusetts that Lieutenant Wulff was "ordered by Governor Andrew to report to Col. Russell 5th Mass Cavalry for recruiting service." On March 17, 1864, by order of the War Department, Wulff was formally discharged from service with the 54th Massachusetts where upon he was mustered in as captain of Company I, 5th Massachusetts Cavalry, on March 26, 1864.[15]

Charles Douglass in writing to his father, weeks after the shooting incident in Baltimore, provided, as will be seen by other accounts, details not only regarding the occurrence but also somewhat of a conflicting report. Douglass wrote, "Lew spoke of Captain Wulff shooting a man he did in Baltimore the way it happened is this he ordered all to fall in line which we did except Sergeant [Amos F.] Jackson he stayed out, he was a little drunk but not drunk enough to not know what was right. The captain fell us in to tell us that he was agoing to let us go around and if we were insulted to go in with a will and defend ourselves, so turning around he saw Jackson out of the ranks. He merely took him by the arm and told him to keep in the ranks when Jackson cursed him, the Captain then ordered him to take off his stripes which he refused to do and to let anybody else do he said if they took off his stripes that he would have to be shot first. The Captain then said I will shoot you then and immediately drew his revolver and shot at Jackson's head, Jackson dodged his head and the ball passed through the heart of Albert White, the one H. O. Waggoner brought out of bondage no more at present."[16]

Douglass' letter provides a greater understanding of the individuals involved. For instance, in the altercation Captain Wulff confronted Private Amos Fields Jackson. Jackson was born in Haddam, Connecticut, and was working as a farmer when he enlisted at West Brookfield, Massachusetts, February 29, 1864, having mustered into service March 26th. It seems that Jackson had been given the rank of sergeant; however, he was not officially mustered in under the rank as indicated in his service records. Furthermore, Albert White was twenty-eight years old, born in Platte County, Missouri, and was recorded as a farmer when he enlisted into the regiment March 11, 1864.[17]

Charles Douglass notes that the man H. O. Waggoner had "brought out of bondage" was Albert White. Henry O. Waggoner, or Wagoner, was born in Hagerstown, Maryland, on February 27, 1816, to a free African American mother and a father of German descent. Primarily self-educated, he was regarded as one of the leading spokesmen for the African American community and the abolition of slavery. By the 1850s Wagoner had established himself as an owner of a saw mill in Chicago, Illinois. While residing in Chicago he befriended men like John Jones and Allan Pinkerton. Along with being hired by Frederick Douglass to be his Chicago correspondent of the Rochester, New York, newspaper *North Star*, Wagoner became well-acquainted with the radical abolitionist John Brown. During one of Brown's raids into Missouri in December 1858, Brown was successful in freeing eleven slaves. Traveling through Chicago on their escape east to Canada, Brown harbored his band of freed slaves in Henry O. Wagoner's saw mill. Wagoner's mill was destroyed by fire in 1860, prompting him to relocate to Denver, Colorado, for a year where he took up his abolitionist cause. Wagoner then returned to Chicago where Illinois governor Yates appointed him to recruit for the 29th United States Colored Troops. Governor Andrew also called upon Wagoner to recruit men for the 5th Massachusetts Cavalry, Albert White being one of those enlistees.[18]

Douglass' letter was not the only account provided in regard to the shooting incident. Found among Private Albert White's military service records is an unattributed newspaper clipping, possibly from the *Baltimore Sun*, providing further knowledge of the shooting which took place at the soldiers rest. It states, "It appears that a battalion of the 5th Massachusetts Cavalry (colored troops) reached this city yesterday, and were marched to the Soldier's Rest to obtain refreshments. Co. I, commanded by Capt. Wolfe, was drawn up in line in the yard of the Rest building, and Capt. Wolfe approached the orderly sergeant of the company and ordered him into line, &c. Some words ensued between the orderly sergeant (who is a colored man) and Capt. Wolfe, when the latter drew his revolver and fired at him. The ball missed the sergeant, but struck a private in the company, John Johnson, killing him almost instantly." Although misidentifying the private who was killed, the newspaper successfully furnished information regarding what happened immediately following the discharge of Captain Wulff's pistol: "The ball entered near the region of the heart. The dead soldier was carried to the Camden Street Hospital, from whence he was buried. The affair was fully reported to the military authorities, who have taken the proper steps in the matter. Capt. Wolfe with the battalion subsequently left the city, *en route* to their destination."[19]

The matter did not merely go away once the battalion, along with Captain Wulff, proceeded to Washington. Between the months of June and July orders were sent between the Adjutant General's Office, Washington, D.C., referring the matter to Major General Lew Wallace, commanding the Middle Department, headquartered in Baltimore, "for thorough investigation and full report." Furthermore, Assistant Adjutant General of Volunteers Charles W. Foster requested an investigation and report from Major General Christopher C. Augur, which implicated Captain Wulff to be the probable officer responsible for the alleged shooting. Part of the service record of Captain Wulff is a collection of statements provided by many of the enlisted men and officers who were witnesses to the shooting of Albert White.[20]

"I was present at the time in the yard of the 'Soldier's Rest' in Baltimore on the 11th of May last at about 11 o'clock a.m.," reported Joseph T. Cook in his witness affidavit. According to Cook's recollection, Company I was "in the yard waiting for orders." He follows with a detailed accounting of the incident:

> Captain Wulff came in to the yard very much intoxicated. Sergt. Jackson was then looking at some pictures. Captain Wulff ordered the company to fall in. Sergt. Jackson continued looking at his pictures. Capt. Wulff took hold of him, jerked him round and ordered him to fall in. Jackson said he must not take hold of him he had been pulling the man round long enough. Capt. Wulff called for a knife to cut off his chevrons Jackson said he would be Goddamned if he could cut off his chevrons without carrying him to the adjutant. Capt. Wulff then called Daniel Lee a private [a 27-year-old from Medford, Massachusetts] of the company and told him to cut them off. Jackson said no God damned man of the company could take them off. Capt. Wulff repeated his order to cut them off. Jackson said he would have to shoot him before he could take them off. Capt. Wulff said that then he would shoot him. He then drew his revolver, cocked it and levelled it at him. Jackson struck it aside, it went off, and the ball went through the breast of Albert White a private of the company who was standing in the ranks about six or eight feet off. He staggered about six paces and fell dead. Jackson then submitted and Private Daniel Lee cut off his chevrons. Jackson then fell into the ranks as a private. Jackson was very much intoxicated during this time. Nothing further was done with him. Capt. Wulff staid [sic] with the body a few minutes. The company was then marched to the Depot under command of 1st Lieut. Jackson [Patrick T. Jackson] and left for Washington. I staid [sic] with the body long enough to take a memorandum of the effects of White which were taken possession of by Sergt. [James T.] Wormley. Capt. Wulff joined the company at the Depot. The body of White was delivered to the Provost Marshall.[21]

Besides Joseph Cook's account, five other men—Sergeants Richard Johnson and George R. Johnson along with Corporals Henry Tillman and Charles Offord, and Private William Harris, all members of Company I, claimed and swore to the above affidavit. Furthermore, 1st Lieutenant Patrick T. Jackson, in providing his sworn affidavit, stated, "I went out into the yard of the Soldiers Rest immediately after the pistol was fired by Capt. Wulff." Lieutenant Jackson further recounted:

> The adjutant had just told me that the company was to start. I saw Capt. Wulff standing with his pistol in his hand. The men were gathered around the body of White. I ordered them to fall in. Capt. Wulff came up to me and said he was in command of the company. I told him I had received orders from the Adjutant to have the company fall in. Major Bowditch ordered me to take the company to the Depot and ordered Capt. Wulff to stay with the body of White. Capt. Wulff rejoined the company at the Rail Road Station. Capt. Wulff appeared to be intoxicated he was in habit of drinking too much.[22]

Accordingly, Major Henry P. Bowditch supported and swore to the same affidavit which Lieutenant Jackson provided. Discrepancies exist in the recording of Private White's cause and date of death. In several instances Private White's service records list his cause of death as "Accidentally shot dead in Baltimore, Md.," with dates ranging from May 10th through May 12th. Filed among the records is a form entitled "Record of Death and Internment" recorded by the Camden Hospital stating that the soldier was "Unknown, name supposed to be John Johnson" along with the note that "Supposed to be Private Co. I 5th Mass. Colored Cavalry" with further indication that he was buried in grave "No. 96 Laurel Park."[23]

In the end, according to records, neither Amos Jackson nor Captain Wulff were charged with a crime or act of insubordination; based on Jackson's military record he remained a private in the ranks when the regiment embarked for the Virginia front. Captain Wulff, on the other hand, might have been feeling pressure by higher authorities investigating the incident or among the ranks of Company I, because on June 5th, he wrote to Major General Benjamin F. Butler, commanding the Department of Virginia and North Carolina, tendering his resignation. However, his reason for resigning was "that having left my native country, Sweden, nearly two years since with the design of gaining experience in the Army of the United States, and having already remained in this country much longer than I originally purposed." Wulff further added that his country was at that moment in a war and his service to his country was in his opinion greatly needed. General Butler by Special Orders #181 dated July 6, 1864, accepted Wulff's resignation.[24]

It had been little more than a month since he resigned his position with the 5th Massachusetts Cavalry when, on August 16th, Erick Wulff, not having returned to Sweden, sent a letter to Major General George G. Meade, commander of the Army of the Potomac, saying, "Sir, I have the honor to apply for the position of Volunteer Aide-de-Camp on your staff." Wulff further writes:

> I am a regularly educated Officer of the Swedish Army, and have served in the Army of the United States for two years past—till I resigned my position as a Captain of the 5th Mass. Cav., for the purpose of going home, to accept a Commission in the Danish Army, at the time fighting against Germany, for the very existence of Denmark as an independent kingdom. Peace is now very soon to be declared between Denmark and Germany; my service will not be needed there. Being very desirous to learn as much as possible, of the Military Art, in your great Army, before I, at the end of the present year, return to my native country, I take the liberty of introducing upon you with this my application. Colonel E.D. Townsend A.A.G. has kindly promised to write to you in my behalf.[25]

General Meade must have wondered who this young former captain was inquiring into a position on his staff. Meade received a communication from Edward D. Townsend at the Adjutant Generals Office in Washington, D.C., on August 22nd. Townsend informed Meade, "The statement of the Swedish officer who writes the enclosed letter agrees with our records. I do not know him, but he appears to be gentlemanly and a good officer." However, Townsend further goes on to state the matter regarding the shooting of Albert White, informing Meade that according to the enlisted men he was intoxicated but that based on Wulff's "own statement is that his regiment in passing through Baltimore to the south was very mutinous and that he intended to shoot the first sergeant for the open mutinous conduct, resistance and disobedience of his orders." Townsend further imparts a brief accounting of the shooting and closes by stating that "the only difference in the official statement and his own is in the coloring given to the facts, he maintaining that he only did right in trying to suppress the mutinous spirit owing as he says from the men not having been paid; and the official statement imparting his cause to intoxication of himself and the sergeant." It seems General Meade had heard enough information to conclude that Captain Wulff would not be granted a position upon his staff.[26]

The journey to Washington, D. C., was proving to be very eventful for the 5th Massachusetts Cavalry. On May 8th, the Second Battalion, consisting of companies E, F, G, and H, having left Baltimore at eleven in the morning and being within twenty miles of Washington, found itself in a precarious predicament: a major, life-threatening train derailment. Private Fitzgerald explained as he wrote in his diary that evening, "A bundle belonging to our company fell on the track and threw the wheels off and a dreadful smashup which I escaped only by a miracle. I was thrown from the car down an embankment and then into a gutter ... but none [soldiers] was killed. Three cars were knocked all up and pushed from the track, arrived in Washington at six o'clock."[27] The men, along with their baggage and equipment, were loaded into seven rail cars for the journey from Baltimore to Washington. Charles Bowditch in writing to his mother recollected, "Our battalion was placed in seven covered cars (common baggage cars fitted with seats lengthwise) and mighty old cars at that. This made about forty men to a car, which crowded them so that many got on top. Every thing went serenely till about twenty miles from Washington when the axle of the forward wheels of the car which contained my men broke in halves and being pushed back tore off the trucks and wheels of other cars, smashing up two behind and one in front."[28]

Having come out of the derailment unscathed, Charles Bowditch, Private Robert Fitzgerald, and the rest of the second battalion gathered themselves along the tracks. Bowditch recalled that "no one was killed, though about a dozen got their joints sprained and faces cut," gratefully noting, "It was the luckiest escape I ever knew." The battalion took to working on clearing the tracks to continue their travels south. Bowditch, in explaining to his mother the scene of wreckage that faced the men, wrote, "Here were 150 men in the four cars, two of which were piled up over the broken wheels and trucks, while another was resting flat on the ground with no wheels at all and no one seriously injured," adding, "We set to work in a little while and in a couple of hours we had cleared the tracks and were on our way to Washington, where we passed the night."[29]

"We are allowed nothing but shelter tents here though there is a prospect of the officers living in barracks," Captain Bowditch described in writing to his mother on the 10th of May, further observing, "There are at present some 1200 men in camp here (all colored) besides our own. They are the most undisciplined mob I ever saw. They have no more respect for officers than nothing at all. I have not seen more than a couple of men salute since I have been here. The officers are about as bad."[30] Now the regiment had established itself and started the process of settling into camp life at Camp Casey outside of Washington. Although Henry Russell retained his title as colonel of the 5th Massachusetts Cavalry, Russell was given command of the provisional brigade of colored troops. Having moved up to command the brigade, Major Horace N. Weld thus took charge of the regiment in his absence.[31] In writing a letter from Arlington Heights, Virginia, on May 10th Charles Bowditch quipped to his mother, "Just think of our being here in Camp Casey, turned into infantry and about to drill in Casey's tactics. Horrid isn't it? It is all very well to die for one's country but to be turned from cavalry to infantry for one's country is a very different thing." Bowditch further remarked, "It is merely a temporary arrangement however, to last only while all the troops are fighting big battles at the front and to prevent any untimely guerrilla raid in the rear."[32]

Captain Charles Bowditch along with Major Zabdiel B. Adams and Captain Hiram E. Clark began the process of establishing and staking out the arrangement of the cavalry camp. "We have got a very nice camping ground with a gentle slope and large enough for ten companies," Captain Bowditch stated in describing the appearance of the camp, further remarking that, "We staked the whole camp out, and I tell you, when it is finished, will make a mighty nice appearance. Our camp here is about three miles from Washington over Long Bridge." Bowditch further expounded, "I have found out the advantage of having a full complement of officers. The day we started I was pitched on to supply the officer of the Day and Adjutant of the battalion from my company, just because I had three officers. Now Mr. Mallory [1st Lieutenant Abner T. Mallory] is acting as Quartermaster and Mr. Whittemore [2nd Lieutenant Curtis H. Whittemore] as Adjutant and I am left alone. However, it will last till the other battalion comes."[33]

The 12th day of May dawned cold and rainy as the entire regiment encamped on Arlington Heights outside the capital. On this day, Franklin Jennings, at age 26, was living in Washington, D.C. He, like forty-nine other men, was recruited while the regiment was stationed at Camp Casey, Jennings mustering into Company B. Jennings' life story is an extraordinary parallel of American history and deserving of a full account here.

In 1799 a slave, Paul Jennings, was born at Montpelier, Orange County, Virginia, the estate owned by the fourth president of the United States, James Madison. As a young boy, Paul Jennings would take on the role of being a life-long personal servant to Madison and accompany the newly elected president and his wife, Dolley, to the White House in 1809. In 1814, during Madison's second term and at the height of the war with Britain, Jennings, at the age of fifteen, was witness to the flames engulfing the White House as British troops ransacked

Washington, D.C. Jennings would be instrumental in assisting Dolley Madison with saving the famous Gilbert Stuart painting of George Washington.[34]

Paul Jennings would later marry Fanny Gordon, a slave, in 1822. To this union three sons John, Franklin, and William were born. Later in life, Fanny would succumb to illness and die August 4, 1844. That same week Dolley Madison, facing financial ruin, sold Montpelier, including the slaves on the property. In 1845, Jennings' freedom would be bought from none other than the noted orator and statesman Daniel Webster. Jennings would establish his residency in Washington, D.C., among other former slaves of ex-presidents Washington and Jefferson. Later in life, Paul Jennings would author and publish *A Colored Man's Reminiscences of James Madison* (1865), noted for being the first White House memoir. With the selling of Montpelier and the death of wife Fanny, Paul Jennings' children were sold to Charles Howard, of Howard Place in Orange County, Virginia. Jennings would visit and reacquaint with his children often on the estate. Ultimately, on January 16, 1856, Charles Howard would manumit and emancipate Franklin Jennings, the last slave he would free before dying two months later.[35]

With the authorization to enlist African Americans to fight in the Union army, Franklin along with his other two brothers, John and William, sought enlistments in regiments of color. Franklin's oldest brother, John, was working as a laborer in Greenfield, Highland County, Ohio, when he enlisted July 7, 1863, and mustered into Company E, 127th Ohio Volunteer Infantry, later to be reauthorized as the 5th United States Colored Troops. William, the youngest of the Jennings brothers, was working as a waiter in Philadelphia when he enlisted February 25, 1865, into the 24th United States Colored Troops.[36] Franklin, a free man for nine years, now joined the fight to release others still in bondage. He fell in as a private with the 5th Massachusetts Colored Cavalry as the unit prepared to depart the capitol.

Having stayed but a few days at Arlington Heights, Virginia, with the three battalions organized into one complete regimental force, the 5th Massachusetts Cavalry was directed by orders from Major General Silas Casey, commanding the Department of Washington, to turn in all horse equipment and be armed and equipped as infantry with orders to report to Fort Monroe, Virginia, May 13th by way of Alexandria, Virginia, aboard the steamer *Webster*.[37] "Raining this morning our tents afford but little shelter from the rain, it beats through, our things are all soaked," recalled Private Fitzgerald. "The regiment moves today we have turned our sabers in and are to be used as infantry for thirty or probably sixty days. 6 P. M. are now at Alexandria, Virginia, were [sic] we take ship.'[38] The *Boston Daily Advertiser* published May 20, 1864, the following account provided by the war correspondence of the *New Bedford Mercury*:

> The Fifth Massachusetts Cavalry.
> [Correspondence of the New Bedford Mercury.]
>   On Board Transport Webster,
>   On the Potomac, May 14.
> The 5th Mass. Cavalry left Camp Meigs, Readville, by rail for Washington in battalions. The first started May 5th, and arrived in Washington safely on the 7th. The second left on the 6th and arrived on the 8th. This battalion was not as fortunate as the first, an accident occurring on the Baltimore and Ohio Railroad, injuring fourteen men. There is great need of a double track on this road, as there is a vast amount of transportation to our capital. The third battalion left camp on the 8th and arrived in Washington on the 10th: one man was accidentally shot dead while in Baltimore. There were only two cases of desertion from our regiment: one man jumped from the cars while they were going twenty miles an hour.
> Every where [sic] on the route we were cheered in a most fantastic manner: on the whole we had a pleasant journey. I must not forget to mention our kind treatment in Baltimore and Philadelphia, where they had bountiful refreshments for us, as they do indeed for all soldiers passing through their cities, thus showing a true patriotic spirit.
> The first battalion, the only one having received horses before leaving Readville, were soon dismounted after reaching Washington. The whole regiment are now armed with muskets. It is hard to convince the men that government has not broken faith in enlisting them for cavalry and then making infantry of them; it does appear like injustice at first thought, but a few moment's reflection of the emergency in so doing. I am very happy to say, that the officers take this view of it, and are determined to do their best under the present circumstances, trusting the government will equip them as cavalry when the present emergency is over. Most of the officers have been in the government service and are not acquainted with infantry tactics. It has been the wish of the friends of the regiment to make it one of great efficiency and no expense has been spared to accomplish this object. No one appears as much disappointed as our Colonel (H.S. Russell) who has been very active during the war. He was taken prisoner at the battle of Cedar Mountain, and in the Libby Prison several weeks. The regiment went into camp called Camp Casey, about four miles from W [Washington, D.C.] and remained two and a half days. We were then ordered to Fortress Monroe for orders and shall probably proceed up the James river. Our passage has been very pleasant thus far: we are in company with a portion of Col. Baker's Independent cavalry, three companies of which, are now in the battle-field under Gen. Meade. The portion of it with us are from the State of Maine. They are armed with Henry's patent carbine, capable of firing sixteen shots without reloading. You will hear good account of them when engaged in a fight.'[39]

   Major General Benjamin Butler's Army of the James had previously on May 5th begun its campaign against Richmond, Virginia, from the southeast along the peninsula between the James and Appomattox rivers. Butler informed General Grant at 9 o'clock on the evening of the 5th from City Point, Virginia, "We have seized Wilson's Wharf, landing a brigade of Wild's colored troops there; Fort Powhatan, landing two regiments of same brigade. Have landed at City Point Hincks' division of colored troops, remaining brigades and battery." Butler goes on to state that the Eighteenth and Tenth Corps were in the process of off-loading men and supplies at Bermuda Hundred, north of the Appomattox River and that it had been "apparently a complete surprise" to the enemy as no opposition was encountered.[40] Having received no news from General Grant, Butler wired Secretary of War Stanton on May 7th requesting that if General Grant "has been in any degree successful, then can we not have here 10,000 of the reserves? They can be here in ten days after the lieutenant-general gives the order. Transportation is at Annapolis for them. If the Army of the Potomac is unsuccessful, then we want them here for the safety of our country. Please send them forward."[41] Stanton wired back to Butler that nothing was known regarding the situation with General Grant other then what was being published in the newspapers. He informed Butler regarding his request for reinforcements from the reserves that "there are none at the disposal of the Department. General Grant has with him all the troops, and you will have to depend only upon such as may have been provided in your programme with him." Stanton assured Butler however, that his dispatch "will be forwarded to him to appraise him of your condition and for his instructions."[42]

With encouraging prospects by General Butler's two corps in advancing upon Richmond from the southeast while General Grant was occupying and contending with General Lee's forces near Spotsylvania Court House, Grant advised Major General Henry Halleck back in Washington, "If matters are still favorable with Butler send him all the re-enforcements you can. The enemy are now moving from our immediate front either to interpose between us and Fredericksburg or to get the inside road to Richmond. My movements are terribly embarrassed by our immense wagon train. It could not be avoided however."[43] In response, Halleck wired General Butler on May 12th, "The Fifth Massachusetts Colored Regiment (about 1,200 men) and the First Connecticut Heavy Artillery, Colonel Abbot (about 1,800 men), have been ordered to report to you at Bermuda Landing. Colonel Abbot's regiment has been designated by General Grant for a special service, and, in the mean time, will be used by you to hold your defenses, but will

City Point, Virginia. City Point was the key stepping off point for Union troops in the opening campaign against Petersburg, Virginia (Library of Congress Prints and Photographs Division Washington, D.C. LC-DIG-cwpb-01855).

not be sent into the field, as the lieutenant-general may, at any moment, order them to be detached for special service."[44]

Upon arriving at Fortress Monroe May 15th, the 5th Massachusetts Cavalry was immediately sent to City Point on the James River, arriving the next day. City Point, Virginia, located at the junction of the James and Appomattox rivers, is approximately eight miles northeast of Petersburg, Virginia. City Point was the key stepping-off point for Union troops in the advance on Petersburg. Here, upon Doctor Richard Eppes' ancestral plantation home, Appomattox Manor, General Ulysses S. Grant established his headquarters during the winter of 1864 to 1865. Upon its arrival, the 5th Regiment Massachusetts Volunteer Cavalry (Colored) was assigned to Edward W. Hinks' (3rd) Division, William F. Smith's (18th) Corps.[45]

While stationed in and around what has become known as the Bermuda Hundred of Virginia, a geographical area south of Richmond and north of Petersburg, the 5th Massachusetts Cavalry was engaged in reconnoitering expeditions and on picket duty during the latter part of May and early weeks of June 1864. Unfortunately, picket duty was a very necessary but annoying duty to have been detailed for in the military. They were the soldiers ordered to stand guard outside the perimeter of an encamped army as a first line of defense against attack. In effect, it would be the 5th Massachusetts Cavalry's duty to picket along the roads and forests near the route of the armies' line of march to protect it from enemy attack. Writing to his father from City Point, Virginia, May 23rd, Captain Bowditch communicated, "Dear Father— For a little while at any rate, we are definitely established here and we are endeavoring to make ourselves as comfortable as possible. I rather think that you would consider we had something else to do than guard prisoners if you saw the way we have to work." Bowditch further explained, "Regularly every morning we have to get up at three A.M. and turn out our companies under arms. After calling the roll they stack their arms and go to sleep in the rear of the stacks until five, one officer remaining with the men and keeping awake. At five another roll-call and men have to keep their equipments on till seven. Then there is an order for five hours drill, which makes nine hours a day for the men to keep their equipments on."[46]

Private Robert Fitzgerald of Company F details in a timely framework the events that transpired for the regiment during the latter weeks of May and early part of June 1864. The diary entries provided by Fitzgerald present a chronological glimpse into the life of the enlisted men and what they were encountering during this period. Fitzgerald writes on May 16th:

> We lay near the Head Quarters of Gen. Butler within 20 miles of the rebel capital. We can here the booming of heavy artillery. South West from this. They say it is at Fort Darling which our forces are about to capture. 3 P. M.–The battalion is safely landed at city point some distance below where we were yesterday. There is a great excitement here. Our picket are coming in & from the masthead of a war vessel they are watching the movements of a heavy force of rebs, that lay to our rear. The 5th Mass. cavalry are unarmed. There are several regiments of colored troops here. With some cavalry and artillery.
>
> 6 P. M.–have had muskets issued to us with ammunition the infantry are in line I have seen one of their pickets that was killed this Afternoon. After noon he was first shot in the calf of the leg which disabled him they then came up to him and broke his skull with the butt of their muskets. His brains are scattered over his face and head. Can such men eventually triumph, God forbid.[47]

May 17, 1864:
  Clear and hot were called out in line with muskets last night at 4 o'clock and stood from that till day. There is fighting among the pickets, drilling with muskets today. We have pitched our camp in the midst of a wheat field. There are entrenchments thrown up all around here. We lay on a point that the rebels occupied a fortnight ago. Under cover of our gun boats.[48]

May 19, 1864:
  Cloudy with some rain. Drilling today. We are called out about 3 this morning and we were under arms till 7 A. M.–waiting for the attack from Lee's forces. The enemies forces have been heard all day in the direction of Fort Darling Virginia. There has been some picket fighting today but no heavy engagements.[49]

May 20, 1864:
  Today clear and very warm. Turned out at 3 this morning and are to continue so until further orders. General Butler captured 1000 rebs and ten pieces of cannon last night. Hear cannons while I write.[50]

May 21, 1864:
  Lay by our arms from 3 A. M. till 7. Heavy fighting all night and this morning the roaring of heavy cannon fire still plainly heard in the direction of Richmond and Petersburgh [sic]. The muskets and infantry accoutrements used by this regiment were inspected yesterday by the general inspecting officer. A new line of pickets were thrown of last night.[51]

Captain Bowditch, commanding the company to which Private Fitzgerald was assigned, remarked, "Entrenchments have been thrown up here and there with pickets and the natural conformation of the ground renders this place somewhat secure." Further mentioning that his brother, Major Henry Bowditch, "is out now in charge of all the pickets which now consist entirely of our regiment, except one or two mounted videttes," adding, "Our men being new are of course seeing things where there is nothing to be seen, and last night there was a continual firing all along the line."[52] There was, however, a likelihood that the regiment would encounter the enemy at a moment's notice, and it was becoming a daily occurrence for the men of the 5th Massachusetts Cavalry. Fitzgerald continues on May 23rd:

Beautifully clar [clear] and warm this morning. 8 A. M. I started out on picket our line lay about 1 ½ miles from our entrenchments. We captured a rebel last night armed with knife and revolver had on his person rebel scrip greenbacks gold & silver saved him. This morning 2 contraband boys came into our lines which say the rebels lay about 4 miles farther out had 1 of my company shot. Saw a rebel out side & out of gunshot.[53]

Captain Charles Bowditch, made mention of the wounding and subsequent death of one of the sentinels to which Private Fitzgerald recorded as being shot "4 miles farther out." Bowditch wrote, "Last night we sent out a picket of 300 men and this morning one of my corporals is brought in wounded in the thigh. The bone is broken and I don't suppose that he will ever get well."[54] Bowditch's observations were correct, as Corporal John Gambol, a Boston native, at age thirty-one succumbed to his wounds eight days later on May 31st at the Post-Hospital, City Point, Virginia.[55]

Private Fitzgerald on May 24, 1864, goes on to state that the day was "clear and fine. A terrible fight last night suspected to be with Longstreets corps. This morning all is still. Gen. Butler visited our regt. he is a fine old fellow. He speak in high terms of our regt. and says we must soon be mounted. I feel very well satisfied with this kind of service."[56] Captain Bowditch's observations of General Butler were decidedly different from those of Private Fitzgerald. Bowditch observed, "He is by all odds the most shocking and disreputable looking man I ever clapped my eyes on." Bowditch continues, "He had his hat perched sideways on his head and looked more like a New York 'Blood-tub' or a 'Plug-ugly' than anything else."[57]

Major Zabdiel B. Adams in command of the Second Battalion took to the water along the Appomattox River. Having boarded transports on the 28th of May the battalion traveled five miles up the river without making contact or engaging Confederate forces. Captain Bowditch recalled that the 2nd Battalion consisting of companies E, F, G, and H were at 6 p.m. with two days' provisions "put on board a transport with one wagon for our baggage." Bowditch further indicated with disgust, "We had got all the companies ready to land, when up comes a dispatch boat from City Point ordering us back again to camp. We were pretty well disgusted, I can tell you, especially as just then the head of the army began to cross the bridge to the South side of the river. However there was nothing to be done except to obey orders, though it did make us feel, as Col. Russell said, like 'a shirt collar with all the starch taken out.'" Bowditch concluded in writing about the expedition up the Appomattox, "So back we steamed to City Point again, pulling off a boat, that had ground, on the way down and got back to camp by nine p.m. Thus ended the first cavalry, steamboat, infantry raid of the 5th Mass."[58]

On June 7th, adjustments to the line of Federal entrenchments were made along with the movement of the 5th Massachusetts Cavalry camp. Captain Bowditch afforded his thoughts regarding the new location the regiment was placed in stating, "We have got moved into our new camp, which affords a very nice swamp for our men to live in, though the officers' quarters are on higher ground. A ditch runs diagonally across the company street, which in our street has been covered over with boards. However, it is not so bad as if the men did not have board floors for their tents." Bowditch further remarked, "For the last four or five days there has been no firing of any importance heard in the direction of Grant, while previously the firing was very distinct and heavy. We can hardly look for the evacuation of Richmond yet awhile however. Lee isn't a man to give up easily."[59] Again, on June 8th, Major Adams along with five companies of the regiment was ordered to proceed up the Appomattox River to Spring Hill to relieve elements of the 6th United States Colored Infantry posted as pickets. Before arriving back at City Point, Virginia, on June 10th, the detachment assisted a battery of Union artillery engaged at Fort Clifton the previous day.[60]

Throughout their time in late May 1864 at City Point, Virginia, the officers of the regiment, besides taking charge of the enlisted men along the picket lines and providing leadership during excursions up the Appomattox River, were assigned to other details, some consisting of sitting on general court-martial proceedings. Along with these details, down times during their day consisted of gathering at their respective officer quarters to be social and merry, playing card games such as euchre and often foraging at the local residences and farms. Captain Charles Bowditch hoped to enjoy his stay at City Point, recalling, "I expect for some time to enjoy myself and not to have much hard work to do, since Gen. Hinks has just shown that he possesses a large amount of sense by putting me upon a General Court martial for the trial of whatever cases come up and of which Col. Russell is President." Bowditch's thought regarding the assignment was "very jolly as it relieves me of all duty of all sorts in the regiment." He added, "I do not have to go on as Officer of the Day, (nor on picket) nor get up to attend roll-call, nor nothing." If there was any doubt among the officers as to whether they should be given such a relaxed assignment while others were ordered to take charge of the pickets along with the day to day duties of the regiment, Bowditch opined, "As it was given me without any suggestion or asking on my part, I feel no scruples about accepting it. Lieuts. Adams [Edward H. Adams] and Higginson [Francis L. Higginson] of our regiment are also members besides quite a number of officers from other troops."[61]

Besides attending to court-martial proceedings, Bowditch along with the other officers of the regiment, were often invited guests to 3rd division commander General Edward Hinks' headquarters for social gatherings to partake in one another's comradery and to discuss old times and current issues of the day. Captain Thomas Livermore, aide-de-camp to General Hinks, stated, "In the heat of the day, when not otherwise occupied we used to be on the lawn under the trees, whose shade, with breezes from the river, delightfully tempered the heat; and there, with the broad James and the Appomattox and the busy fleet plying their waters before us, affording a changing and enlivening view with the meadows and woods in the distance, we took solid comfort in our siestas, or with the iced julep, and tobacco for those who liked."[62] Charles Bowditch wrote to his mother on May 25th, "Thursday I was invited to Gen. Hinks' to tea," adding, "I found the General playing euchre with Capt. John White (his expected brother in-law) in the latter's room. Gen. H. was very sociable and I had quite a pleasant conversation."[63] Thomas Livermore remembered, "In the evening we often had a regimental band at headquarters to play for us, and the officers of our command, particularly of the 4th and 5th Massachusetts Cavalry, came there to chat or make merry with us."[64]

As in all wars, soldiers often seek to supplement their daily rations and creature comforts of camp through scrounging and foraging for both military and non-military essential goods. Lieutenant Curtis Whittemore, it was observed, had the uncanny knack of procuring the finer luxuries so coveted by an army on the march. Previously, in the early part of the month, Captain Thomas Livermore stated that the division had upon disembarking at City Point found it "to consist of a bluff some fifty feet high at the point of where the Appomattox River empties into the James; the remnants of a wharf which had been consumed above the piles of by fire; at the foot of the bluff a few shabby houses ranged along two or three short lanes or streets; and the spacious grounds and dilapidated house of one Dr. Eppes." Livermore further recalled, "The people, except the negroes, had all fled, I believe. We disembarked our troops and encamped them just outside the place, after a reconnaissance for a mile or so toward Petersburg without finding an enemy except a few pickets, or those we had driven out of City Point, and took up our own quarters in Dr. Eppes's house and grounds."[65] Charles Bowditch noted that Lieutenant Whittemore was "a very good hand at foraging," recollecting, "He brought in a medicine chest, a chair, coffee pot, salt cellar, a saddle and half a dozen novels, which latter are very acceptable indeed." Captain Bowditch indicated, "There is an order against foraging, but as he [Whittemore] turned over the medicine chest to the surgeon who pronounced it exactly what he wanted, as his had not come, I don't think that any trouble will come from it." Bowditch added, "It makes me disgusted to see the mild way that secessionists are treated."[66]

This would have all been acceptable, however, Dr. Eppes had taken it upon himself to prepare an itemized accounting of the goods taken by the occupying forces on his property and sent it to the Federal command to have procured and restored to his ownership. Word must have reached and moved throughout the camps regarding Dr. Eppes'

request, as Captain Bowditch wrote on May 28th that "Dr. Reps (or some such name) was the owner of the grounds here on City Point and was taken by us on our occupation. He was taken to Fort Monroe and afterwards released and sent to Richmond. He now sends up a schedule of the property which he says he had which he wishes to be sent after him and Gen. Butler has ordered Gen. Hinks to collect all the property and have a report made on its condition preparatory to turning it over to the Doctor." Bowditch added, "In the schedule are four slave and one Confederate flag. Gen. Hinks says that these two articles will not give him much trouble, since he does not recognize slave as property and he has no knowledge of there being a Confederate nation which has a right to have a flag."[67] Captain Livermore concluded the matter regarding Dr. Eppes' request stating, "We got some few

First Lieutenant Curtis Whittemore was recognized by Captain Bowditch for his excellent foraging skills, saving the day on more than one occasion with his unique finds. After the war he relocated to the south, settling with his wife and family in Pulaski County, Arkansas. He served a stint in the Arkansas House of Representatives and subsequently as Pulaski County, Arkansas, treasurer (author's collection).

articles of property here, such as tents, and also a horse which a rebel courier from Petersburg had there, and this property was afterwards demanded as exempt from capture. We returned all the tents which we could find, I believe, but the horse General Hincks kept."[68]

The 5th Massachusetts Cavalry would continue to provide daily picket duty in front of their encamped army, every day witnessing an increase in the amount of enemy movement and contact. The men of the regiment eagerly anticipated the chance to prove their mettle in the face of the enemy and to show the country that they were true stalwart American soldiers.

3

Seeing the Elephant

"We had gone but a short distance before we came upon the ambulance train, then I knew that some of us were not coming back again."

—Sgt. Charles R. Douglass

Private Fitzgerald expressed on May 31st, "We can see the fight at Fort [illegible] quite plainly. It is distant only 3 miles and one can see the flash & the course of the shell as it makes its horrid circuit through the air." Fitzgerald continues, "The 4th, 5th, 6th & 22nd Col. Troops are participating in it & I almost begrudge them the honour [sic]. Though it is a solemn sight."[1] With General Grant's army entangled in conflict around the Confederate capital of Richmond it became evident that a sweeping campaign to take the city of Petersburg, south of Richmond, would be the Union's next strategic plan. Major General Butler's Army of the James was supposed to capture the city. On June 9th, Major General Quincy A. Gillmore was ordered to lead 1,800 men of the X Corps combined with part of Brigadier General Edward W. Hinks' Colored division against Petersburg, an engagement which would go down in history as The Battle of Old Men and Young Boys. Three cavalry regiments commanded by General August V. Kautz led the vanguard bringing the attacking force to 4,500 men.[2]

Private Robert Fitzgerald recorded in his diary on June 9th, "All bustle this morning. Butlers troops are engaged near Petersburgh about 500 of our Regt. sent to assist. 4. P. M. Wounded coming in by dozens."[3] It was 5:00 a.m. when General Gillmore directed Hinks to lead his division along the Jordan Point Road following Kautz's cavalry in the lead. Gillmore advised Hinks that "unless the attack is made promptly and vigorously there will be danger of failure as the enemy will reinforce their lines." General Gillmore was to commence his attack when he

74

heard General Kautz's guns from the south. He further instructed that if Hinks happened to "penetrate the town before Gen. Kautz, who is to attack on the Jerusalem Road," then he was to take "the public buildings, public stores, bridges across the Appomattox, depots, and cars" and destroy them.[4]

By 12:30 that afternoon Gillmore advised General Butler that General Hinks was unsuccessful in carrying the works towards his front stemming from the fact that "since he [Hinks] arrived there at 7 a.m. two more regiments have been added to the intrenchments [sic], coming from the city," relating that, based on reports by Confederate prisoners, "our movement was known at 1 this morning, and that reenforcements arrived by railroad." With uncertainty in hearing the sound of Kautz's guns, Gillmore mistakenly led his troops back towards Bermuda Hundred, informing General Butler, "Distant firing on my extreme left has been heard for the last hour and a half. I, therefore, judge that Kautz finds himself opposed. I am about to withdraw from under fire in hopes of hearing from him." According to Gillmore, Hinks stated that the last he heard of firing in the vicinity of General Kautz's troopers was at 12 p.m., "apparently just where it commenced." Thus Gillmore recalled, "Gradually withdrew to Baylor's, and then waited until 3:30 o'clock." In the meantime, General Kautz began his assault along the Jerusalem Plank Road leading to the city.[5]

Petersburg was lightly defended by General Henry A. Wise, commander of the First Military District of General Pierre Gustave Toutant Beauregard's department. A force gathered up of local boys, old men, convalescents from the city hospitals, and prisoners from the local provost jails made up the city's meager defense—such units as Major Fletcher H. Archer's Militia, the Petersburg City Battalion under the command of Major Peter V. Batte, and William Hood's Virginia Reserve Battalion composed mostly of employees from the city factories and railroads. General Wise also had at his disposal approximately 500 men of the 46th Virginia Infantry.[6] One Petersburg resident recalled the morning alarm which sounded throughout the city "when, as though our city were blessed with a patent fire-telegraph, all the available bell metal in the corporation broke into chores [sic, chorus] with so vigorous a peal, and a clangor so resonant, as to suggest to the uninitiated a general conflagration."[7] General Beauregard had for days pressured those in Richmond to send supporting troops to defend Petersburg from an attack. Beauregard expressed his concern to General Bragg that he believed Grant would move south of the James to operate against Richmond. Beauregard's telegraphed pleas to Bragg, Lee and even President Davis, regarding not having enough able bodied men to hold off an impending coordinated attack upon his defenses by the enemy, continued to be dismissed and taken lightly.[8]

General Wise positioned his forces, stretching from the east of Petersburg starting at the south shore of the Appomattox River heading south and then wrapping west of the city, along the Dimmock line of earthen fortifications. Major Peter V. Batte's Reserve Battalion and Major William Henry Hood's Virginia Reserve Battalions took position along the works east of Petersburg between Batteries Two and Seven. Followed to the south of them along the line, Wise deployed the 46th Virginia Infantry to Battery Sixteen

Henry A. Wise, the pre-war governor of Virginia, would go on to join the Confederate army and command the First Military District, Department of North Carolina and Southern Virginia. He had charge of the Confederate defense of Petersburg, Virginia, on June 15, 1864 (Library of Congress Prints and Photographs Division Washington, D.C. LC-DIG-cwpb-06502).

with the support of four heavy guns. Deploying between Batteries Twenty-six and Twenty-Eight, with a view to the south of Petersburg along the Jerusalem Plank Road, was Major Fletcher H. Archer's Militia. Protecting to the west of Petersburg through a mile of open fortifications were stationed two guns of Sturdivant's Virginia Artillery.[9] Describing the fortifications around Petersburg, Brigadier General R. E. Colston, temporarily the ranking Confederate officer within the Cockade City, who was waiting for a permanent command assignment recalled, "With the exception of a few lunettes and redoubts at the most commanding positions, they were barely marked out, and a horseman could ride over them without the least difficulty almost every-where, as I myself had done day after day for weeks just before the fight."[10]

In recounting the actions taken upon General Wise's front, Wise indicated that, "They pressed hard upon the left, for three or four hours, and then suddenly attacked the militia on my extreme right, with a detachment numbering one thousand [Kautz's cavalry], which were handsomely received by Archer; but they broke through his line, one half of them taking the road to Petersburg, and the other the road leading to Blandford." Wise's meager forces of invalids and prison inmates were doing all they could to fend off the Federal onslaught. Wise recalled, "The two companies of 'Patients' and 'Penitents' moved out on the Blandford road, while I advanced with three companies of the Forty-sixth [Virginia] from our left; and the enemy on that road, seeing the head of the column of 'P.P.'s' advancing in their front, and my three companies bearing on their right flank, wheeled to the right-about at once retired; and Graham's Battery repulsed the other party advancing upon the city."[11]

General Kautz's men faced an untimely encounter along the Jerusalem Plank Road near the outer defenses of the city's works with Captain Edward Graham's Petersburg Artillery. Graham's artillery had arrived from Chesterfield County over the Pocahontas Bridge and opened fire atop Reservoir Hill. With the arrival and ultimate counter-attack by Confederate brigadier general James Dearing's cavalry, General Kautz, with no support from General Gillmore, was pushed back from the city limits and ordered his troops to retreat toward the main Federal lines at Bermuda Hundred. In the final analysis of the conflict the Federals lost around 60 men and the Confederates approximately 100. General Wise immediately reinforced his defensive position with the Twenty-sixth Virginia Infantry and nine companies of the Thirty-Fourth Virginia Infantry.[12]

Beauregard continued to press for troops, telegraphing General Braxton Bragg from his headquarters at Swift Creek on the morning of June 14th, "Movement of Grant's across Chickahominy and increase of Butler's force render my position here critical. With my present forces I cannot answer for consequences. Cannot my troops sent to General Lee be returned at once?" With no response, Beauregard wired Lee, "A deserter from the enemy reports that Butler has been reinforced by the 18th and part of the 10th Army Corps." Still without receiving a suitable guarantee of support Beauregard dispatched his aide, Colonel

Samuel B. Paul, to meet with General Lee, carrying instructions to explain the situation presenting itself in front of Petersburg. Ultimately, Beauregard would receive reinforcement from Richmond by way of General Matt Ransom's North Carolina brigade and General Archibald Gracie's Alabama brigade strategically stationed to reach Petersburg in case of a renewed threat to the Petersburg defense.[13]

It all but seemed that in a matter of days a larger scale conflict was going to transpire. Previously, on June 14th, Generals Grant and Butler conferred at Bermuda Hundred. At that time orders were issued for an all-out attack on the vitally important railroad center in hopes of capturing Petersburg and ultimately putting pressure on Richmond. The Eighteenth Corps, under Major General William F. "Baldy" Smith, was given command of the operation, to which Hinks' all black division was assigned.[14]

After a delayed movement compounded with changes in marching orders and points of rendezvous as well as difficulties on the waterways, two of General Smith's XVIII Corps divisions, led by Brigadier General William T. H. Brooks and John H. Martindale, on the morning of June 15th, were finally in position on the south side of the Appomattox River; with added support from General Kautz's cavalry and General Hinks' division. Private Fitzgerald recalled, "A battle expected. The pickets driven back but no fight. The boys very much tried for they were anxious for a fray."[15] The morning of the 14th of June dawned clear and warm. Fitzgerald took to writing in his diary, "Fell in with the boys for a reconnoiter at about ten this morning marched to line of pickets furthest out on the road leading the river." He added, "Fell back was reinforced by the 4th Mass. Cav. & advanced on the road to the left. Marched through woods over land plantations and through slave quarters up narrow glens and halted in a shady nook under a hill as a reserve. The main body going on but found no enemy save two rebel officers belonging to the signal corps."[16] Captain Bowditch recalled that the regiment had "started out at half past one o'clock from City Point" on the morning of the 15th. He continues, "Marched till about six or seven with an interval of two or three hours rest. Somewhere about seven or eight we were formed in line and marched through fields and over a railroad gully and through dense woods till we came to an open field, where we found a line of infantry drawn up some little way in front of us. When we first formed line, some shell came over our heads with a rather disagreeable accuracy of fire, one of which damaged some of the horses of the 4th [Massachusetts] Cavalry."[17]

General Wise's forces commanding the Dimmock Line batteries on the morning of the 15th consisted of Colonel Powhatan Robertson Page's 26th Virginia Infantry, Col. John Thomas Goode's 34th Virginia Infantry, and the 46th Virginia Infantry under the command of Colonel Randolph Harrison, one company of the 64th Georgia Infantry, the 23rd South Carolina, Major Fletcher H. Archer's Militia, Major Peter V. Batte's Reserve Battalion and Major William Henry Hood's Virginia Reserve Battalion, Major Thomas H. Bond then in command, and Sturdivant's (Virginia) and Slaten's Macon (Georgia) light artillery batteries. William B. Tabb's 59th Virginia Infantry would subsequently be called up and come on line during the night of the 15th.[18]

Brigadier General Edward W. Hinks was commander of the 3rd Division, 18th Corps, to which the 5th Massachusetts Cavalry was assigned during the campaign against Petersburg, June 15, 1864 (Library of Congress Prints and Photographs Division Washington, D.C. LC-DIG-cwpb-04473).

While the morning of June 15th found Secretary of War Edwin M. Stanton in Washington, D.C., preparing to designate Arlington Heights outside of Washington officially as a military cemetery, shortly after daybreak Union columns one hundred thirty miles south approached the City Point and Petersburg, Virginia, turnpike at a place known as Baylor's Farm.[19] As part of Holman's (Provisional) Brigade, Hinks' (3rd) Division, the soldiers of the 5th Massachusetts Cavalry would come under their long anticipated baptism by fire or, as the soldiers referred to it, seeing the elephant.

The assaulting USCT infantry force consisted of Colonel Samuel A. Duncan's 2nd Brigade, Hinks's 3rd Division, taking the lead and forming in line of battle from right to left, the 5th U.S.C.T, Colonel James M. Conine commanding; 22nd U.S.C.T., Col. Joseph B. Kiddoo; 4th U.S.C.T., Lt. Col. George Rogers and the 6th U.S.C.T. under the command of Colonel John M. Ames. Holman's Brigade, consisting of the 1st U.S. Colored Troops, Lt. Col. Elias Wright; 5th Massachusetts

Cavalry, Colonel Henry S. Russell; two companies of the 4th Massachusetts Cavalry, under the command of Lt. Col. Francis Washburn and Captain Francis C. Choate's Battery B, 2nd Regiment Light Artillery, United States Colored Troops brought up the second line of attack.[20]

On the early morning of the 15th before sunup, General Kautz's cavalry, in all 2,500 men, were sent to make a reconnaissance of the enemy to their front. "We came upon the enemy's pickets on reaching the City Point Railroad," recalled Kautz, "We drove them in, capturing one line of obstructions, an abatis across the road at the [Perkinson] saw-mill." Kautz's troopers came upon a second line of rifle pits manned by "three pieces of artillery and an infantry support, commanding the road which debouched from a dense wood." General Kautz then deployed several of his troopers to hold the road until infantry could come up to support.[21] Captain Thomas Livermore, aide-de-camp to General Hinks, remembered, "No skirmishers were thrown out, as General Smith's orders were to advance without delay, and the work before us had been deployed by the cavalry, who had entirely withdrawn, leaving some on our left in the woods, I believe. I carried the orders to Colonel Duncan, who was to see in this his first battle, and well recollect the rather pale but determined face with which he received and set about executing the order."[22]

Within moments of the stepping off, the two Federal brigades under Hinks' command came under fire from a Rebel battery. The guns belched forth upon the Federal troops behind a line of heavy wooded thickets. This battery position was held by Brigadier General James Dearing, consisting of two infantry regiments, several companies of cavalry, and four twelve-pound cannon. The 4th North Carolina Cavalry, under the command of Colonel Dennis Dozier Ferebee with the support of Captain Edward Graham's Petersburg Artillery, had established in Baylor's farm fields an advance picket position from the Confederate main Dimmock line of defense, thus impeding the advance of the Federal assault.[23] Captain Livermore again recalled, "Our infantry entered a piece of woods about a quarter of a mile wide, through which the road ran, and crossed these woods under a very severe artillery fire which the enemy, who were posted in open ground beyond the woods out of our sight, poured into us."[24] Captain Bowditch, leading the men of Company F, recalled that the line officers having dismounted "sent the horses to the rear, thinking it preferable to keep their horses all straight than to have to walk on all the marches of the regiment."

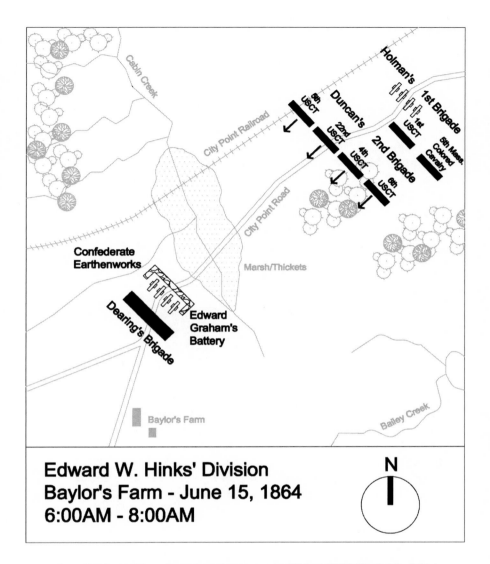

Battle at Baylor's Farm. Opening movements of Edward W. Hinks' 3rd Division against James Dearing's Confederate forces on the morning of June 15, 1864 (drawn by Becky LaBarre).

Bowditch further remarked, "After getting into the open and having a few shells pitched at us, the line in front of us moved on and we followed suit. We entered into a thick wood, just as full of underbrush as it could be, rendering it almost impossible to keep in line. We did our best however and succeeded pretty decently in places."[25]

What made the terrain difficult, according to Colonel Samuel A.

Duncan, leading his 2nd Brigade, was that the entrenched Confederates opposing them were positioned on a "crest of rapidly rising ground 300 yards in rear of an exceedingly difficult wood." Making special mention of the woods in the brigades' front, Duncan ascertained that it was of considerable width of approximately six hundred yards. Accordingly the ground was "traversed by a turnpike and a railroad in directions diagonal to that to be followed by an attack upon the enemy's works." With the roads causing deep cuts in the direct line of march and a marshy and obstructed floor of fallen timber, dense thickets of vines and bushes "twenty feet high" according to Duncan, made for a serious stumbling block to overcome in the movements of the assault. Duncan had ordered each regimental commander of his brigade when reaching the farthest skirt of woods to "open a heavy fire upon the enemy" and to reform the brigade in line of battle to await the command to charge the enemy works.[26]

Recalling the movement of the 5th Massachusetts Cavalry and the second line of assault, Sergeant Charles R. Douglass noted, "At two o'clock the next morning [June 15th] everything was ready for a march which was soon ordered, and about 400 of our regiment—the 5th Massachusetts—were soon into line, that being all we had left in camp, the rest being on picket duty. Our brave colonel took command of the battalion, and we started out of camp."[27] Douglass lamented, "We had gone but a short distance before we came upon the ambulance train, then I knew that some of us were not coming back again."[28] Private Robert Fitzgerald noted in his diary, "Aroused this morning at 2 o'clock by the harsh command 'to Arms' 'fall in.' 10 A. M. engaging the foe with infantry & artillery. Driving him slowly from a line 4 deep the woods so thick that no mortal can see more than 15 or 20 yds. grape, canister & shell whizzing in every direction. Emerged from the [woods] in the face of a terrific fire and in front of the rebel breastworks. A falter, our noble colonel wounded but mounts his horse & a charge upon the fort. It is ours but few prisoners taken, have sent a brass 12 lb Howitzer down to City Point drawn by 50 of the boys."[29] Captain Bowditch had ascertained that "the front line had driven the rebs out of the woods and they began to play pretty sharply with grape and canister, and the sharpshooters letting us have a good share of rifle bullets, while the shell burst around altogether too freely to be amusing."[30] Surely, there was now no doubt the cavalry troopers were beginning to see the elephant.

Charles Douglass provided additional information as to the movements of the 5th Massachusetts Cavalry at Baylor's Farm in writing to his father:

> We marched on until we struck the Petersburg road; then proceeded up the road until daylight, when we halted, being about five miles from Petersburg.... We moved forward down the hill into a wheat-field; formed two lines of battle. Sending out our skirmishers, we soon met the enemy's advance pickets, and drove them back through two pieces of woods. Our regiment was in the second line of battle. As we came through the second piece of woods, the enemy opened on us with solid shot and shell. We kept on, however, until we reached the next piece of woods. Then we were only about a quarter of a mile from the enemy, they being drawn up in line of battle behind their breastworks. All this time we were under a withering fire from the rebel batteries. The underbrush was so thick in the woods that we could not form a line of battle; but we got into line as soon as we could, and waited to see what the first line of battle would accomplish. We had not long to wait before the first line of battle fell back upon us under a galling fire, which killed several of our men in the second line.[31]

Bringing up the men of the second line of attack, Colonel Holman ordered the 1st U.S.C.T. to "clear the way for the advance of the column, and upon arriving at the bridge, about one mile, where the enemy had been previously intrenched [sic], and deploy to the right of the road."[32] Sgt. Douglass recollected the day after the assault that "immediately after the first line fell back, we were ordered by our colonel to fix bayonets and charge, which we did in good style, driving the enemy from behind their first line of breastworks, and capturing one piece of artillery from the Johnnies. There we had only twenty men from any company in the fight, and we were right in front of the line, a little to the left of the center."[33] Casualties began to be inflicted upon the men of the 5th Massachusetts. Colonel Russell was hit and command devolved upon Major Horace N. Weld. Charles Douglass wrote of the wounding of Colonel Russell,

> Col. Russell was just in front of me, about a couple of yards; he cried out, "Come on, brave boys of the 5th!" and soon he was struck in the shoulder by a rifle-ball, merely taking off the shoulder-straps. In an instant our men began to fall around us pretty fast but we drove the enemy off the field, into the woods, on toward Petersburg. After we had started the rebels, the white troops were ordered forward to keep them going. This was within about three miles of the city.
>
> Col. Russell then ordered Lieut. Mallery, myself, and 50 men, to take the piece of artillery that we had captured, and proceed on to camp, where I now am at present, though our regiment is at the front yet. I kept close to the Colonel during the whole of the engagement, and when he was wounded, I went to gather him some currants. Although wounded, he could not be persuaded to leave the field until the Surgeon insisted upon it. Major Adams was struck in the side by a piece of shell, and it is said that it may prove fatal. Capt. Clark, the officer I had to report my company to, was hit on the knee-pan, and suffered considerable pain.

African American soldiers of General Edward Hinks' division parade a captured Confederate artillery piece on June 15, 1864. Charles Douglass recollected that Colonel Russell had ordered "Lieut. Mallery, myself, and 50 men, to take the piece of artillery that we had captured, and proceed on to camp" (Frank Leslie, *The Soldier in Our Civil War, v. 2*, p. 277).

> While I am writing we have got orders to return to the front, to escort the bodies of officers that fell yesterday.[34]

Captain Bowditch added that "Captain Clark, Co. G. was hit soon after entering the wood by a splinter, which knocked him down and lamed him doing him no serious damage, so that he kept on the ground till after the affair was over." Bowditch recalled that upon emerging from the woods that what lay before the regiment was "a mass of men in front of me firing apparently at random and now and then cheering," adding, "After a while and before I reached them, they turned round and ran for the woods. You can judge of the effect such a course would have upon our men, just coming out of the woods, and seeing others running helter skelter back upon them."[35]

Holding out for most of the morning against repeated Federal assaults and with a supply of ammunition having been expended, the 4th North Carolina Cavalry and Graham's Artillery retreated toward the inner defenses of the Petersburg works. By late morning and into mid-afternoon the 5th Massachusetts would be deployed, half of the regiment taking a supporting role in reserve and the other half stretched along the left flank of the brigade to stand guard against an enemy movement in that direction.[36]

As early evening approached orders were sent to all brigade commanders to prepare for a determined all-out assault of the enemy works. Holman's (Provisional Brigade) and Duncan's 2nd Brigade advanced with skirmishers to the front against the fortified rebel battery emplacements numbered 7 through 11; the 5th Massachusetts Cavalry was held back from participating in the assault. Over the evening of the 15th and into the next day, under withering fire from fortified infantry and artillery fire, the infantry regiments of the two brigades were successful in flanking and enveloping the battery positions, all while advancing from battery to battery inflicting casualties, securing prisoners and ultimately capturing one artillery gun with caissons and horses.[37]

Contradictions arise in the telling of the fighting that took place at Baylor's Farm. Even during and immediately after the battle conflicting reports of who accomplished what was being filed. In Edward G. Longacre's work *Army of Amateurs* (1997), he relates that, "With Hinks incapacitated, command passed to Colonel Duncan, who had not led a charge in his career." Longacre contends that the 5th Massachusetts Cavalry was willing to do its duty but "Duncan's inexperience showed in his choice of a unit to lead his assault: a dismounted cavalry regiment made up of raw recruits and only recently attached to the division." Longacre concludes that "under the accurate shelling of Dearing's twelve-pounders, the dismounted troopers broke for the rear in panic."[38]

Theoretically, cavalrymen during the American Civil War were trained to fight from the saddle and were often armed with a carbine, saber, and sidearm. However, frequently cavalry corps during the Civil War fought as dragoons or mounted infantrymen; they rode to battles on horseback but dismounted to deploy and fight using the latest infantry formations and tactics. As Longacre pointed out, we need to remember that at this time the soldiers of the Fifth were raw recruits, dismounted and only recently attached to the division as infantrymen. Colonel Duncan explained that the "Fourth Regiment was the first to reach the open field. The center companies of this regiment, injudiciously and without orders, and before any attempt at a correction of the alignment, started forward for the works with cheers." The two companies were ordered back into line which in effect caused the rebel artillery to open up with a "destructive fire of canister from all his guns." Duncan asserted that the inexperience of the men coming under fire with the added difficulty of terrain caused confusion. All of this was hampered with the added increase "by the second line in the excitement of the moment opening fire upon the first line." Panic arose as the 5th Massachusetts Cavalry broke for the rear, catching up with parts of the Fourth U.S.C.T. who stampeded to the rear in turn, followed on their heels by the Sixth U.S.C.T.. This allowed for two other black regiments in Duncan's brigade, the 5th and 22nd U.S.C.T., to fight their way across the open field and successfully construct a determined thrust upon capturing the Confederate works.[39] Captain Bowditch asserted, "Our officers set to work and tried to rally them [i.e., the 6th U.S. Colored Troops which had broken] but could do nothing with them till they were in the woods, where our men and the 6th were mixed up all together. We got them up again and out of the woods, and formed line again in the open field, but in the mean time Col. Russell had been shot in the shoulder and Major Adams in the breast and we were all under the command of the Lieut. Col. of the 6th, who was more like a fool than anything else."[40]

Captain Thomas Livermore sheds light upon the confusion encountered by the division and that of the 5th Massachusetts Cavalry, recollecting, "The officers of the 5th Massachusetts Cavalry said that their men were demoralized by the conduct of one of the field officers in the first brigade, who, as they alleged, just as that line emerged from the woods turned to the rear and madly gesticulating urged them to retreat or halt, and I think the 6th Regiment, was affected by his conduct. We had great charity for the 5th Massachusetts Cavalry. It was officered by a gallant set of men, but was indifferently drilled for foot service and was discontented and spiritless because it was not mounted." With hindsight, Livermore questioned the deployment of the brigades in line, further expounding, "There might, perhaps be a shadow of reason for doubting the wisdom of sending the second line so close upon the first rather than deploying it on the same line or holding it farther in the rear, as, I believe, some of the 5th Massachusetts Cavalry, did but General Hincks's orders from General Smith were peremptory to put his whole division in at once. He did not suppose, and the event proved him correct, that there was need of a greater front than that of one brigade, and it is probable that the second brigade was of greater value where it was, to give courage to the first and stop any breach that might occur in the line of the latter, than it could be if retained to charge if the first line was repelled."[41]

Captain Bowditch recounts that the 5th Massachusetts Cavalry had "got into line behind a hedge and were in a good position to start a charge, when were moved forward to a position where there was not a mite of cover and where the rebs had a slanting fire on us." Charles Bowditch was adamant upon writing of the whole affair, "By charging at this time we could have taken the battery as easily as possible, but the Colonel of the 6th ordered us to lie down, and then moved us by the flank somewhat to the rear and flank of the battery." Bowditch concluded that "luckily for us the battery was charged from the other side and the rebs left. Otherwise they could have taken in the battery, which gun we hauled into City Point."[42]

Charles Torrey Beman, a private in Company C of the 5th Massachusetts Cavalry wrote a letter to his abolitionist father, Pastor Amos Beman, on June 20, 1864, from Point of Rocks, Virginia. He relates the action taken by the regiment at Baylor's Farm on June 15:

> Since I last wrote, almost half of the 5th Massachusetts Cavalry have been in several engagements, and about thirty have been killed and wounded. The first notice I had of going into the engagement was about 1 o'clock, a.m., Wednesday, the 15th. We heard the bugle, and sprang to our arms, and, with two days rations, we started towards Petersburg, and when about four miles on our way toward that city, at a place called Beatty's House [Baylor's Farm], we came in front of the rebels' works. I was with some thirty of my Company. We had to pass through the woods; but we kept on, while the shell, grape and canister came around us cruelly. Our Major [Zebdiel Adams] and Col. [Henry S.] Russell were wounded, and several men fell—to advance seemed almost impossible; but we rallied, and after a terrible charge, amidst pieces of barbarous iron, solid shot and shell, we drove the desperate greybacks from their fortifications, and gave three cheers for our victory. But few white troops were with us. Parts of the 1st, 4th, 6th and 22nd [USCT] were engaged.
>
> The colored troops here have received a great deal of praise. The sensations I had in the battle were, coolness and interest in the boys' fighting. They shouted, "Fort Pillow," and the rebs were shown no mercy.[43]

Paradoxically, Sergeant Major Christian A. Fleetwood of the 4th U.S.C.T. provided the *Anglo-African* newspaper with a dissimilar account of the action taken on June 15, 1864: "Our regiment [4th U.S.C.T.] was the first to clear the woods and met with a heavy enfilading fire from the rebel work which was discovered on our right. Nevertheless our boys charged at a double quick until our reserve, the 5th Massachusetts Cavalry, who were not yet out of the woods, fired a heavy volley, which took effect upon the rear of our left wing, which, with the fire of the enemy, threw it into confusion." Having orders to withdraw back into the woods and reform, Fleetwood expounded, they "fell back accordingly, re-formed, and again advanced, in time to lose several more men killed and wounded, before the final capture of the work." Fleetwood was adamant that "it was the 22nd U.S. Colored Troops that took the work when we fell back, and not the 5th Cavalry."[44]

The official report filed by Brigadier General Edward W. Hinks immediately following the engagement on the 15th of June ties together and reinstates the factual events that occurred. General Hinks stated that the 5th Massachusetts Cavalry's awkwardness in maneuver that day was based on the fact that the unit was "composed of new recruits and drilled only in Cooke's single rank cavalry formation and was entirely unfitted to act as infantry in line."[45] Notwithstanding, General Hinks also affirms in a later correspondence the specific role the 5th Massachusetts Cavalry took in the final assault on the evening of the 15th of June:

> In forming line of battle in the morning, for the attack upon the enemy's works near Baylor's house, I placed the Fifth Massachusetts Cavalry (dismounted) on the left of the second line of battle, and its awkwardness in maneuvering delayed my movement fully three quarters of an hour, and finally when it advanced, though nobly and heroically led, it was but little other than an armed mob, which was held up to its work by the almost superhuman efforts of its officers. Its losses were heavy, among being its gallant commander (Colonel Russell) and Major Adams, while its power to inflict injury upon the enemy was nominal. I could but commend its gallantry, but considering its inefficiency, decided that to further engage it with the enemy would be a reckless and useless exposure of life to no purpose, and accordingly withheld it from participation in the final attack upon the enemy's works, which were carried by the five-well drilled infantry regiments of the division.[46]

Charles Bowditch in writing to his mother on June 18th indicated the final action taken by the regiment and his observations regarding the conduct and performance of the men in the regiment, writing, "Our men behaved very well indeed though it is not the most favorable way of going into a first action with another regiment breaking through them."[47] Bowditch further informed her that after the brigades were able to reform and the enemy was falling back upon the inner defenses of Petersburg "we were marched and counter-marched and at last were ordered to support a battery of ten guns which was going to take part in the attack on the Petersburg entrenchments. We were put in various positions and kept getting shelled out of all." Bowditch recalled, "In one, a round three or four inch shell, after hitting the ground, rolled along to the front rank of our men, without exploding. At another time an elongated shell ricocheted and, bouncing over and over, made a jump across the gully through which the road ran, just escaping by six inches Capt. Kaler [Cornelius Kaler], who dodged in time, and passing through his company. The shell came so slowly that they had full time to get out of the way." Thus, Bowditch along with

Captain Cornelius Kaler. During the opening days of the siege of Petersburg, an "elongated shell ricocheted and, bouncing over and over, made a jump across the gully through which the road ran, just escaping by six inches Capt. Kaler, who dodged in time, and passing through his company (author's collection).

the rest of the regiment "lay in support of the battery till night, and heard the engagement by which the forts were taken, and marched up and passed the night just outside one of the forts."[48]

"Before you receive this, you will no doubt hear of the fall of Petersburg, for our forces are at the last line of intrenchments [sic], a quarter of a mile from the city. The colored troops last night captured Fort Clifton, and several hundred prisoners," wrote Charles Douglass.[49] Unfortunately, the opening days of combat had not provided the Federal forces a breakthrough of the Confederate defense line. They had been pushed back closer to their base, but the Confederates had held. It has been disputed that if General William F. Smith had advanced the XVIII Corps farther into the defenses on the opening night, Petersburg would possibly have fallen on June 15th or 16th. Smith recollected years later, "I ... knew that reinforcements had been rushing in to [sic]

Petersburg since two o'clock, and had every reason to believe that the enemy's force equaled or exceeded my own. I knew nothing of the country in front. My white troops were exhausted by marching day and night, and by fighting most of the day in the excessive heat. My colored troops, who had fought bravely, were intoxicated by their success, and could hardly be kept in order."[50] Confederate general P.G.T. Beauregard recalled, "Petersburg at that hour was clearly at the mercy of the Federal commander, who had all but captured it, and only failed of final success because he could not realize the fact of the unparalleled disparity between the two contending forces."[51] As a result, the continued advance into the heart of Petersburg had not been accomplished and the campaign against the Cockade City would unfold throughout a nine-month siege, dragging out to be a relentless combination of ghastly bloodshed and boredom.

Thus, contradictory reports appear throughout personal reminiscences at the time and in post war years. Official war records and modern historians on the subject have expressed many varying opinions about what had transpired during the conflict at Baylor's Farm. Psychologically, one man standing next to another on a battlefield could have totally differing views of what each had sensed took place. One must remember that many personalities were represented on the field, and boasting bravado was just as commonplace one hundred fifty odd years ago as it is today. Everyone wanted his fair share of fame and glory—not to be looked upon as cowardly but as fearless and courageous. As veterans returned to civilian life in the post-war era, further removing themselves from the actual moment of conflict, the fog of war could often cloud their recollections of what transpired on the fields of battle. Only by taking these accounts as a whole and exploring them further can we garner a concise and overall sound perspective as to the actions taken by these regiments and more specifically the fighting men themselves.

Whether or not General Smith could have taken the city of Petersburg, after having failed to exploit the advantage, and brought the Union army one step closer in destroying the rebellion is irrelevant for us to analyze, for history had already been written and the Federal army would go on to fight. What *can* be said is that on June 15, 1864, whether they were criticized or praised for their role at Baylor's Farm, the men of the 5th Massachusetts Volunteer Cavalry became combat veterans. They in turn could ultimately go on to say that they had collaborated in the opening campaign on Petersburg. It was for the African

American soldier the first time in the war in which they performed, to the extent of a division, in battle. In this single day's action the casualties inflicted upon the 5th Massachusetts Cavalry were four dead and nineteen wounded. Those killed were Private Thomas Williams of Company D along with Private William Edwards, Company G, and Privates Daniel Carter and Henry Johnson both of Company I. Among the wounded were Colonel Henry Russell, who suffered a hit to the left shoulder; Major Zabdiel Adams, shot in the chest; and Captain H. E. W. Clark, who was slightly injured in the leg. With the incapacitation of Russell and Adams, Major Henry P. Bowditch assumed command of the regiment.[52]

Charles Douglass related to his father, "Gen. Grant is here; he passed our camp this morning with his staff and body-guard, on his way to the front. I saw him from my tent." Douglass continued:

Major General William F. Smith commanded the 18th Army Corps in the opening assaults on Petersburg. He would declare, "To the colored troops comprising the division of General Hinks… The veterans of the Eighteenth Corps, they have stormed the works of the enemy and carried them, taking guns and prisoners, and in the whole affair, they have displayed all the qualities of good soldiers" (Library of Congress Prints and Photographs Division Washington, D.C. LC-DIG-cwpb-06368).

I am yet unhurt, but am much worn out; my shoulders are raw, from the straps of my cartridge-box, as I had forty rounds in my box, two days' rations, canteen, blankets, and musket. I can see red flags flying from every old church, barn, or house on the point, and our wounded are coming in rapidly. Col. Russell and Major Adams are in the hospital. Sergts. Cook, Wormley, and myself are all right. I will write again soon; I am writing now in a hurry, just to let you know that I am unhurt as yet, although several of our company fell around me.[53]

Private Fitzgerald wrote on June 16th, "In line in sight of Petersburgh [sic] our forces are sending in a terrible fire upon the city. Have captured enemy line of breastworks this side of Petersburgh [sic]. I hope the colored troops may always be kept together the 1st, 4th, 5th,

6th, 22nd U.S.C. Troops & the 5th Mass. Cav. fought together in this battle."[54] A fitting tribute to this feat would be the expression of admiration General William F. "Baldy" Smith stated to a reporter, "To the colored troops comprising the division of General Hinks.... The veterans of the Eighteenth Corps, they have stormed the works of the enemy and carried them, taking guns and prisoners, and in the whole affair, they have displayed all the qualities of good soldiers.[55]

4

The Bottom Rail
Had Got on Top

"The post here is established on a low, sandy, malarious, fever-
smitten, wind-blown, God-forsaken tongue of land."
                              —Charles Francis Adams, Jr.

"We have had our first fight and I have got out all right," wrote
Captain Charles Bowditch to his mother after the engagement at Baylor's Farm.[1] The 5th Massachusetts Cavalry, having been placed in a
reserve position and taken out of the evening attack of Wednesday,
June 15th, were merely witnesses to the assault made by the remaining
regiments of the U.S.C.T.. Writing to his sister Charlotte from Point of
Rocks, Virginia, on June 18th, Bowditch informed her of the attack
made by the U.S.C.T., stating, "They rushed on over a long open plain
on which they were exposed to a cross-fire from three batteries and
charged the centre [sic] fort…. How our troops managed to take them
I can't imagine, for it would be almost impossible if there had been a
large force to defend them. As it was the men rushed over the plain
with a cheer and fired a volley. The left was evacuated without much
trouble to us." Bowditch further expressed, "The forts were very
strongly built, but not by any means so well as many of ours. Some
dozen guns were captured in the two right hand ones, but I believe the
left hand one had all the guns taken from it before our forces took possession." That evening the 5th Massachusetts Cavalry was ordered to
take shelter and bed down "just outside the left fort," according to
Bowditch. This left the men of the regiment that night in a precarious
position among the carnage of the day's fighting. In describing the horrid conditions in which the regiment was exposed throughout the night,
Captain Bowditch continued, "The ground in front of the fort was

covered over with tall weeds and some underbrush, and in places it had been impossible to bury the dead, and the result was the most awful stench."[2]

On the morning of the 16th, the regiment was awoken and formed into line to prepare to march some distance to the rear of the army. Captain Bowditch recalled that the regiment "started and marched down to the right of the line nearer the river [Appomattox] and lay up on a ridge till about noon."[3] Writing to his father, Bowditch expressed in further detail the regiment's encounter with the enemy while resting upon the ridge: "About noon we encamped in the woods, near enough for the enemy to see us perfectly, which they evidently did, for they threw one shell into us which did no damage however, passing some fifteen feet over our heads and exploding harmlessly."[4] By afternoon, having broken ranks and ordered to rest, the regiment was again back on their feet in column of march, proceeding to make their way to Rushmore Farm near Spring Hill to position itself as a reserve.

Now, however, the 5th Massachusetts Cavalry encountered what so many soldiers throughout history have grumbled about—the notion of hurry up and wait. When they did finally move, it was often a fatiguing march and countermarch over the same ground. Bowditch expressed that "this time our regiment marched back exactly the same track that they had come, for some mile and a half or two miles."[5] While on their march to the area of Rushmore Farm, Captain Bowditch indicated that they had "stopped near the Brigade team of Gen. Stannard [George Stannard] and got some jolly good ice-water."[6] In writing to his father, Captain Bowditch seemed to harbor some remorse in the fact that the Union troops were marching to and fro over pristine fields of grain untouched so far by the hard hand of war. This observation would, in the long run, play out in the coming months of the campaign against Petersburg. Bowditch wrote, "Splendid pieces of open field and nicely planted with corn and oats are lying all round loose," adding, "It seems rather hard to spoil such fine fields of grain by marching through them with horses and men, smashing down the grain without compunction, but it has to be done and can't be helped."[7] Upon coming to final rest, Bowditch noted, "We camped in the orchard and close to the house of some people calling themselves Union, and whose property was therefore respected."[8]

This was the farm of forty-three-year-old Thomas Rushmore and his wife, Julia, along with their five children, one being their 18-year-old daughter, Julia Augusta, who Captain Bowditch would refer to in the many letters he sent home. The Rushmores were transplanted natives of New York. On the eve of the American Civil War, Thomas Rushmore, through agricultural pursuits, had amassed a real estate property valued at $12,000 along with another $10,000 in personal property, mostly from the ownership of thirteen slaves, 6 male and 7 female. Previously, during the assault on June 15th, the Rushmore estate had been turned into a field hospital. S. Millett Thompson provides a detailed accounting of the occupation by Federal forces on the Rushmores' property. In his post-war regimental history of the 13th New Hampshire Infantry, Thompson recounts the assault made by the regiment upon Confederate Battery # 5 and that several of the men, including himself, had been taken to the farm to tend to their wounds. According to Thompson, the farm lay "near the Appomattox river, a little over a mile northward from the battlefield." Based on his understanding, Thomas Rushmore, along with his ten-year-old son, was seized by the Confederate Army "and imprisoned in Petersburg." Confederate general Henry A. Wise, in his efforts to fortify the city with local boys, old men, convalescents from the city hospitals, and prisoners from the local provost jails might, in fact, have impressed Thomas Rushmore and his young son to take up arms unwillingly to strengthen the fortifications.[9]

Captain Bowditch, along with other officers of the regiment, was able to procure and purchase from the Rushmores some added morsels of food to supplement the two days' worth of rations they and the enlisted men had been given before marching into battle on the morning of the 15th. He remembered, "We bought some hens however and potatoes and eggs and had a jolly chicken stew and roast chicken." Bowditch added he was able to procure for himself "a large pailful of milk and had two or three jolly tumblers full of milk fresh from the cow, going down to see the cows milked for the purpose." Adding to the fact that there was an icehouse on the premise, in Bowditch's estimation, the evening dinner "we had was pretty good." S. Millett Thompson, in writing his 13th New Hampshire regimental history, substantiates the ease by which the soldiers were able to procure food and other provisions from the loyal Union inhabitants all while occupying the Rushmore residence. Thomas Rushmore's wife, along with his two daughters, Julia Augusta and Virginia, were "up all night caring unceasingly for the wounded," according to Thompson, adding, "They tear up all suitable cloth in the house, even to sheets and underclothing, into bandages; and bring milk, coffee and food without stint so long as there is any left to bring." Thompson further adds, "Augusta brought to the officers of the Thirteenth a good supper, and next morning a breakfast; and when the ambulance took them away on the morning of the 16th, she appeared with two or three quarts of ripe cherries and handed them up to the officers of the Thirteenth, who soon rode away eating them."[10]

Before the day was out on the 16th the 5th Massachusetts Cavalry was put in place as a reserve to the forward skirmish line as a "guard against a flank attack which of course never came," according to Captain Bowditch.[11] On June 17th the regiment crossed over the pontoon bridge stretching across the Appomattox River at Point of Rocks, reporting to General Turner, Tenth Army Corps. While at Point of Rocks, Private Joseph Jackson of Company L, a carpenter born in Northumberland

Point of Rocks, Virginia. During the later weeks of June 1864, the 5th Massachusetts Cavalry continued to fortify their position east of Petersburg and along the Appomattox River. On a number of occasions they crossed the pontoon bridge over the Appomattox River at Point of Rocks. The regiment reported to General Turner, Tenth Army Corps, along with re-crossing near Spring Hill and occupying a position at Rushmore Farm (Library of Congress Prints and Photographs Division Washington, D.C. LC-DIG-ppmsca-32744).

County, Virginia, having enlisted just a little over two months prior on April 11, 1864, received a gunshot wound Monday, June 20th, to the thorax. Private Jackson's circumstances were not detailed, however. His military record indicates that he was "wounded accidently in camp, Point Rocks, Va." Having been sent to the hospital at Fortress Monroe, he never fully recuperated from his wound; Joseph Jackson would die on July 18th in Hampton General Hospital.[12] By the 21st of June the regiment was back on the march this time within Hinks' Division of the Eighteenth Corps, crossing over the Appomattox River near Spring Hill and again occupying a position at Rushmore Farm.[13]

Throughout the last weeks of June the Federal army dug in along the earthen fortifications facing Petersburg and the opposing fortified Confederate forces under General Beauregard to their immediate front. Captain Bowditch remembered there was a report circulating that "Grant had demanded the surrender of Petersburg on threat of shelling it," further stating, "We certainly heard some very heavy firing in that direction. Heavy firing has been going on all the morning."[14] Between June 21st and the 23rd, elements of the Union 2nd Army Corps under the command of Major General David B. Birney along with portions of the 6th Corps led by Major General Horatio G. Wright, made a determined attack on the Weldon and Petersburg Railroad line immediately south of the Cockade City. Encountering Confederate forces under Major General Cadmus Wilcox within Lieutenant General A. P. Hill's corps along with Brigadier General William Mahone's division west of the Jerusalem Plank Road, the Federal forces were caught off guard. In the aftermath of battle, the Confederate forces were able to control a large portion of the Weldon Railroad line. However, several days later, under a combined force of brigadier generals James Wilson and August Kautz, the Federal cavalry was successful in destroying and tearing up railroad track throughout the south and southwestern region opposite Petersburg which held a significant juncture with the city. As a result, the Federal army was able to further extend the line of entrenchments around Petersburg.[15]

The 5th Massachusetts Cavalry, besides taking cover inside the entrenchments east of Petersburg and around the Rushmore residence, continued providing picket duty along the banks of the Appomattox River. "On picket on the Appomattox, June 25, 1864" was the heading Captain Charles Bowditch penned in a letter to his mother. Bowditch, having been put in command of placing the forward pickets stretching along the Appomattox River after two days, now took a break from his duties to write and describe the terrain and enemy forces the regiment was encountering, "The other bank is held by the rebels and we can see them very easily walking quietly along, without heeding in the least that we are within good shooting distance of them." Bowditch continues, "The rebs have got fortifications opposite the left of our line, from which they amuse themselves shelling back. Some of the shells which have been provided with poor cartridges drop down very uncomfortably near our picket line. Between where our line runs and the river is a dense swamp some one-eighth or a quarter of a mile wide."[16]

Captain Bowditch further provides a detailed understanding of the geographical terrain and physical conditions which the men on picket endured all while coming under enemy shelling. "Yesterday about six p.m. we were ordered to throw the whole line out upon the banks of the river. Some of the posts could be placed very easily, but three of them, which I had to post, had to be pushed through a dense jungle of grape vines and all other sorts of vine intervening, which had to be cut away with a knife in order to make any progress. Then would come a swamp of alders, really leaving no space larger than a foot wide between the stalks." Bowditch further explained, "Every now and then we would come to ditches and the ground was most disgustingly swampy for the whole distance. I posted the three pickets, however, though it took a couple of hours to do it, and was pretty well played out afterwards." Having successfully placed his pickets on line and thoroughly exhausted, Bowditch found that "a drink of whiskey and a night's sleep made me all right however." In closing Bowditch informed his mother, "We have put up a battery just behind Rushmore's house, which is expected to open on the rebs soon and to make the rebs open their eyes."[17]

On Monday, June 27th, having dug in and seemingly begun to adjust to the daily regimen of life inside the earthen entrenchments, supplies and baggage had made their way from Point of Rocks, Virginia. Captain Bowditch recalled that he had just been relieved of picket duty the day before and had "got back to camp in time to put up my A tent, which had just arrived from Point of Rocks." The guns which Bowditch had previously spoke of when writing his mother a few days earlier, placed to the rear of the Rushmore house, had, on Sunday the 26th, opened fire on the Confederate works. "Yesterday our forces opened from a battery of four 30 lb. Parrott guns, which they have put up just on our left," wrote Bowditch to his sister Charlotte. Bowditch explained, "The third shot dismounted one of the reb guns and drove the defenders of the redoubt helter skelter out of the work." The Confederate artillerists responded by accurately sending "one shot hitting the parapet and another passing directly over the fort." During the day, Eighteenth Army Corps commander General William "Baldy" Smith made his way down to inspect the fortifications and gain a better perspective of the enemy fortifying in his front. Bowditch recalled, "He was taking a view of the country round about and was accompanied by a little fellow—a captain on his staff, I suppose." Bowditch observed that General Smith "has a rather a round face with a light colored mustache and imperial and is a very solid substantial sort of man, one who lives well, I guess, when he is able." For General Smith's "edification" the artillery battery, according to Bowditch, were ordered by Smith to open fire "he being desirous of shelling a bit of woods where a rebel battery was supposed to be." Bowditch added, "but as half the shells did not explode and the other half burst up in the air, no great harm was done, I imagine."[18]

Subsequently, after operating as dismounted cavalry on the Petersburg and Bermuda Hundred fronts, the 5th Massachusetts Cavalry was directed to report to Point Lookout, Maryland, to guard Confederate prisoners of war. Sergeant Bartlett Yancey Malone, Co. H, 6th North Carolina Infantry, took pen in hand to write in his diary while imprisoned at Point Lookout of their arrival, "Saturday, July 2nd, 1864. Clear and very warm. Gold is worth from one forty to fifty in New York. A new regiment of Negroes called the 2nd [sic 5th] Mass. Cavalry arrived today. Several Hundred prisoners left for Elmira New York today. Others are expected to follow."[19]

Officially reporting July 1, 1864, the soldiers of the 5th Massachusetts Cavalry, one thousand strong, relieved the 36th United States Colored Troops. The 36th U.S.C.T. had been sent in February to garrison and guard Confederate prisoners at Point Lookout. Their colonel, Alonzo Granville Draper, was overall commandant of the post until the 36th U.S.C.T. was relieved and sent back to the Petersburg front. Draper seemed to have been left in the lurch and wondering what he should do regarding the transfer of the regiment and the subsequent replacement of the 5th Massachusetts Cavalry to take their place. All while the 5th Massachusetts was waiting aboard the transport ship to disembark on the shores of Point Lookout, Colonel Draper immediately shot off a wire to Secretary of War Edwin Stanton. From Headquarters St. Mary's District, Draper expressed, "The Fifth Massachusetts Dismounted Cavalry (colored), 1,000 strong, have reported here to relieve the Thirty-sixth U.S. Colored Troops, 1,000 strong, who are ordered by General Butler to report to his headquarters. I am in doubt whether to obey the order. The transports are here waiting for the Thirty-sixth."[20] The confusion was resolved that same day when Colonel Draper was provided orders from Major General Christopher C. Augur directing, "You will relieve the Thirty-sixth U.S. Colored Troops by the Fifth Massachusetts Dismounted Cavalry, and send the former regiment to General Butler. You will remain in command at Point Lookout until the arrival of General Barnes, who will relieve you."[21]

Confederate B. T. Holliday expressed his feelings regarding having black troops as guards: "During my imprisonment at Point Lookout negro troops took the place of white guards. They were the first negro soldiers I had seen. It was a bitter pill for Southern men to swallow, and we felt the insult very keenly." Reminiscing years later Holliday added,

> They were impudent and tyrannical, and the prisoners had to submit to many indignities. I saw two prisoners with barrel shirts on and linked together by a rope after the manner of the Siamese twins. A negro guard was behind them, walking them up and down in the hot sun. I saw a negro run the point of his bayonet into a prisoner who crossed his beat to go into the cook house to get his ration. Ludicrous things happened. A negro soldier, recognizing his former master, who advanced toward the fence to speak to him accosted him after this manner: 'How'e, Messa Robert! Mighty glad to see you, but the white folks say you mussen' come across that line.[22]

In addition, prisoner Luther Hopkins, formed his impression of the prison camp upon arrival:

> I think there were about fifteen thousand prisoners at this camp guarded by negro troops, which made our southern blood boil. As the darkies use to say, "The bottom rail had got on top." I imagine there was about twenty acres of ground, surrounded by a high board fence, probably about fourteen feet high. Just below the top was built a platform about three feet wide, and on this platform the guards walked to and fro with their guns on their shoulders. From this position they could guard inside the camp, while artillery and regiments of infantry were stationed near the camp to guard it from outside attack, and one or more gunboats patrolled the waters that nearly surrounded the camp.[23]

For the Rebel soldiers who were captured, their first stop on the road to prison would be a holding area behind the battle line. They would be guarded by armed soldiers and each prisoner would report to an officer his name and unit, which, in turn, would be written down. After leaving the holding areas by train or boat the prisoners would report to depot prisons. From the depots Confederate prisoners would ultimately be sent to larger, established prisoner of war camps within the interior of the Northern states, such as Elmira, New York; Rock Island, Illinois; Camp Douglas, Chicago, Illinois; and scores of others. Here the men's names were once again checked against a list, and from there they would spend the balance of the war, although a Confederate soldier would always hold a hope that he would be exchanged for a Union prisoner.[24]

On July 20, 1863, in the aftermath of the Union victory at the Battle of Gettysburg, a brief letter was written by Montgomery C. Meigs, quartermaster general, to General Daniel H. Rucker, chief quartermaster, U.S. Army, Washington, D.C., initializing the establishment of what would ultimately become the largest Federal prison for captured Confederates. Ironically, the prison is probably the least recognized and studied for the significant role it played during the War of the Rebellion. General Meigs expounds:

> General—It is proposed, as I am informed, by the General-in-Chief to establish a depot for prisoners of war at Point Lookout [Maryland]. The officer to command has not yet been designated, but it is proper to make provisions in advance. The depot will probably ultimately be constructed for 10,000 prisoners; for the present 5,000. Old tents should be sent from those in depot and necessary camp and garrison equipage, lumber to erect kitchens and store houses, and large cast-iron boilers for cooking. The labor will be performed by the prisoners themselves, but preliminary arrangements should be made by this Department.
>
> Have you an officer disposable for it to send there to establish the depot? If not, Captain Edwards, Post Quartermaster, should be called upon to receive the property. Lumber should be obtained by requisition from Baltimore. Colonel Donaldson will fill your requisition.[25]

Point Lookout, Maryland, is at the extreme tip of St. Mary's County, on the barren peninsula where the Potomac River joins the Chesapeake Bay. The Point attracted attention from the onset of English colonization in America for its prime location to view incoming ships. Captain John Smith explored the Point following his voyage during the first decade of the 17th Century. In 1632, the land consisting of the point was included in the grant from King Charles I to George Calvert, Lord Baltimore.[26]

Point Lookout began as part of St. Michael's Manor. It was one of three landed estates owned by Leonard Calvert, George Calvert's younger son, the first governor of Maryland colony. During the American Revolution, and again in the War of 1812, it was the subject of British raids. It was a key American lookout point for a watchman to convey news of British fleet activity in the lower bay. In 1830, the Federal government erected a lighthouse on the tip of the Point.[27]

Point Lookout, Maryland. View of Hammond General Hospital & U.S. General Depot for prisoners of war (Library of Congress Prints and Photographs Division Washington, D.C. LC-DIG-pga-02593).

In the years preceding the Civil War, it had become a popular summer resort for city dwellers seeking respite from the hot summer months. The surrounding land consisted of beach cottages, a large wharf and a lighthouse. In 1857, William Cost Johnson bought much of the land and developed it as a business venture. With the onset of war, people's attention turned away from recreational activities and the summer resort owners' financial status suffered greatly.[28]

Following General George B. McClellan's failure during the Virginia Peninsular Campaign to capture the Confederate capitol of Richmond, the United States government, requiring a hospital to house casualties of the Northern armies, leased the Point Lookout resort. Therefore, Hammond General Hospital was built and received its first Union army patients on August 17, 1862. By early 1863, authorities ordered a small number of Confederate prisoners to be confined to the hospital grounds; many were southern Marylanders accused of helping the Confederacy. Point Lookout, Maryland, was strategically located to make escape difficult by its isolation having the Potomac River and Chesapeake Bay flanking its sides. Yet, the mere fact that it was so close to the proximity of battle made it the largest depot prison established during the entire war. The site became officially known as Camp Hoffman; however, among many soldiers it was simply referred to as Point Lookout Prison.[29]

There are no surviving records indicating who designed the unique spoke-wheeled hospital wards or the placement of facilities on the barren sand peninsula, only five feet above sea level, which would become Point Lookout Prison Camp. It is, however, known that Brigadier General Gilman Marston assumed command of the prison depot and of the St. Mary's Military District. With General Marston's arrival at the Point, a formal program with full dress parade was initiated. As soon as the formalities were over, Marston lost no time in getting down to the business of establishing the prison depot. In less than one week Point Lookout Camp was established to receive prisoners of war.[30]

The mode of housing for the prisoners consisted mainly of Sibley tents and cracker box houses. The Sibley tent was 18 feet in diameter and 12 feet high, supported by a single pole which rested on an iron tripod, by means of which the tent could be tightened or slackened at will, making the tent appear like an Indian teepee. At the top of the tent was a circular opening, about a foot in diameter, which served the double purpose of ventilation and of passing a stove pipe through in cool weather. At Point Lookout each of these tents housed 14 men.[31]

Cracker box houses were constructed from scrap wood collected from the surrounding area by prisoners with the permission of the commanding officer. Nearly one whole division of the camp was composed of these ramshackle-looking structures. These particular quarters provided housing for up to a dozen men. The prisoners soon realized that the clay soil on which the camp sat could be utilized for the production of sun-backed bricks. Ultimately, these bricks were implemented in the use of fireplaces for the tents and cracker box houses. Of course, obtaining any such suitable firewood on the sandy isolated stretch of land was a whole other issue faced by the prisoners.[32]

Captain Bowditch, in writing home from Point Lookout, expressed that he would send home "fans made of wood and all cut out of one piece," further acknowledging that "they are made by the rebel prisoners and are very nice pieces of handicraft." According to Bowditch the Confederate prisoners held at Point Lookout would craft rings out of buttons or gutta-percha (a hard composite made from rubber plants) inlaying the jewelry with "little pieces of plate." Along with this, the prisoners made other items like watch chains. Having run across a prisoner who was captured a year earlier at the Battle of Gettysburg, Bowditch recounted that he had been "working as carpenter on the new hotel" being constructed along the Point. Accordingly, Captain Bowditch stressed that the Confederate prisoners confined at the Point were not required to work. However, he pointed out, "If they do work for the Government, they get extra rations and perhaps some tobacco. They also work for private individuals and get something extra for it." Bowditch concluded that it was "rather a contrast to the way our men have been treated in Richmond prisons," adding that he felt it "very pleasant however to see these rebels working under the charge of negro guards."[33]

Upon receiving fans made from the hands of Confederate prisoners, there must have been some concern from Captain Bowditch's family regarding the ease with which prisoners were able to fashion their camp trinkets using tools, specifically knives, with no regard to potentially overpowering the sentries at their posts. Captain Bowditch addressed these concerns with his mother when he wrote home on August 7th. He assured his mother that the only instruments the prisoners were able to use in creating their crafts were a knife and that "they would not be able to do much with that." Bowditch further explained the way in which the prison grounds were enforced and the means by which the guards along with the regiments stationed at Point Lookout would come down upon the prisoners if any potential threat of uprising or escape was executed:

> The guards are placed on a platform which runs round on the outside of the fence, some ten or twelve feet from the ground and a knife would be of little use against these. To be sure there are several guards on the ground inside the pen, but these could easily be overpowered, knife or no knife. In the night eight or nine men armed with revolvers patrol the camp, to prevent collections of prisoners or passing from one tent to another. After all, the main reliance is to be placed on the fact that the prisoners as a body seem disinclined to escape. One or two try it now and then and generally get caught for it. Two are in the guard house now for attempting escape, there would be in the first place the whole guard on the platform in a very short time (160 men) firing into them. Then there are three regiments close by which would be under arms within ten minutes, and ours would come into play in not over fifteen minutes. Then there are four field pieces which would be brought to bear on them, and the iron-clad *Roanoke* and several vessels, which would pitch shell into them without delay.[34]

Time hangs heavy on one's hands when in prison. Accordingly, life for the men of the 5th Massachusetts developed its own tedious rhythm. Along with this the men's morale would descend to a low point with the realization that the 5th Massachusetts Cavalry had been ordered there by General Butler to perform more menial tasks than that of a fighting soldier. Butler looked to restructure his black regiments within the Army of the James; thus the 36th U.S.C.T. was ordered to the division under the command of Brigadier General Charles J. Paine. In so doing, Butler looked to fortify his troop strength with well-trained infantry for assistance in breaking the Confederate stronghold around Petersburg, Virginia.[35]

The 5th Massachusetts Cavalry, if not standing guard over Confederate prisoners, was detailed to assist in prisoner exchanges and in digging fortifications. For a full strength cavalry regiment to have been sent off the front lines and ordered to take charge of guarding prisoners was indeed a rather hard pill to swallow, however, the men took to their newly assigned duties. Captain Bowditch expressed that he "never knew why this was done." He believed that "our men had been discharging their duties very well."[36] Rumors soon abounded throughout the prison camp as to the true reason the 5th Massachusetts Cavalry had been sent to Point Lookout. Confederate prisoner Anthony M. Keiley's opinion was less than flattering, writing on Friday, July 1st, in his diary, "To-day one of the negro regiments that has been guarding us—the Thirty-sixth United States Colored—left this point for the front, their places being taken by the Fifth Massachusetts Colored Cavalry and another black regiment, ordered here, it is said, by Butler, for cowardice in the presence of the enemy (good joke for Butler.)" Although these rumors persisted, spirits were still high among the men of the Fifth Cavalry. Taking these allegations in stride, many expressed hopes of soon returning to the front lines to show their fighting prowess. Determined to prove themselves, Private Gustavus Booth expressed to the *Anglo-African* newspaper, "We shall show ourselves one of the best cavalry regiments in the service."[37]

"The difference between our present mode of life and that which we have had is something remarkable," wrote Captain Bowditch to his mother. On July 3rd, the regiment had begun the process of settling into their new mode of life in the service to their country along with adjusting to their new living quarters. Bowditch offers a glimpse into the luxuries afforded the officers. Having procured a canvas wall tent, which provided a comfortable interior to stand, Bowditch explained to his mother that he "used my A tent to make a porch in front." In decorating and making his home-away-from-home more to his liking, Charles said, "A Kidderminster, or 3 ply, or something of the sort of carpet, half covers my floor, while the boards appear in the other half." He regarded the having of a board floor to be a "luxury," because "there are only one or two in camp." Along with having a board floor, the quarters was equipped with a wood framed door holding a hinged frame of four panes of glass which allowed Bowditch "to sleep with my window open or shut." He added a few army chairs along with a "pine table stained red" to add to what he called the "luxuriousness and comfort of my apartment." During down times in their daily routines the men would venture out into the waters of the bay to swim and bathe. Along with this, local citizens living north along the Point would venture down to the military camps bringing with them "berries, chickens, onion, etc.," as Bowditch recalled, "so that we shall be able to live like fighting cocks."[38]

On Sunday July 3rd, the regiment was relieved from having to turn out for a morning inspection, but rather, was given the opportunity to get their equipment into order for an evening inspection followed by a full dress parade. The following day the men of the 5th Massachusetts Cavalry would celebrate their first 4th of July in the service with a ceremony in raising the American flag over the camp. General Barnes had officially arrived to relieve Colonel Draper from command over the regiments serving at Point Lookout. Captain Bowditch, in writing to his father regarding General Barnes' arrival, remarked, "I suppose that we shall have to be reviewed, inspected and tortured in every way his ingenuity can devise to keep us employed." That inspection would come soon enough, as on July 23rd Bowditch informed his mother, "Yesterday we had an inspection of the regiment by the Inspector General of Gen. Barne's Staff." Bowditch's impression of the regiment upon their turning out in formation was that they "looked as well as could be expected considering the amount of hard duty they have had to perform." Having been on campaign in front of Petersburg since early June, it took time for all the requisitions to be processed thus resupplying the men through the quartermaster. Bowditch indicated that for the enlisted men, "Their clothes were pretty dirty and worn but new ones can be got for them and then they will make quite a reputable appearance."[39]

Within the last weeks of June and early weeks of July, Abraham Lincoln had formally accepted the nomination for president, campaigning to serve a second term in office. Along with this, Confederate general Jubal Early was organizing his army of 14,000 into two corps in an invasion of the North to put pressure on and in hopes of ultimately capturing Washington, D.C. Heading north from the Shenandoah Valley, his troops seized or destroyed property throughout the Maryland countryside. Early's corps crushed a small Federal force near the Monocacy River on July 9th and in two days came within five miles of the Union capital. Unfortunately for Early, his advance stalled at Monocacy giving Washington time to man its lightly fortified fortifications, and Early withdrew back into the Shenandoah Valley. Within this offensive by General Early, Confederate general Bradley T. Johnson attempted a daring raid on Point Lookout Prison. His overall plan was to liberate the prisoners, arm them, and march on Washington with Early. Union authorities caught wind of this plot and made preparations, resulting in Johnson abandoning his plan when the Confederate authorities found out that their intentions had been published.[40]

Rumors of Early's advance on Washington, D.C., had been spreading throughout the prison camp. "During my imprisonment there were many rumors of an exchange of prisoners, which raised our hopes only to be dashed to the ground," lamented B. T. Holliday of Chew's Battery. Having been incarcerated at Point Lookout, Maryland, "At the time of General Early's advance on Washington City in July, 1864," Holliday wrote, "there was a rumor that he [General Early] would make an effort to release us, but he was unable to accomplish it. Had he succeeded in doing so, he would have augmented his army by twenty thousand men. After his raid ten thousand prisoners were sent from Point Lookout to Elmira, N. Y."[41] Captain Bowditch wrote on July 15th, "A little while ago an orderly came in from the front, (the idea of our having a "front" down here in this corner of the world!), announcing that the rebs were within twenty miles of here. Immediately a great hubbub among Headquarters people and a fortification which they are building was immediately hurried up. I guess that it is only a small scare." Bowditch added, "The *Minnesota*, steam frigate has steamed up abreast the fortification and is prepared to throw broadsides into any rebs that may appear."[42] On July 28th, the cavalry camp was again aroused at a potential Confederate raid upon the prison camp. Captain Bowditch continues, "The monotony of this place was relieved last night by another scare, which originated from a dispatch received from our scouts up the country. We got under arms, sent our reinforcements for the pickets and then went to bed." Bowditch quipped, "It doesn't take anything at all to get up a scare on the most improved style, rebels and other fixins complete."[43]

"There rose a thunder cloud early in the morning and raind [sic] very hard," remembered Bartlett Yancey Malone from his confines within the rebel prison walls, "there was a whirlwind just out sid [sic] of the Prison on the point it blew the Comasary [sic] house and Shop down and seven other Buildings, it destroyed a good deal, wounded four senternels [sic] broak [sic] ones leg there was but littel [sic] wind inside of the Prison.[44] Captain Bowditch wrote his father that day, "The Point received an unaccustomed visitor this morning," adding, "A very heavy thunder shower came up just after reveille and a strong wind from the sea at the same time. The latter I suppose caused a water spout which came just over the end of the Point." Describing the resulting damage from the storm, Bowditch informed his father that, "it passed over the bow of the boat in which Capt. Kaler and Higginson were embarking but did them no damage. It knocked down a sentry on the wharf and nearly killed him, bending his gun up, and three planks and half of the wharf into the water." Confirming what prisoner Malone had witnessed, Bowditch recalled that it "demolished the Commissary building, Adams Express Co's abode and two or three small hospital buildings."[45]

The storm which cut a swath of destruction wasn't the only "whirlwind" brewing and causing havoc throughout the camp of the 5th Massachusetts Cavalry. "How Negro Troops are Treated by Yankee Officers," read the headlines in the *Daily Age*, August 4, 1864. Quoting from an unknown correspondent of the *Anglo-African* newspaper the *Daily Age* wrote:

A Louisiana correspondent, who furnishes it [*Anglo African*] with the following case of horrid treatment of a negro soldier by a Massachusetts Yankee officer. The sufferer was a member of the 5th Massachusetts Cavalry. The writer says:

We were, a few days ago, eye witnesses of an act, a most atrocious crime, perpetrated on an inoffensive creature, a private of this regiment—George Washington, of Co. L. The poor fellow was tied to a pole by his two thumbs, his feet scarcely touching the ground. The distance was not less than seven inches. All his efforts at stretching to gain a resting place for his expanded body in order to keep his weight from severing his thumbs were vain. His arms and legs ached from his exertions. He felt that his strength was gradually passing away; his stern heart and stout resolutions refused sympathy with the approaching weakness of his outstretched form. The little strength which trench digging, throwing up breast work, and heavy marches had left, soon became exhausted. The new seagrass twine cleaved to his thumbs pressing them like a vice, cutting with razor sharpness.

The pain becoming so excruciating, he struggled vainly to release himself; his mouth became opened; his eye-balls were almost forced from their sockets by the great agony he suffered. He felt as if he could live but a few minutes longer. A horrible pain it was, for his own leaden weight seemed to be against his having any relief. He could no longer support himself and falling unconscious to the ground, he left his flesh cleaving to the new seagrass twine!—a spectacle of horror to his fellow soldiers! How tightly wrapped it was! Agony—heart-rending agony! He was taken up insensible, and the doctor arriving, his wound was dressed; his consciousness, his natural sight, sense and feeling returned, and he felt relieved. The murderer, the carniverous[sic] miscreant whose savage intentions was gratified, was present, and with fiery eyes gazed upon the foul work he had so cowardly done. A cold shudder would have run through the veins of the most hardened mortal witnessing the scene.

The real cause of this punishment was that the poor worn-out creature had hid himself, or could not be found when wanting to go on duty. The regiment had just arrived from the front and had gone into quarters, which the 36th U. S. C. T. had just evacuated; the men were busily engaged in removing the rubbish which had accumulated.

The 5th Massachusetts Cavalry is suppose to be from a Christian State—is supposed to be commanded by Christians—by men of uncontaminated morals and good standing, but we see daily occurrences of crime. At the moment of my writing many are suffering living deaths—aye, worse than crucifixion! These offenders—these American criminals, worse than those engaged in the massacre of St. Bartholomew, are permitted to continue their duties in defiance of justice!

Oh, Goddess of Justice! Wilt thou not hasten the time when these may be brought to know that thine edicts must be trampled under foot with impunity! Yes! Methinks I hear the distant roaring of thy chariot wheels! Methinks thy annihilating thunderbolts are near and ready to fall. Withhold not thy power, but come with the destructive strength of the whirlwind, and save us from the havoc which those lawless miscreants have inaugurated.

It would be far better to be in the bonds of accursed slavery, than to breathe the breath of freedom in such a withering atmosphere. It would be better to be in the State prison than to be soldiers sustaining the banner of a country that has always kept us for its union aggrandisement[sic]—that has always used us only because the etoffe was genuine.[46]

The Bridgeport, Connecticut, *Republican Farmer*, of August 12, 1864, further corroborates and reveals details not previously mentioned:

MASSACHUSETTS HUMANITY—The N. Y. Express contains the following account of the manner in which a negro in Louisiana was treated by one Lieut. Gilmes [Lieutenant Francis L. Gilman] of the Fifth Massachusetts Cavalry.

It appears that he had the poor fellow tied to a pole by his two thumbs, his legs vainly endeavoring to touch the ground.[47]

Although he did not deny the charges, Major Horace N. Weld took exception to the *Anglo-African* publishing the anonymous report regarding the incident between Private George Washington and Lieutenant Gilman. In writing to Robert Hamilton, the editor of the *Anglo-African*, he scolded the paper saying that it was fostering "a mutinous feeling among the enlisted men of this command." Furthermore, Major Weld insisted Hamilton reveal the name of his contributor so that "proper steps may be taken in this regt. to prevent similar letters being sent to the press." Weld's threats were ignored by the editors of the *Anglo-African* newspaper which resulted in Major Weld arguing his case before the provost marshal of New York City on August 1st. Weld demanded that the provost marshal take steps in forcing the paper to cease publication of letters transmitted by the soldiers. He exclaimed, "The Anglo-African is extensively circulated in this regiment and if such letters are allowed to appear in it a few unscrupulous men may produce very great mischief in the command." Despite Weld's efforts to combat the reports being published, the *Anglo-African* continued as before.[48]

Confederate prisoner Bartlett Yancey Malone recorded in his diary for August 7th, "The knight of the 7th A Negro Senternel [sic, sentinel] Shot one of our men and kild [sic] him for no cause attall [sic]."[49] Captain Charles Bowditch writing to his sister Charlotte, on August 11, 1864, noted, "One of our men shot a rebel prisoner the other day for refusing to obey the prescribed regulations. The officer of the guard entirely exonerated the man from blame yet he was put in the guard house and still continues there. It is a pretty way to urge men to do their duty."[50] Prisoner Malone again took to writing in his diary on the 28th of August, "a senternel [sic] shot a nother [sic] one of our men wounded him very badly it is thought that he will die."[51] With what seemed to be further tensions mounting within the camp, it seemed that the regiment was lacking true leadership from the one person the men of the regiment most respected, that being their colonel, Henry Sturgis Russell. Bowditch wrote on August 14th to his father, "How is Col. Russell coming on? I hope he will recover soon so that he may come here, for the regiment needs him exceedingly."[52]

Throughout the 5th Cavalry's time at Point Lookout, continued racial tensions among the enlisted men and officers resulted in several heated confrontations. Private John H. Hackett of Company K was slapped across the head with the flat of Second Lieutenant John W. George's sword for not forming ranks properly. Hackett retaliated by bringing his rifle to the charge bayonets position and declaring, "God damn you! You would not strike me that way." Hackett was tried in a military court of law and sentenced to prison for six months.[53]

Company F witnessed two incidents' of open conflict among the men in the ranks. Private Joseph Stafford, a native of Natchez, Mississippi, who volunteered to enlist on July 28, 1864, and forwarded to the 5th Massachusetts Cavalry camped at Point Lookout, refused Sergeant William Carter of Company C's order to fall in. In so doing, Sergeant Carter struck Stafford. While both Carter and Stafford were locked in a scuffle another private pulled Carter away. Sergeant Carter testified that Stafford "kept walking along close beside me, cursing me, and calling me a 'damned yellow nigger, etc.'"[54]

In December, Private Abraham H. Williams reported drunk to company drill and was escorted to the guardhouse. Colonel Russell, having by this time arrived back with the regiment, instructed Lieutenant A. I. Mallory to "handcuff the Prisoner, and gag, and tie him up so that his toes should just touch the ground." Private Williams lashed out at Mallory as he approached declaring that no "God-damn white son-of-a-bitch shall put irons on me." At which point, Lieutenant Mallory swung the cuffs hitting Williams in the head and causing him to fall to the ground. While the incident ensued Private James Finley of Company H proceeded to round up a band of armed soldiers announcing, "Come, boys, get on your equipment, I'm going to the Guard House to release that man." All the while as Finley was rounding up his posse, Sergeant James H. Cornish intervened and ordered Lieutenant Mallory not to "strike that man [again], don't you touch him." The heightened tension among both the officers and enlisted men ultimately subsided and concluding with Private Williams being found guilty of drunkenness and contempt and eventually returning to duty. Private Finley, convicted of being mutinous, served four months in prison but was returned to the ranks following an appeals court review which deemed the charge of mutiny unfounded. Sergeant Cornish was found guilty of "contempt and mutinous language" and reduced to the rank of private.[55]

Two soldiers of the regiment, Private William A. Underhill serving in Company E and Private George Butler of Company D, were both involved and charged in sexual misconduct incidents while the regiment was stationed at Point Lookout in February 1865. Author Thomas Lowery provides further details related to these occurrences in his book *Sexual Misbehavior in the Civil War* (2006) and that are substantiated through the service records and Court-Martial Case Files, Records of the Office of the Judge Advocate General (Army). In regard to Private Underhill, Lowery writes that he went to a citizen's home "where he beat up a man and offered money for sex to Eliza and Anne Carnes." Furthermore, "Underhill was acquitted of attempted rape, but was fined six months pay for indecent and disorderly conduct." Private Butler, who Lowery explains accompanied Underhill, "entered a citizen's home where a mother and her son and daughter lived. Butler forced the son to drink whiskey before beating him." Lowery continues, "He then threw the daughter on the bed, chocked her and attempted to rape her, 'acting the part of a dog or a hog [coitus a tergo?].' The mother poured a chamber pot over Butler to make him stop, whereupon Butler punched her in the head. He was sent to prison for twenty years."[56]

Amid much of the turmoil in the ranks, a lawyer from Quincy, Massachusetts, Charles Francis Adams, Jr., was commissioned July 15, 1864, and mustered in September 8, 1864, as lieutenant colonel of the 5th Massachusetts Cavalry. Upon hearing of Adams' appointment, Captain Charles Bowditch in writing from Point Lookout on July 28th supposed that this was "Col. Russell's doings," further adding, "but I should not think that Capt. Adams would wish to join the regiment until it is mounted." Bowditch noted, "Most of the officers of the 1st [Massachusetts Cavalry] are delighted to have him come here."[57] The son of President Lincoln's ambassador to Britain, Charles Francis Adams, grandson of President John Quincy Adams and great-grandson of John Adams, Charles, Jr., was born May 27, 1835, in Boston. Adams was a graduate of Harvard, class of 1856, with a literary mind that made him a prolific researcher and writer.[58] At the outset of war he was a member of the 4th Battalion of Massachusetts Volunteer Militia. His experience with the militia provided the catalyst to higher military service. He had enlisted with the 1st Massachusetts Cavalry in 1861. Adams fought at Antietam and Gettysburg, where he acquired

Charles Francis Adams, Jr., son of President Lincoln's ambassador to Britain, was the grandson of President John Quincy Adams and great-grandson of John Adams. He was commissioned July 15, 1864, and mustered in September 8, 1864, as lieutenant colonel of the 5th Massachusetts Cavalry (Library of Congress Prints and Photographs Division Washington, D.C. LC-DIG-cwpb-03797).

DC Public Library

Title: Duck soup (Motion
picture)
Item ID: 31172088041645
Date charged: 11/21/2016,20:
28
Date due: 12/27/2016,23:59

Total checkouts for session:1
Total checkouts:10

Thank you for using the
DC Public Library

DC Public Library

Author: LaBarre, Steven M., 1976-

Title: The Fifth Massachusetts Colored Cavalry in the Ci

Item ID: 31172092418474
Date charged: 12/17/2016,14:11
Date due: 1/7/2017,23:59

Thank you for using the
DC Public Library

the knowledge and understanding to lead a cavalry unit. With Colonel Russell being incapacitated from wounds received at Baylor's Farm, Adams assumed temporary command of the regiment.[59]

Like his grandfather, John Quincy Adams, who Charles remembered as an old man, "always writing ... with a perpetual inkstain on the forefinger and thumb of his right hand," Charles would write often to his parents and to his brothers while serving with the 5th Massachusetts Cavalry.[60] Many of the letters he wrote gave open and unreserved insight into his feelings for the unit, men, and overall surroundings that he encountered while serving with the regiment. "My stay at these Head Quarters and my connection with the 1st Massachusetts Cavalry draws, according to all appearances, towards its close. A day or two since my commission as Lieutenant Colonel of the 5th reached me, and now I only wait for Flint's return to get leave to go to Washington and immediately afterwards I shall join my colored brethren," wrote Charles Francis Adams, Jr., to his mother on August 12, 1864. "I am fortunately once more perfectly well; in fact I haven't felt better for a year. Thanks to a greater degree of exercise and quinine I have completely gotten rid of my jaundice and the malaria, have a superb appetite and a sufficiency of energy."[61]

Three months prior, the 5th Massachusetts Cavalry had turned in their cavalry arms and horse equipment along with a portion of the regiment relinquishing their cavalry mounts upon receiving marching orders as infantry to the trenches of Petersburg. Now, Adams went to Washington, D.C., during the latter weeks of August to try and carry out a plan that he had of fully mounting the 5th Massachusetts Cavalry. Again he wrote to his mother on August 27, 1864:

> My business in Washington was to try and get the government, as they would not mount the 5th Cavalry on new horses, to give them enough old horses unfit for present service, owing to severe work in the present campaign, and to let them build them up while doing their present work at Point Lookout. The officials by no means approved of me or my scheme, or, I thought, of General Grant.... I am getting nervous and restless and discontented. For the time the 5th will serve me as a new object of interest and in working over that I shall hope for a time to keep myself contented and quiet in the service and when that plays out, I must look for something new; but I am very tired of the war.[62]

Having reported to the cavalry camp of the 5th Massachusetts, Adams writes to his brother Henry on September 18, 1864, his impression of the black soldiers under his command:

> The week has n't [not] been very exciting here; in fact, they rarely are. I am in command of the Regiment and very busy and so keep contented. I am organizing

now and, while I see things all around daily growing and improving, I am quiet and satisfied.... As for the "nigs" they are angelic in all respects ... my first impression of this poor, humiliated, down-trodden race is both favorable and kindly. They lack the pride, spirit and intellectual energy of the whites, partly from education and yet more by organisation; [sic] but they are sensitive to praise or blame, and yet more so to ridicule. They are different and eager to learn; they are docile and naturally polite, and in them, I think, I see immeasurable capacity for improvement.... Patience, kindness and self- control have not been my characteristics as an officer, any more than they have been characteristics of ourselves as a dominant race. I fear I shall often find myself pursuing towards them a course in which I have no faith, and I have little hope for them in their eternal contact with a race like ours. However, closer acquaintance will lead to increased knowledge.[63]

Adams further states in a letter dated September 23, 1864, to his brother Henry:

Here everything is quiet all day long, and every day I live surrounded by my "nigs" and very busy, for everything is to be done and be done by me. I no longer am surrounded by skilled white labor and am forced to study subjects which I don't know anything about. For instance, with 700 horses here I did n't [not] have one tolerable blacksmith. Before a horse could be shod I had to go to work and show the smiths what a good horseshoe is. So it is with almost everything. Owing to Colonel Russell's long absence and my delay in reporting, the Regiment has fallen sadly into arrears, and the officers have never been under one able commander long enough to become homogenous. The result is that I am pulling things to pieces and building up with all my might. If left alone, I should see no reason to doubt my ultimate success; but, as Colonel Russell will soon be here, he may go to work anew in his way, perhaps better than mine, but still another and unfortunate change.[64]

During the fall months of 1864, the regiment was able to complete the filling of many vacant officer positions, vacancies which had been left unfilled when the regiment departed Boston earlier that year. Having obtained a supply of horses for purposes of building them up for rigorous military campaigning along with allowing the troopers to acquire further training and handling to become proficient as a cavalry force, a regimental veterinarian was much sought after and implemented into the non-commissioned officer ranks. Forty-two-year-old James M. Cutting mustered into service September 16, 1864, as the regiment's veterinary surgeon. Furthermore, promotions and juggling of officers into the various companies were implemented. One of note was the vacancy made by the promotion of George A. Fisher to Company C. Edward Jarvis Bartlett, who was working in the offices of the United States Sanitary Commission and who earlier in January 1864 been denied a commission into the regiment, even though he had backing from men like George L. Stearns and Ralph Waldo Emerson, was finally provided a commission as second lieutenant in Company E.[65]

Not only had the 5th Massachusetts Cavalry been able to procure further men to fill vacancies and needed positions within the pool of officers, an influx in new enlisted recruits streamed into the camp at Point Lookout, in September 1864. Charles Waters, for instance, was born about the year 1843 in New Harmony, Indiana, located northwest of Evansville along the banks of the Wabash River dividing Indiana from Illinois. The town had been founded by a German religious group named the Harmony Society.[66] Previously on July 4th, President Lincoln had signed an act entitled, "An Act further to regulate and provide for the enrolling and calling out the national forces and for other purposes." Lincoln declared in the act, "Now, therefore, I, Abraham Lincoln, President of the United States, do issue this my call for 500,000 volunteers for the military service: *Provided, nevertheless,* That this call shall be reduced by all credits which may be established under section 8 of the aforesaid act on account of persons who have entered the naval service during the present rebellion and by credits for men furnished to the military service in excess of calls heretofore made." Lincoln added, "Volunteers will be accepted under this call for one, two, or three years, as they may elect, and will be entitled to the bounty provided by the law for the period of service for which they enlist."[67] Charles Waters, now residing in Chicago, Illinois, would formally enlist in September 1864, having done so under the July 18, 1864, call for enlistments' being assigned as a farrier in Company A.[68] One must wonder if Chicago's black community leaders such as John Jones provided a guiding hand in assisting Waters in his enlistment and journey east to join the cavalry regiment.

A total of 52,264 prisoners, both military and civilian, was held captive at Point Lookout. Although initially designed for ten thousand prisoners, during most of its existence the camp held 12,600 to 20,000 inmates at any one time. The topography, poor drainage, extreme heat in the summer and cold in the winter, inadequate food, clothing, fuel, housing, and medical care resulted in approximately three thousand prisoners' deaths over the twenty-two months of existence.[69] Charles Francis Adams, Jr., in writing a letter to his father, provides us with a well-documented description of Point Lookout's appearance when the 5th Massachusetts Cavalry was detailed there. On November 2, 1864, from company headquarters, Adams wrote:

You all appear to entertain curious ideas of Point Lookout and my duties while here. A safer residence or one to my mind less inviting could not well be found. The Post here is established on a low, sandy, malarious, [sic] fever-smitten, wind-blown, God-forsaken tongue of land dividing the Chesapeake Bay from the Potomac River. It is remarkably well adapted for a depot of prisoners, as it is not only notoriously unhealthy, but most easily guarded. The prisoners' pens and public buildings are situated on almost an island, and, while only a narrow beach at two points connects this with the main, the whole establishment quietly reposes under the broadsides of various gunboats which garnish this shore. Thus but a poor chance for escape or outbreak is offered to the prisoners. Nor do I think that any very strong desire to get away exists among them as a mass. To be sure they do not here live in luxury, but neither do they starve, and, judging by appearances, for they look tough and well, imprisonment does not disagree with them. The prisoners' pens are large enclosures, containing several acres, surrounded by a board fence some fifteen feet high, round the outside of which, and four feet from the top, runs a gallery on which sentinels are posted. From this vantage ground they observe the proceedings of our captive and deluded brethren and shoot them, if necessary. Inside, the pens are nothing but large camps, for the prisoners have canvas tents and the devils are more ingenious in making themselves comfortable than I ever supposed southern men could be.... Some of those men have been here eighteen months—one man I captured myself more than a year since—and many of them came here wounded and still more chronically sick. In the hospital there are some 2800 patients, but I do not know what the average of mortality is. Heavy or not, with a view to encourage new comers, I presume, there is always, kept piled up close to the main entrance some eighty or one hundred ready made coffins....

Our camp is not on the Point where the pens are, but further up the shore and some mile or so from them. Here we look after our horses, build houses, dig wells and stagnate.[70]

As previously mentioned, one of the more noteworthy African American soldiers to embody the ranks of the 5th was Sergeant Charles R. Douglass, son of Frederick Douglass. While stationed with the 5th Massachusetts Cavalry at Point Lookout, Charles Douglass was again so seriously ill that it prompted his father to write President Abraham Lincoln, August 29, 1864, on Charles' behalf: "I hope I shall not presume too much upon your kindness ... but I have a very great favor to ask. It is ... that you will cause my son Charles R. Douglass ... to be discharged."[71] Upon receiving this letter, the president gave Special Order #301, dated September 10, 1864, Adjutant General's Office. This expressed the simple endorsement of: "Let this boy be discharged. A. Lincoln."[72] This authorized the discharge of Charles R. Douglass on September 15, 1864, as first sergeant.[73] The rest of the 5th settled into a rhythm of tedium, guarding prisoners and all the while wondering when they would once again, if ever, face the enemy on the fields of battle.

* * *

Life for the soldiers in the 5th Massachusetts Cavalry was not always plagued with a rhythm of tedium. By the end of November 1864, the unit would celebrate the newly formed tradition of Thanksgiving. A proclamation had been declared on October 3, 1863, in which President Lincoln announced that the last Thursday of November shall be set aside as a day of thanksgiving. The unit gathered together as a family within their camp at Point Lookout for a day of festivities, comradeship, and a meal fit for a king. On December 17, 1864, a summary of the event which took place on November 26th was published in the *Weekly Anglo-African Newspaper*. This letter was presumably written by Sergeant Amos Webber of Company D:

> Permit me to inform you of the doings on Thanksgiving day in and about the Fifth Massachusetts Cavalry camp. It was the first holiday that we have witnessed during the eleven months in service. Our officers determined to have some sport most congenial to the feelings of their men, and sumptuous turkey dinner for each Company; wines excepted.
>
>
>
> PROGRAMME OF THE DAY
> Reveille—Full Band, 10 a.m.
> Horse Race, for officers, at 12 o'clock m.
> Thanksgiving Dinner
> Sack Race, 1–1/2 o'clock
> 1st prize, 1 turkey; 2d prize, bale of tobacco.
> Climbing Greased Poles; 2 o'clock
> 1st prize, 1 goose; 2d prize, plug of tobacco.
> Foot Race; 2–1/2 o'clock.
> 1st prize, pair of gauntlets; 2d prize, pair of spurs.
> Wheelbarrow Race; 3 o'clock.
> One Prize—a box of Cigars
> A Jig Dance—Prize, pair of Mexican spurs.
> A greased pig will be let out every half hour.
> Music by the band at intervals during the exercises.
> Committee: Maj. H[enry] P. Bowditch of the 2d Battalion;
> C[harles] C. Parsons, Captain of Co. D;
> F[rederick] G. Parker, Assistant Surgeon in Hospital.
>
>
>
> The day proved as clear and fine as an autumn day in the North, and all got ready to see the events of the day as it was ushered in bright and clear. According to programme, the exercises commenced at 12 o'clock. The officers entered the course for the race, and after a spirited run, Lieut. [Curtis] Whittemore's horse won the prize.
>
> Dinner—The turkey dinner was served up to each Company fine style. I noticed Cos. C, D, and E had large table spread out in the Co.'s street, about 40 feet long, and the men were all seated around the table, eating away for life, on turkeys, oysters, turnips, onions, bread without butter, etc.
>
> Sack Race—The parties entered for the race with their heads just out of the

sack. It was a laughable affair to see them jumping along for the prize. Sergt. Wm. Holmes, Co. G, won the 1st prize; David White, Co. E, the 2d.

Greased Poles—There were two greased poles. On the top of one hung the goose; on the other a plug of tobacco. After many attempts, John Miller, Co. M, succeeded in getting the tobacco; others failed and left the goose high and dry.

Foot Race—1st prize won by William D. Cooper; 2d by Boyd Hyde, both of Co. E. Wheelbarrow Race—Won by Peter Smith of Co. D.

Turkey Shooting—The following men shot a turkey for their prize: Sergt. Wm Holmes, Co. G; Corp. David Walker, Thos. Bell, Westley Rhoades, all of Co. I; Franklin Jennings of Co. B, and Another whose name I could not learn.

Jig Dance—Prize won by Richard Holmes, Bugler of Co. A.

Pig Chase—One caught by Alexander Ware, Co. H; one by Alexander Davis, Co. D, and by others, names unknown.

Second Foot Race—The officers and visitors, being anxious to see the sport of another Foot Race, soon made up a donation for the prizes. 1st prize, Sergt. James Treadwell, Co. M, $25.00; 2d prize, James C. Greenly, Co. G., can of turkey; 3d prize, James Moulton, Co. D, box of collars and $4.75.

Second Jig Dance—Corp. Ray of Co. E received $5.00 and $4.00 2d prize on the first Jig Dance.

Thus the day was well spent in sport and pleasure to their satisfaction. During the time, Capt. [Horace] Welch of Co. C. was recipient of a handsome saber, two scabbards and a silk sash, all neatly finished. It was presented to the Captain by Sergt. John Davis (Orderly Sergeant) in an eloquent speech. The Captain lifted his hat and responded in a brief manner.

The evening was well spent, to the enjoyment of all. The band poured forth volumes of music from their great horns, during the day and evening, for which they received great credit.

The Chief Bugler of the regiment, Sergt. Rueben Huff, was recipient of a handsome cavalry jacket and saber-belt, presented to him by the buglers of the regiment as a token of respect to their Chief.[74]

A new year dawned on 1st of January 1865 in the camps of both sides. The war was eagerly coming to a close; weeks previously on December 16, 1864, Union forces had successfully broken Hood's Army of Tennessee outside of Nashville. This would be the last major battle it would fight during the war, for Hood's army was hastily making a retreat into Alabama. Subsequently, General William Tecumseh Sherman had also successfully cut a swath of destruction from Atlanta to the sea and had presented President Lincoln the city of Savannah, Georgia, as a Christmas gift. Telegraphing Lincoln, Sherman announced, "To His Excellency President Lincoln, Washington, D.C.: I beg to present you as a Christmas-gift the city of Savannah, with one hundred and fifty heavy guns and plenty of ammunition, also about twenty-five thousand bales of cotton."[75] Lincoln in writing to congratulate Sherman on his success stated, "My Dear General Sherman: Many, many thanks for your Christmas gift—the capture of Savannah." Having reminded

Sherman how he had left the general to his own deportment with no interference by the President, which along with noting General Thomas' successes in Tennessee, he now asked of Sherman, "But what next?" Lincoln followed up the question with what seemed to be the overall answer to defeating the Confederacy: "I suppose it will be safe if I leave General Grant and yourself to decide."[76] Indeed, the hopes of the Confederacy were slowly drawing to a close; it would only be a matter of months before the great rebellion would totally crumble.

From Point Lookout, Maryland, January 23, 1865, Corporal Amos F. Jackson, Company I (who as will be remembered was involved in a confrontation with former Captain Wulff in Baltimore, Maryland), penned a letter to Mrs. Dolly Hazzard in Brookfield, Massachusetts, relating the daily goings-on in camp and current conditions for him and Mrs. Hazzard's sons:

> My Dear Friend
> Mrs. Hazzard
>   It is with pleasure that I now take this opertunity [sic] write you a few lines to let you know how we are getting along and you must excuse me for not writing to you before you know that I am rather slack [sic] but it is difrent [sic] now that Emm [William Hazzard] is here and you can't here [sic] from us as before so I thought that I would write and let you know how wer [sic] getting along. We are well, thank God. Alfred [Hazzard] has got to keeping house out here and Lorenzo [Hazzard] draws his rations and Emm cooks it for him so it makes it better for him for he gets it cook clean and it is better for him and he is getting fat. I am having very good times here but I would like to come home and see you all once more. We have not had any very colde [sic] weather hear [sic] Water has not frose [sic] more than one inch and a half thick here this winter and We have had about one / 2 inches of snow this winter here. But we have good deal of rain but it is not colde [sic] Emm and Alf are well and send there [sic] love to you James [Hazzard] is well and harty [sic]. I have not got much news to write this time for I suppose that you know more about the war than I do for you can get papers and they tell you more than I can. Lorenzo is on guard to day he is well. Capt. Howe reach here last night But I have not seen him but Alf sed [said] that he had but not to speak to him. No more at present. Write me soon please and tell me how you and all the folks get alonge [sic].
>   I wish that you have good health and may the Blessing of the Lord ever be present with you and prosper you in your undertakings and I ask you to pray for me for I need the prayers of the church that I may be more faithfull [sic].
>   [Postscript] Give my love to all inquiring friends.[77]

On February 14, 1865, Lieutenant Colonel Charles Francis Adams, Jr., received word from Colonel Henry S. Russell that he was resigning his command of the 5th Massachusetts Cavalry. The Boston abolitionist newspaper *The Liberator* published February 24th a testimonial to Colonel Henry S. Russell:

TESTIMONIAL TO COL. HENRY S. RUSSELL.
        Point Lookout, (Md.) Feb. 17, 1865.
    My Dear Mr. Garrison—The following testimony to the remarkable fidelity and
high military and personal merit of one of whose invaluable services the country
is now unfortunately deprived, seems to deserve the permanent and general
record of your columns. To the wise and thoughtful friend of the colored race, few
will seem entitled to more of grateful admiration and praise than they who, in
simple and unostentatious fidelity to duty, have devoted their best energies to the
work of developing and disciplining the military capacities of the colored man;
and among those to whom such praise justly belongs few, if any, will deserve a
higher place or a heartier recognition than the late Colonel of the 5th Massachusetts Cavalry.
    Every friend of civil justice and equality will confess, that the patient endurance
and steady valor shown by so many of our colored troops have done very much to
establish, among friends and foes, the *manhood* of the negro. Very few, whether of
the doubtful or the unfriendly, who know the true soldierly qualities of the Massachusetts colored regiments, can longer doubt or deny that, tried by one of the
severest tests of individual or national character, the colored man has won an
incontestable *right* to share with the white race every civil right, every civil pre-
rogative, and every civil emolument. And yet it is certainly true that this result is
largely due to the earnest moral courage and military skill of a comparatively few
who were willing to put their most cherished reputation at risk to promote so
great a cause. While we crown with unfading honors those who with voice and
pen have maintained this long and momentous anti-slavery struggle, this purpose
to make our Republic truly Republican, let us not forget how much a few large-
hearted and clear-headed officers have done, at a most critical hour, both to *save
our own manhood*, and to establish and vindicate the manhood of the colored
man. And in his record the faithful chronicler will award a highly honorable place
to Col. Russell. Without self-seeking, and averse to all forms of ostentatious notoriety, in the simple rectitude of a true hear and a wise head, he has done a work of
organization and discipline which will be the model to all his successors and his
own best praise. As friends of justice and equality, as friends of our own, not less
than of the colored race, let us recognize such services and honor such names.

———

                Camp 5th Mass. Cavalry,
            Point Lookout, (Md.,) Feb. 5th 1865.
    Col. Henry S. Russell:
    Dear Sir:—The undersigned, officers of your regiment, have learned with the
most sincere regret of your determination to resign your present position and to
leave the service, which, for a long period, you have honored and adorned. We
cannot allow you to leave us without an expression of our appreciation of your
services to us, and to this regiment.
    From our earliest association under your command your conduct, whether in
moments of excitement and danger or of dissatisfaction and despondency, has
been our sure guide and faithful support; teaching us to meet danger and suffering, or to endure disappointment, with cheerful and manly courage. We feel that
the impartiality and high sense of honor and duty which you have envinced
toward us as officers, and ever patient and watchful attention which you have
bestowed upon the interests of the regiment, deserve our heartfealt [sic] gratitude

and respect. Whatever may be the future history of the regiment, we feel that the skill and wisdom displayed by you in its organization, and during the first year of its existence, have given it a character and reputation which it will be our constant endeavor to sustain.

In the fullest confidence that the step you now take is dictated by the same fidelity to duty which we have marked in all your conduct as an officer and a man, we beg you to accept this expression of our most cordial respect and friendship, together with our warmest wishes for the future welfare and success of yourself and family.

We remain dear Colonel, ever your faithful servants and friends, [Signed by all the officers present with the regiment,—thirty-seven in number.][78]

Adams now assumed command as colonel of the regiment. He and the regiment returned to the Petersburg front in time to participate in the closing campaign of March and April 1865.[79] The preceding movement of the regiment was captured in the official correspondence between participating Union generals. On March 20, 1865, at 4:30 p.m., Lieutenant General U.S. Grant sent a dispatch to Major General Christopher C. Augur, asking: "Is the Fifth Massachusetts Colored Cavalry longer needed at Point Lookout? If not, send it to the Army of the James." In reply from Washington, D.C., Major General C. C. Augur related, "The Fifth Massachusetts Cavalry (Colored) will be sent, as you have directed, as soon as they can exchange their muskets for carbines and transportation be obtained."[80]

On the following day, Brigadier General James Barnes, commander of Point Lookout, Maryland, received a dispatch from Augur asking, "General Grant wants the Fifth Massachusetts Cavalry. Can you spare it? General Hoffman thinks 1,000 men there will be sufficient. By bringing in your detachments, except at the Government farms, will you not have more than that number? Please let me know at once." Receiving the dispatch, Barnes relayed the message back to Augur that "I should recommend that the Fifth Massachusetts Cavalry be ordered to the front. I will make the best disposition of the force left here, and if necessary it would be far better to fill up the regiments of the Veteran Reserve Corps. As cavalry the Fifth Massachusetts are of no use here. It will make a good regiment in the performance of their regular duty as cavalry." With this disposition of the regiment Augur requested to know, "How many men and how many horses will there be in the Fifth Massachusetts Cavalry to send?" Barnes' reply later that afternoon related, "The Fifth Massachusetts Cavalry will have 1,200 men and 900 horses, camp and garrison equipage, and six wagons."[81]

With this, Augur sent the final disposition of what the 5th Massachusetts Cavalry would encompass to Lieutenant General Grant. On

March 22, 1865, Grant received this report: "The Fifth Massachusetts Cavalry numbers 1,200 men. They have 900 horses. Shall I send them as they are, or supply them with complement of horses? They are armed with muskets. Shall they be furnished with carbines instead? Shall they take wagons with them?" From City Point, Virginia, approximately an hour later, General Grant sent the simple order, "You may send the Fifth Massachusetts Cavalry as it is, transportation and all."[82]

5

The Day of Jubilo

"Richmond Negroes were beside themselves with joy."
—Benjamin Quarles, *The Negro in the Civil War*

After months of being stationed at Point Lookout, Maryland, with orders in hand, the men of the 5th Massachusetts Cavalry embarked on their journey toward the trenches of Petersburg. Galvanized by word of General Philip Sheridan's success at the battle of Five Forks, Virginia, General Grant launched a concentrated assault on the weakened Confederate defenses in and around Petersburg. Petersburg fell, but its surrender came at a heavy price. In the absence of complete records the exact casualties will never be known, but in the nine-month campaign at least 42,000 Union troops had been killed, wounded, and captured, while the Confederates had suffered losses of more than 28,000. Grant was able to utilize the great resources at his disposal, and he turned the Petersburg campaign into a form of relentless beating which the Southern army was not able to withstand.[1]

The final days of March 1865 found the Union army and the men of the 5th Massachusetts Cavalry knocking on the door of the capital of the Confederacy. Major General Edward Otho Cresap Ord handwrote two telegraph blanks to Major General Godfrey Weitzel, commander of the Twenty-fifth Corps, Army of the James, who was in the field on March 27, 1865:

General:
   If an evacuation occurs [Richmond] during my absence lookout for torpedoes and mines—it is now reported that large numbers of the former are put down on Chaffin's farm and Bermuda front—don't let your columns take the roads—keep them in the woods and bypass—send cattle and old horses up the roads first—tonight and tomorrow keep campfires going as usual in empty camps—and the usual picket on make as little change as possible at conspicuous points—if you can

do so, cover the prominent part of the evacuated camps with shelter tents—for a day or two—or old newspapers; go on with drills and parades in sight as usual—5 Mass. col'd cavalry is on its way to Deep Bottom—may arrive tomorrow or day after—better camp them near where McKenzie's outside camps were—it is very full—besides this, I leave about 500 cavalry of McKenzie's Division—command'g officer to report to you—Birney's Division will move very quietly soon as 'tis dark, cross at Aiken's, thence cross at Broadway, behind Turner—both put waggons in front—

Yours & c.,
E. O. C. Ord[2]

As Ord indicated, the 5th Massachusetts Cavalry was placed under the command of Major General Weitzel at the Bermuda Hundred front on March 28, 1865. In later years General Weitzel recalled that the "Fifth Massachusetts Colored Cavalry was a fine regiment of about 900 strong commanded by Colonel Charles F. Adams, Jr."[3]

The morning of April 2, 1865, found Confederate president Jefferson Davis sitting in his customary pew No. 63 at St. Paul's Episcopal Church on Grace Street, Richmond, Virginia. Sexton William Irving had just received an urgent telegram from the War Department which he expediently forwarded to the president. Davis, upon leaving St. Paul's Church, opened the slip of paper to read the telegram:

Petersburg, April 2, 1865
His Excellency, President Davis, Richmond Va.:
    I think it is absolutely necessary that we should abandon our position tonight. I have given all the necessary orders on the subject to the troops, and the operation, though difficult, I hope will be performed successfully. I have directed General Stevens to send an officer to Your Excellency to explain the routes to you by which the troops will be moved to Amelia Court House, and furnished you with a guide and any assistance that you may require for yourself.

R.E. Lee[4]

As early as 1862, the Confederate capital of Richmond had devised a general plan of evacuation if deemed necessary. The *Richmond Dispatch* reported the announcement in the publication on May 5, 1862, to the citizens of Richmond:

It has been deemed advisable, in case a necessity should arise for the destruction of the manufactured tobacco now stored in this city, that it should all be gathered together in certain prescribed warehouses, so that its destruction might certainly be assured if we are ever so unlucky as to have a visit from the Yankee vandals. When this course was determined on, all owners were notified that they could remove their tobacco from the city, but would not be permitted to spread it about in small lots for the purpose of retaining it here and evading the order respecting it. Yesterday, Assistant Provost Marshal Alexander caused a lot of it to be seized which was being distributed in the wrong way.[5]

With the fall of Petersburg on April 2, 1865, General Robert E. Lee and the Army of Northern Virginia retreated towards Appomattox, Virginia, and on their heels in hot pursuit were General Ulysses S. Grant and the Army of the Potomac. With the subsequent evacuation of Richmond by the Confederate troops remaining under General Richard S. Ewell's command and government officials, the city became a site of disastrous plunder, looting, pillaging, and fiery inferno. The *Richmond Whig* of April 4, 1865, heralded an astounding account of the destruction and devastation that laid waste to the city:

> The evacuation of Richmond commenced in earnest Sunday night [April 2nd], closed at daylight on Monday morning with a terrific conflagration, which was kindled by the Confederate authorities, wantonly and recklessly applying the torch to Shockoe warehouse and other buildings in which was stored a large quantity of tobacco. The fire spread rapidly, and it was some time before the Fire Brigade could be gotten to work. A fresh breeze was blowing from the South, and the fire swept over great space in an incredible short space of time. By noon the flames had transformed into a desert waste that portion of the city bounded between 7th and 15th streets, from Main street to the river, comprising the main business portion. We can form no estimate at this moment of the number of houses destroyed, but public and private they will certainly number 600 to 800.
>
> At present we cannot do more than enumerate some of the most prominent buildings destroyed.—These include the Bank of Richmond; Traders Bank; Bank of the Commonwealth; Bank of Virginia; Farmers' Bank, all the banking houses, the American Hotel, the Columbian Hotel, the *Enquirer* Building on 12th street, the *Dispatch* office and job rooms, corner of 13th and Main streets; all that block of buildings known as Belvin's Block, the *Examiner* office, engine and machinery rooms; the Confederate Post Office department building, the State Court House, a fine old building situated on Capitol Square, at its Franklin street entrance; the Mechanic's Institute, vacated by the Confederate States War Department, and all the buildings on that Square up to 8th street, and back to main street; the Confederate Arsenal and Laboratory, [and] 7th streets.[6]

Meanwhile, sleep came uneasily for the troops of the Twenty-fifth Corps under the command of General Godfrey Weitzel as they waited for the dawn of the day that would give them the Confederate capital. According to General Weitzel, on April 3rd, he received a dispatch delivered by cavalry courier, from Lieutenant General Grant, reading in part, "I do not doubt that you will march into Richmond unopposed. Take possession of the city and establish guards and preserve order until I get there. Permit no one to leave town after you get possession." In the meantime Grant expounded to Weitzel, "The army here will endeavor to cut off the retreat of the enemy."[7] When dawn broke over the camps of the Army of the James on the morning of April 3rd, Colonel Charles F. Adams, Jr., and his 5th Regiment Massachusetts Cavalry broke camp and moved out beyond their picket line. Lieutenant Edward J. Bartlett, of Company E, remembered that it was approximately six in the morning as they rode out only a short distance when a command was given to "halt, dismount, and prepare to fight on foot."[8]

Adams communicated in a letter to his father that at dawn he received a dispatch from the picket line that the enemy was not to be seen and he moved his command to the Darbytown road. He relates:

> After fretting, fuming and chafing for an hour, I had the satisfaction of getting in motion at last. I had about one thousand mounted men and a battery. I got out to the Darbytown road and by this time heavy explosions were heard towards Richmond, like the sound of heavy, distant fighting. Finding the enemy's lines deserted and no orders coming I concluded that something was up and it was best to push ahead; so we went through the lines and took the Richmond Road. Then came an exciting march, not without vexations; but nine o'clock found me in the suburbs of Richmond.[9]

Major General Godfrey Weitzel commanded the 25th Army Corps and took charge of the surrender of Richmond, Virginia. He remembered that "Colonel Adams asked as a special favor to be allowed to march his regiment through the city, and I granted it. I was told that this fine regiment of colored men made a very great impression on those citizens who saw it" (Library of Congress Prints and Photographs Division Washington, D.C. LC-DIG-cwpb-07632).

Undoubtedly, what Adams and others heard on the morning of April 3rd were the sounds of the city magazine, an accumulation of military munitions and powder stored in Richmond, to which the torch had been placed. A chilling and ghastly record of events was recorded by the *Richmond Whig*:

> It will be recollected the magazine was blown up by the Confederates just before sunrise on the morning of the 3rd instant—eleven inmates of the city almshouse and one old colored man living on 2d street being killed by the explosion, and thousands of panes of glass in the city smashed by the concussion. We have no means of ascertaining the quantity of powder in the magazine at the time it was blown up, but presume it must have been several tons. The magazine, a

small brick building, twenty feet wide, by thirty long and twenty high, surmounted by a steep slate covered roof, and surrounded at the distance of six feet by a thick brick wall which rose above the eves, was situated on the southern slope of a hill one hundred yards east of the northern extremity of Shockoe Hill Cemetery, and about the same distance north of the buildings occupied by the Superintendent of the Poor and the city paupers.—The building faced due north and south. On the morning of the evacuation, the Superintendent and inmates of the Poor House somehow became aware that the magazine was to be blown up, and all hustled out and ran in their night clothes over the neighboring hills and stopped in what they considered places of safety. Having waited some time, and no explosion taking place, a number of them determined to return and save their clothing. About the time they reached the places where they had left their clothing and whatever other little property they possessed, the explosion occurred. The four walls of the magazine were blown not equally in every direction, but in four volleys towards the four cardinal points of the compass. One of these volleys raked the Almshouse premises, making a wreck of one-half of the main building and utterly demolishing several of the smaller buildings. Eleven of the paupers were killed outright either by flying brickbats or the concussion, and several others seriously injured.—Another volley was thrown westward up the hill toward the cemetery, about twenty yards of the wall of which was knocked down level with the earth.—Many of the bricks and other rubbish were thrown much farther westward, to Second street and beyond. An old colored man, lying asleep in the upper story of his house, on Second street, was killed by a brick which passed through the roof and struck him in the temple. The other two volleys, flying east and north, expended themselves on the hills. Nothing but a long narrow trench in the ground, looking like a grave of a resurrected giant, marks the spot where the magazine stood.—It is astonishing into what atoms the brickbats and timbers of the building were for the most part blown. They have more the appearance of having been ground in a grist mill or quartz-crusher than blown up. None of the rubbish fell back into the foundation. From each side spreads out over the green hills the pulverized brickbats, like four enormous pale red faces.

By this explosion the City Hospital and the new Poor House had most of their glass broken, but received no other considerable damage. Had the magazine not been situated somewhat in a ravine, the injury to the city and the loss of life resulting from its being blown up must have been much greater. We have not learned the name of the individual who applied the torch. We wish we were able to state that he lost his life by the exploit.[10]

Throughout the annals of history the morning events of April 3, 1865, have been debated, analyzed, and pondered concerning whether the 5th Massachusetts Volunteer Cavalry was the first unit to enter the fallen Confederate capital of Richmond on that momentous day. Authors and historians, past and present, have come to the overall conclusion that the 5th Massachusetts Cavalry was the first *black cavalry* regiment leading the vanguard of General Godfrey Weitzel's 25th Army Corps into the burning ruins of Richmond.[11]

Major General Weitzel stated: "Before daybreak I felt pretty well convinced that the enemy were evacuating Richmond, and therefore

Federal army entering Richmond (*Harper's Weekly*, April 22, 1865).

as soon as day dawned I sent Maj. A. [Atherton] H. Stevens, 4th Massachusetts Cavalry, and Maj. E. [Eugene] E. Graves, aide-de-camp, both of my staff, with forty of my headquarters cavalry, belonging to Companies E and H, 4th Massachusetts Cavalry, to receive the surrender of the city, and to direct the authorities and citizens to cause all liquor to be destroyed and to preserve order until my troops arrived."[12] Major Graves and his detachment had successfully entered Richmond and arrived at Capitol square where they were met by Mayor Joseph Carrington Mayo and received the surrender of the city. Weitzel further elaborated:

> At daybreak I started General Kautz's (First) division, Twenty-fifth Corps, up the Osborne pike, General Devens' (Third) division, Twenty-fourth Corps, up the New Market road, and the cavalry under Col. C. F. Adams, jr., Fifth Massachusetts Cavalry, up the Darbytown and Charles City roads, and directed them all to halt at the outskirts of the city until further orders. I then rode ahead of the troops along the Osborne pike and entered the city hall, where I received the surrender at 8:15 a.m. Majors Stevens and Graves had entered a little after 7 a.m. I found the greatest confusion, pillaging and disorder reigning, and the city on fire in several places. ... The first troops to reach the city were the two companies (E and H) of the Fourth Massachusetts Cavalry who were the escort to Major Stevens and Graves, and their guidons were the first national colors displayed over the city. Next came the pickets of the Twenty-fourth Corps. After that, as I was in the city and not on the outskirts, I do not know what came, and is a matter of dispute, both divisions claiming the credit.[13]

According to the *Richmond Whig* of April 4, 1865, it recounts further testimony to the destruction that awaited the coming of the Union army upon its march on Richmond:

At sunrise on Monday morning [April 3rd], Richmond presented a spectacle that we hope never to witness again. The last of the Confederate officials had gone; the air was lurid with the smoke and flame of hundreds of houses sweltering in a sea of fire.

The streets were crowded with furniture, and every description of wares, dashed down to be trampled in the mud or burned up, where it lay,—All the government store houses were thrown open, and what could not be gotten off by the government, was left to the people, who everywhere ahead of the flames, rushed in, and secured immense amounts of bacon, clothing, boots, &c.

Next to the river, the destruction of property has been fearfully complete. The Danville and Petersburg Railroad depots, and the buildings and shedding attached thereto. For the distance of half a mile from the north side of Main street to the river, and between 8th and 15th streets, embracing upwards of twenty blocks, presents one waste of smoking ruins, blackened walls and broken chimnies [sic].

After the surrender of the city, and its occupation by Gen. Weitzel about 10 o'clock, vigorous efforts were set on foot to stop the progress of the flames. The soldiers reinforced the fire brigade, and labored nobly, and with great success. The flames east on Main street, were checked by the blowing up of the Traders' Bank about noon.

The flames gradually died out at various points as material failed for it to feed

The Ruins of Richmond, Virginia. The Richmond *Whig* of April 4, 1865, reported, "Next to the river, the destruction of property has been fearfully complete" (Library of Congress Prints and Photographs Division Washington, D.C. LC-DIG-ppmsca-34851).

Federal army entering Richmond. Trooper Charles T. Beman of the 5th Massachusetts recalled, "Going through the city we passed thousands of citizens, colored and white, who cheered and cheered us as we rode in triumph along the streets.... They shouted 'God bless you! We have been waiting for you and looking for you a long time'" (Frank Leslie, *The Soldier in Our Civil War,* **v. 2, p. 372).**

upon; but in particular localities the work of destruction went on until towards 3 or 4 o'clock, when the mastery of the flames was obtained, and Richmond was saved from utter desolation.[14]

Witnessing the horrid scenes that were presented, General Weitzel instructed that General Charles Devens march his division into the city and "endeavor to extinguish the flames."[15] He also ordered "Parson's Engineer company to assist," adding, "I directed Kautz to occupy the detached forts nearest the city and Manchester, and Adams to picket the roads."[16] At this moment Colonel Charles Francis Adams, Jr., presented a special request to General Weitzel. The general recalled, "Colonel Adams asked as a special favor to be allowed to march his regiment through the city, and I granted it. I was told that this fine regiment of colored men made a very great impression on those citizens who saw it."[17]

Trooper Charles T. Beman of the 5th Massachusetts recalled what he witnessed upon entering Richmond: "Going through the city we passed thousands of citizens, colored and white, who cheered and cheered us as we rode in triumph along the streets," recalling, "this is certainly a city of hills for it is going up and coming down all the time. There are many fine buildings and nice-looking colored people here. They shouted 'God bless you.! We have been waiting for you and looking for you a long time.'"[18] Furthermore, Lieutenant Bartlett again recalls the morning events: "In the rear of our battalion was a brigade of colored troops, who marched up the street platoon front, with their drums and fife. It was a grand, triumphal march."[19]

"Long lines of negro cavalry swept by the Exchange Hotel," wrote city resident Sallie Brock,

> Brandishing their swords and uttering savage cheers, replied to by the shouts of those of their own color, who were trudging along under loads of plunder, laughing and exulting over the prizes they had secured from the wreck of the stores, rather than rejoicing at the more precious prize of freedom which had been won for them. On passed the colored troops, singing, "John Brown's body is mouldering in the grave," etc.[20]

Nellie Grey recalled "negroes," who "falling on their knees before the invaders hail them as their deliverers, embracing the knees of the horses, and almost preventing the troops from moving forward."[21] Benjamin Quarles' work, *The Negro in the Civil War* (1969), epitomizes the feeling of local inhabitants of Richmond. One can envision the appearance of the regiment as they rode in column through the fallen Confederate capital:

> Richmond Negroes were beside themselves with joy. Here on horseback and afoot were men of color, in neat blue uniforms, their shoulders erect, their heads high, their eyes confident. The black admirers ran along the sidewalks to keep up with the moving column, not wishing to let this incredible spectacle move out of sight. In acknowledgment of their reception, the Negro cavalrymen rose high in their stirrups and waved their swords. The cheers were deafening.[22]

Chaplain Garland H. White of the 28th U.S.C.T. was witness to the 5th Massachusetts Cavalry riding throughout the fallen ruins of the Confederate capital. "The excitement at this period was unabated, the tumbling of walls, the bursting of shells, could be heard in all directions, dead bodies being found, rebel prisoners being brought in, starving women and children begging for greenbacks and hard tack, constituted the general order of the day," wrote Garland. "The Fifth Cavalry, colored, were still dashing through the streets, to protect and preserve the peace."[23] What a fitting honor it was for Charles Francis Adams, Jr., as he said, "To have led my regiment into Richmond at the moment of its capture," recalling that it "is the one event which I should most have desired as the culmination of my life in the Army."[24] Adams, in writing to Massachusetts governor John A. Andrew on April 5, 1865, expressed his recollections of leading the 5th Massachusetts into Richmond:

> Your Excellency
> Deeming the entry of the regiments, which I have the honor to command, into the City of Richmond, as a part of the column which took possession of that City on the 3rd inst. an incident in the closing events of this war of sufficient moment to justifye[sic] special mention. I have the honor to submit to you the following report. I do so for the additional reason that I believe this regiment was the only one from Mass. in that column & as it is the only recruited Reg. of Colored Cavalry East of the Alleghenies.
> The last detachment of the Reg. arrived before Richmond from Point Lookout Md. late in the day where the whole Regt. Had been stationed during the nine months previous, late in the day on Sunday April 2nd. At the same moment that it arrived orders were received to be in readiness for instant movement. Early in the morning of Monday the 3rd orders came for the provisional brigade of which it was a part, to move out on the Darbytown.
> Incidence of war—a Regiment of black Cavalry from the State of Massachusetts marching amid the wildest enthusiasm into the Capital of the State of Virginia.
> I am happy to be able to state that the conduct of the recruited portion of the Regiment on this occasion was most exemplary. Not only were they guilty of no desorder[sic] or act of pillage, but not one man left his rank & not a single case of intoxication, even, came under my notice. Both in its appearance & conduct the Regiment did credit to itself & the Commonwealth.[25]

For the 5th Massachusetts Volunteer Cavalry, and for all African American soldiers of the Civil War, this was a most fitting tribute to what they had so dearly fought for. It was the final honor that the black soldier enacted in the closing drama of the Civil War. The *Chicago Tribune* reported on April 5th the news regarding the fall of Richmond and the ironic entrance upon the fallen Confederate capital by the United States Colored Troops. "This war has been full of marked coincidence," stated the *Tribune*, "and that by which the representatives of an enslaved race bore the banner of Freedom into the birthplace [Charleston, South Carolina] and also into the capital of the Rebellion, is not the least of the historical compensations of the war. We can imagine the sable warriors of Weitzel, rolling up the whites of their visual orbs, and exhibiting an untarnished display of nature's dentistry, as they passed the offices of our contemporaries of the press—the Richmond Sentinel, Examiner, Whig, and Dispatch. Perchance Richmond hears from their own lips, for the first time, the 'wild warbling strains' of 'John Brown's Soul is Marching On,' or sympathizes opportunely in the sentiment so feelingly expressed by the venerable and aged 'Shady':

'Good-bye, Massa Jeff, good-bye, Massa Steben!'" The *Tribune* declared, "The survivors of those who fell in the disastrous assault on the 'crater' at Petersburg have had the post of honor in the final consummation."[26]

One of the many questions that has arisen over the years has to do with a certain guard being placed at the doorstep of Mrs. Robert E. Lee.[27] It has been mentioned that possibly the guard at the Lee's residents was, in fact, an African American soldier. Taking this query a little further it has been pondered that just possibly this was a member of the 5th Massachusetts Cavalry. The amount of truth or credence held in these allegations should be regarded as relatively slim. The story might easily have been established through a *New York Herald* tabloid of April 13, 1865, reporting the "serious illness of Mrs. General Lee." The dispatches of Mr. Theodore C. Wilson in Richmond reports:

> Mrs. General Robert E. Lee is seriously indisposed at her residence in this city. The reverses attending the rebel arms have unnerved the lady completely. Since the occupation of Richmond the government authorities have acted with the most scrupulous regard for the feelings of Mrs. Lee. At first a colored guard was placed in front of the house she is occupying on Franklin street; but upon it being represented that "The color of the guard was perhaps an insult to Mrs. Lee," they were withdrawn, and a white one substituted. There are some who do not think the change ought to have been made. If colored men are fit to fight down treason and restore the authority of the government of the United States, they are certainly good enough to patrol in front of the residence of the wife of a general who has used his influence and talents to cost this nation thousands of lives and millions of treasure, the matter of feeling to the contrary notwithstanding. Last evening the condition of Mrs. Lee was somewhat improved; but it is said that the shock to her constitution has been very severe, and that there is not much hope for her recovering.[28]

General Weitzel in his memoirs of the entry into Richmond refutes the claims that were alleged by the *New York Herald*. He states:

> My brother, Captain Lewis Weitzel, aid-de-camp on my staff, was riding through the city in obedience to my orders engaged in gathering all the able-bodied men to assist in extinguishing the fire, when he was hailed by a servant in front of a house towards which the fire seemed to be moving. The servant told him that his mistress wished to speak to him. He dismounted and entered the house and was met by a lady who stated that her mother was an invalid, confined to her bed, and as the fire seemed to be approaching she asked his assistance. The subsequent conversation developed the fact that my brother was addressing Miss Lee, and that the invalid was no other than Mrs. R. E. Lee. My brother knew that I was a cadet at West Point, General Lee was superintendent of the academy, and had often heard me speak in high terms of him and his family. He at once, therefore, went to the nearest commander, Col. Ripley, who furnished him with a corporal, two men, and an ambulance from his own regiment, the 9th Vermont. Captain Weitzel ordered the corporal to remain near the house and if there were serious danger to remove Mrs. Lee. These men remained on duty until all danger was

over. These are the facts upon which the lie was based. As I have herein before stated, no colored troops were placed on duty in the city. Devens' division of white troops, having had more experience in extinguishing fires, was alone on duty with Parsons' company of the 1st New York Volunteer Engineers.[29]

Rationally, the *New York Herald* article was written to sell papers! Although the *Herald* was a reputable newspaper of the era, controversial topics were then, as now, what consumers wanted to read about. From reading the news clipping it was definitely a Northern jab at the Southern gentility and General Robert E. Lee in particular. In taking it for what it was worth, General Weitzel's rebuttal of the account made no headway in disarming the myth through the ages.

The morning of Tuesday, April 4, 1865, greeted President Lincoln in the captured Confederate capital. Upon arriving, Lincoln made his way on foot escorted by an entourage of United States sailors through the city streets. There were mixed feelings expressed by the local residents and soldiers who witnessed the occasion. Many, according to Richmond resident Sallie Brock, pushed close "to press or kiss his hand."[30] Others voiced their disgust as Emmie Sublet had; she found the whole spectacle "a monkey show."[31]

The *Richmond Whig* reported, "The President was dressed in a long black overcoat, high silk hat, and black pants, giving to his form a very commanding appearance." Making his way through the city from Rocketts Landing, Lincoln was "enthusiastically cheered by the populace and Federal soldiers," according to the *Whig* correspondent. Proceeding up Main Street to Market and from there to Franklin and to Governor Street, the newspaper reported, "The President and escort moved up Governor to Twelfth street, out Twelfth to Marshall street and the mansion of Jeff. Davis, late President of the Confederate States, and now the headquarters of Major General Godfrey Weitzel," further detailing, "The crowd surrounded the mansion, and sent up cheer after cheer as the President entered the doorway and seated himself in the reception room and reception chair of Jefferson Davis. Three cheers for Admiral Porter were then proposed and given with a hearty good will." After this momentous occasion Lincoln was greeted by staff members of General Weitzel's along with other officers outside the reception room of the fallen Confederate White House. According to the news correspondent for the Richmond *Whig*, "Subsequently the President and suite, with a cavalry escort of colored troops [5th Massachusetts Cavalry], appeared on the square, drawn in a carriage and four, which was driven around the walks, the President inspecting the condition

President Lincoln riding through Richmond, Virginia, April 4, 1865. According to the news correspondent for the Richmond *Whig*, "Subsequently the President and suite, with a cavalry escort of colored troops [5th Massachusetts Cavalry], appeared on the square, drawn in a carriage and four, which was driven around the walks, the President inspecting the condition of the troops and exhibiting an unwonted interest in everything" (Frank Leslie, *The Soldier in Our Civil War, v. 2,* p. 373).

of the troops and exhibiting an unwonted interest in everything."[32] For one private in Company D, 5th Massachusetts Cavalry, Isaiah King, he would reminisce in a post war interview:

> I had seen General Grant a good many times and I was looking forward to seeing Lincoln, but when I did, I didn't know him. The cavalry had a banquet in Richmond to celebrate the victory. I saw a tall, gangly looking man in a silk hat walking up through the aisles between the tables, stooping a little as if he was afraid of touching the ceiling. I asked a waiter who that farmer was, and I learned it was our President.[33]

6

Honorable Soldier,
Honorable Discharge

"The colored soldiers in this four years' struggle have proven themselves in every respect to be men."
                    —Unknown Trooper, 5th Massachusetts Cavalry

After having been ordered to picket the roads into Richmond, the
5th received a surprise order for the troops to return to Petersburg.
On Thursday, April 6th, Adams called in his pickets and made what
he called a "moonlight flitting."[1] It was midnight when the 5th left camp
marching through Richmond's streets where they "found the conquered
city quiet and silent as a graveyard."[2] Upon reaching the scarred ruins
of the siege of Petersburg, Adams again stretched his pickets through
the abandoned earthworks of both the Union and Confederate lines.
Adams recounts the desolation of the battlefield that met his eyes:

> I have ridden through mile after mile of deserted huts, marking the encampments
> of armies ... large houses are gone so that even their foundations can no longer be
> discovered, Forts, rifle pits and abattis spring up in every direction ... the whole
> soil is actually burrowed and furrowed beyond the power of words to describe.
> There it all is, freshly deserted and as silent as death; but it will be years and years
> before nature must bring forth new trees and a new race of men must erect other
> habitations.[3]

As stated by Adams in an earlier quote, the taking of Richmond
was not without vexation. Within days of the 5th's arrival, Charles Francis Adams, Jr., would be court-martialed and ordered to Fortress Monroe for trial. The order read in part:

Head Quarters Department of Virginia
Army of the James
Richmond, Va., April 15th 1865.

Special Orders

No. 101
  Extract
3. Colonel Adams 5th Mass. Cavalry is hereby placed in arrest for neglect of duty in allowing his Command to straggle and maraud and will report to the Commanding Officer Fort Monroe where he will be tried.

By Command of Maj. Genl Ord
(Sg'd) Ed. W. Smith
A.A. General[4]

Having been arrested for negligence of duty in allowing his command to "straggle and maraud," Adams' response was that Headquarters went off "half-cock" with the usual results.[5] The incident that provoked Adams' arrest and the charge of allowing his command to rove in search of plunder most likely took place at the Reverend Richard Ferguson's house near Darvills, Dinwiddie County, where a band of ex-slaves, led by a private in the 5th Massachusetts Colored Cavalry, were captured.[6] General Orlando B. Wilcox heard of "marauders on the Nottoway River" and sent a detachment from the IX Corps out to successfully capture the marauders' camp and wagon loads of plunder on April 16th. This band of marauders was identified as black soldiers belonging to the Federal army. According to author Chris Calkins in *The Final Bivouac: The Surrender Parade at Appomattox and the Disbanding of the Armies April 10–May 20, 1865* (1988), in the resulting capture, "some were killed and the rest were made prisoners."[7] However, Major Robert C. Eden of the 37th Wisconsin recalled that Colonel Samuel Harriman sent Captain Burnett of his staff "accompanied by a sufficient force, to reconnoiter and report on the condition of affairs."[8] Major Eden, not having witnessed the situation that took place at the Reverend Ferguson's house first-hand, nonetheless, wrote of the incident stating:

[We were] in the neighborhood of Black's and White's [Blackstone, Virginia] ... guarding the railroad and the farms and plantations adjoining, and administering, as far as our commissariat would permit, to the wants of the adjacent population.... Deserters from both armies have formed bands of guerrillas for the purpose of plunder and pillage, men from the opposing armies having in some cases associated together for this purpose near Black's and White's.... [We were] informed that a large body of guerrillas had formed a camp in the neighborhood.... [It was] found to consist of about a couple of hundred Guards, &c, duly posted. The commanding officer was a private of the 5th Mass. Colored Cavalry, who had, by some means or other, strayed from his command, and had, like David, "gathered to him every one (of his color) that was in distress and every one that was discontented," and had established a camp in regular military style.

The sable chieftain sat at his tent door as the Captain approached, and while one intelligent son of Africa was carefully cleaning his master's horse, another highly intellectual contraband was blacking his boots.... Poor Cuffee was sent back to his regiment under arrest, and his sable warriors who belonged to the neighboring plantations dispersed to their homes, and their arms, which they collected from the battle field of the Five Forks, turned over to Uncle Sam.[8]

"Poor Cuffee" may refer to Private James Cuffee of Company L. Cuffee was a laborer and resident of Dorchester, Massachusetts, who at the age of twenty-two enlisted on April 15th, 1864. He was mustered out on October 31, 1865, with the regiment. However, more likely, "cuffy" or "cuf" was a common slang term referring to any black male. It derives from the word *kofi*, a name given to boys born on Friday from the Gold Coast of Africa.[9]

From the camp of Company G, 5th Massachusetts Cavalry, Captain Hiram E. W. Clark reported to Brevet Major-General Edward Ferrero his findings regarding reports that soldiers within the Union camps outside Petersburg had been straggling and pillaging among surrounding civilian occupied farmsteads. On April 22, a scouting party led by Clark took to the north side of the Appomattox River. Clark reported, "I took to the river road, sending out parties on all cross roads. At Mr. Gill's I learned that two sheep had been killed at his farm by soldiers on the 20th instant. These men crossed the river in a boat. They were armed with the Spencer carbine." Moving farther on, the scouting party came upon the village of Matoaca. Clark writes, "I learned that soldiers were in the habit of crossing the river at various points in boats and on rafts. Soldiers have often been to Mr. Keesee's, taking such things as suited their fancy. This gentleman lives about nine miles from Petersburg. He had two mules taken on the night of the 20th. It is said they were taken by two of his former slaves." A mile from Mr. Keesee's farm Clark reports that he led the scouting patrol onto the Hickory Road "some three or four miles distant." Detailing his findings further, Hiram Clark states:

> In this district there had been no soldiers. I found that about two weeks ago there had been soldiers at houses some six miles from the city, taking horses and arms, searching trunks, taking jewelry, &c. For the past ten or twelve days there have been no depredations committed north of the River road, as far as I could learn. The testimony of the people goes to show that these depredations are not committed by stragglers, but by men coming across the river from their respective camps. I have found that these men generally come across in the morning and return at night to their camps.[10]

On Sunday the 23rd, the 118th Pennsylvania stacked arms at Sutherland Station, Virginia. It was reported by veterans of the 118th that "a ludicrous incident occurred here."[11] In their front was a cavalry regiment from Massachusetts which had reached the field, this being the 5th Massachusetts Cavalry. The survivors' association of the 118th Pennsylvania published their recollection of the incident:

The Officers of this regiment [5th Mass. Cavalry] were all white, the men all black. A number of our men went up to the tent of their regimental sutler and found he had a large stock of goods such as army sutlers usually sell. The colored soldiers were proud of their new uniforms and put on many airs. Our boys were ragged and rough and had no money—were ready for any kind of a skirmish. They crowded around the sutler's tent. Three negro soldiers on guard ordered them to fall back, but the men didn't feel so disposed and kept increasing in numbers. The corporal of the guard, a big black fellow, wishing to magnify his office, came up and undertook to arrest our men for disobeying orders. The result was that Sergeant Brightmeyer landed the corporal on his back; in a moment all was excitement. The ropes of the sutler's tent were quickly cut, and the men rushed in and carried off boxes of canned peaches, canned tomatoes, sardines, tobacco, cheese, cookies—everything disappeared in a moment. The 20th Maine, 1st Michigan and our boys all had a hand in this plunder. The officers of the colored regiment rushed down with drawn swords to arrest the offenders, but by the time they arrived on the ground there were entirely other men there seeking plunder and participating in the fight with the negro guards (they having now been called out). The officers' swords went flying in the air, and their new hats with cords and tassels were being kicked about like footballs by the men. If the cavalry officers had acted wisely they would have let the matter drop, but, to our surprise, we heard their bugles calling "boots and saddle," and saw the colonel with two or three squadrons of his men come dashing down on the regiments. That officer, in a loud voice, asked what was wanted. The colonel of the cavalry demanded that these men be arrested and punished, and if they were not he would arrest them himself; and suiting the action to the word, he pressed his line forward till their horses stood between our stacks of guns. The boys of the 1st Michigan and 20th Maine had received orders to take arms and fix bayonets. The result was the cavalry was handsomely repulsed with the loss of a number of horses. The colonel's had been bayoneted six or eight times and had to be shot, along with others. The brigade commander advised the cavalry colonel to move his regiment away or some of them might get killed.[12]

In the end no trial or charges were placed against Colonel Charles Francis Adams, Jr., or any soldier of the regiment. Special Orders No. 114 issued by Major General Ord directed as follows:

Head Quarters Dept. of Virginia,
Army of the James,
Richmond, 27th April 1865

Special Orders
No. 114   Extract
3. Colonel Adams Commanding 5th Mass. Cavy. Having Satisfactorily explained the circumstances which led to his arrest and that he was in no wise responsible for the bad behavior of a portion of his regiment; is relieved from arrest and will resume command of the 5th Mass. Cavy. reporting for orders to Major Genl. Hartsuff.

By Command of Major Genl. Ord[13]

As a postscript to all of this strife, in May orders came down for the unit to embark on an expedition to Texas to crush out all Confederate resistance. In December 1861, as the early years of the Civil War were beginning to be waged, forty thousand French troops, including French Foreign Legion regiments serving under the puppet regime of Austrian Duke Maximilian, were landing in Mexico by orders of Emperor Napoleon III. This was a direct response to Mexican president Benito Juarez's suspension of payments of foreign debt. For the United States this was a violation of the Monroe Doctrine and in a greater measure thousands of Confederate soldiers began fleeing towards the Texas-Mexico border, where Maximilian was granting sanctuary and enlisting these bands into his forces.[14]

The first week of May brought to a close the long mournful funeral train procession of the slain President. It had been three weeks since President Lincoln was shot at Ford's Theater on the night of April 14th, succumbing to death the following day at 7:22 a.m. After a public viewing circuit throughout the North, May 3rd found Lincoln's body home at last in Springfield, Illinois, where vast numbers of viewers came to behold the "Great Emancipator" as he lay in state at the capitol building. It was the public's last chance to show homage and respect to their fallen virtuous leader. The following day Lincoln's casket proceeded from the state capitol to Oak Ridge Cemetery where one last funeral ceremony was beheld. In the sorrowful days immediately following Lincoln's funeral in Springfield, the men of the 5th Massachusetts Cavalry left Petersburg, Virginia, on May 6th, moved to Light House Point, Virginia, being assigned by Special Orders, Number 146 to the Cavalry Brigade, 25th Army Corps, on May 30, 1865.[15]

On May 1st orders were sent from Major General Henry Halleck to Major General Ord instructing that all colored troops under his command were to be "assigned to the Twenty-fifth Corps, and that the corps will be put into camp of instruction at City Point or Bermuda Hundred."[16] On the 18th of May, General Weitzel in command of the Twenty-fifth Corps was ordered to "get his corps ready for embarkation at City Point immediately upon arrival of ocean transportation."[17] He was to take to Texas "forty days' rations for 20,000 men, one half of his land transportation, and, one fourth of his mules, with the requisite amount of forage for his animals." Any surplus baggage along with public property was to be "turned over to the depots at City Point."[18] These orders set off a chain of communications between Generals Weitzel, Halleck, and Grant concerning the amount of mules along with forage to be sent, besides this, there were, according to Halleck, "attached to the Twenty-fifth Corps several batteries manned by white troops." Halleck wanted to know from Grant whether these troops were to be sent with General Weitzel because, as he understood it, "they are unwilling to go." Halleck recommended to Grant that because Weitzel "has plenty of colored artillerymen without batteries" that it might be better that "the guns be transferred so as to make his command homogenous." General Grant wired instructions back, clarifying his orders regarding the final amounts that General Weitzel was to take on the sea voyage along with instructions that the white troops connected with the mentioned batteries were to be detached and subsequently mustered out.[19] All the while, the 5th Massachusetts Cavalry prepared for transportation and only awaited final orders when around June 1st Colonel Adams' health again broke down from past ailments. He returned to his home in Quincy, Massachusetts, to recuperate, but his military career had come to a close. His discharge from military service was on August 1st, 1865, after an active service of three years, seven months and twelve days. Upon returning to civilian life Adams became an expert on railroad regulation and management, and from 1884 to 1890 was president of the Union Pacific Railroad. He also would become a prolific author and historian. Passing away March 20, 1915, in Washington, D.C., he was laid to rest at Mount Wollaston Cemetery, Quincy, Massachusetts.[20]

A reporter for the *Army and Navy Journal* stated that Grant had no intention of sending "any Eastern troops of importance to that service [Texas] at present, Weitzel's Twenty-Fifth (colored) corps being the only ones mentioned as likely to go."[21] General Henry W. Halleck proposed and was given approval for the movement of the entire Twenty-fifth Army Corps, approximately 20,000 men to Texas. Halleck reasoned that the black soldiers were ill-disciplined and feared that the occupation of Virginia by African American soldiers would lead to race conflicts in the state. Characteristically, toward the end of the war, the demobilizing of black troops back into civilian life was not as expediently implemented as it was for their white counterparts. As previously stated, African Americans did not begin enlisting into military service until 1863 and 1864. Accordingly, their three-year terms of enlistment had not expired when the Confederacy crumbled with the surrendering ceremony at Appomattox Court House, Virginia, on April 9, 1865. The United States government contended that the Twenty-fifth Corps would be ideal participants in deterring the Confederacy from reestablishing a renewed foothold in Texas and wished to pressure Maximilian and his French contingent to forsake Mexico. General Ulysses S. Grant expressed after the war that by protecting Mexico from a European monarchy and "thus threating our peace at home, I myself, regarded this as a direct act of war against the United States by the powers engaged, and supposed as a matter of course that the United States would treat it as such when their hands were free to strike." Grant further asserted, "After the surrender of Lee, therefore, entertaining the opinion here expressed, I sent Sheridan with a corps to the Rio Grande to have him where he might aid Juarez in expelling the French from Mexico."[22]

Therefore, during the month of May, General Grant sent instructions to General Philip Sheridan stating, "Assigning you to command West of the Miss. [Mississippi River].... Your duty is to restore Texas, and that part of Louisiana held by the enemy, to the Union in the shortest practicable time, in a way most effectual for securing peace." Grant further expressed, "To be clear.... I think the Rio Grande should be strongly held whether the forces in Texas surrender or not and that no time should be lost in getting them [Federal troops] there."[23]

In the coming months the region west of the Mississippi River, specifically Texas, would see a determined Federal presence totaling fifty thousand soldiers and within that amount were an estimated twenty thousand black troops.[24] Thomas Morris Chester, writing for the *Philadelphia Press*, reported on May 22, that "the negro corps [XXV Corps], under General Weitzel, has received marching orders is well known throughout their camps, and they are beginning to put on the war-paint with the impression that they are going to Texas. They look forward to the period of embarkation with a great deal of satisfaction."[25]

On June 13, 1865, the regiment having arrived at Fortress Monroe, Virginia, embarked on U.S. transports sailing from Hampton Roads, June 16th, to the base of supply at Brazos de Santiago, Texas. The *New York Times* informed readers that two days earlier, "Immediately after the departure of the infantry portion of the Twenty-fifth Corps for the point of rendezvous at Mobile Bay, about a dozen large steamers arrived here [Fortress Monroe] for the purpose of transporting the Cavalry Brigade of the Twenty-Fifth Corps, under command of Brig.-Gen. Cole, to the same destination." All of the steamers had been "supplied with twelve days' coal and water, and much of the cavalry has already embarked." The *New York Times* further reported that "the following-named steamers have their full complement of troops, and are now ready to sail, viz.: H.S. Hagan, Dudley Buck, New Jersey, McClellan, Weybasset, and Demolay. The remaining steamers will all be ready in a few days, although the oppressively hot weather prevents dispatch in landing."[26]

The embarkation had proven tumultuous as other black enlisted men, who had arrived at Fortress Monroe to board the transport ships, had mutinied. The 5th Massachusetts Cavalry had the unfortunate circumstance of being falsely grouped into the mutiny incident. A correspondent of the *Philadelphia Inquirer* reported from Fortress Monroe, Tuesday, June 13th:

> A mutinous spirit has been manifest among several of the brigades of the Twenty-fifth Corps and the inauguration of the Texas expedition, and there has been an outbreak or two, but as the cases were individual, and there being no evidence of preconceived action, we abstained from giving publicity to exceptional cases, not wishing to furnish food for the prejudice already existing against the employment of colored men as soldiers. The Colored Cavalry Brigade, consisting of the First, Second and Fifth United States Colored [sic; Massachusetts] Cavalry, made threats at City Point that they would not be "sent to Texas"; "that the government had no right to send them there," &c. No attention was paid to these mutterings by the others, who regarded them as the grumblings peculiar to the African race.[27]

According to the correspondent, the cavalry brigade was ordered to exchange their weapons at City Point, Virginia, and were "furnished with new Sharpe's breach-loading carbines, new accoutrements, new sabres, sabre belts, &c." for the coming deployment to the Texas theater of war. When some of the soldiers of the 1st United States Colored Cavalry were ordered to board the steamer USS *Meteor* they refused, telling their officers that they would not board oceangoing steamers as the government had no right to send them to Texas. With an organized force from Fortress Monroe, consisting of the 3rd Pennsylvania Heavy Artillery, arriving on scene the riotous black soldiers were ultimately quelled and ordered to stand down.[28]

There were other incidents of mutiny reported amongst the U.S.C.T. regiments preparing to sail for Texas. The 29th Connecticut Volunteers (Colored), for instance, rose up against not only their commanding officers but also towards those in their own ranks who were willing to board the ships for Texas. The prevailing fear among most who mutinied was a belief that they would be placed on board ships and sent to Cuba or other parts of the West Indies and sold back into slavery. "I was astonished at the behavior of the soldiers," remarked Alexander H. Newton. "They gave themselves over to all kinds of sports and jestings, which disgusted me most thoroughly. Many were unruly, even threatening the lives of those who favored going to Texas whither we had been ordered for garrison duty. Some of the gang were arrested for their insubordination." Newton observed, "There was quite an excitement on board when it was whispered about that the officers had covenanted together to take the soldiers on board, to Cuba, and sell them as slaves."[29]

The *Boston Daily Advertiser* reported that the "steamer McClellan, having on board Brig.-Gen Cook, commanding cavalry brigade, Twenty-fifth Army Corps, and staff with a detachment of the 5th Massachusetts Cavalry, Lieut-Colonel Weld in command had, arrived at South Pass, Mississippi River, June 23, from Fortress Monroe, on her way to Texas." Detailing further that "the detachment of the 5th Cavalry consists of headquarters of the regiment and 1st battalion, companies *E, F, G* and *I*," furthermore the paper concluded that all were "well on board."[30] Ultimately, arriving off Brazos de Santiago, Texas June 30, 1865, the 5th Massachusetts Cavalry disembarked on July 3rd.[31] After unloading and guarding brigade property, the companies of the regiment joined at Clarksville, Texas (along the mouth of the Rio Grande River) as a unit to begin its assignment in Texas.[32] At Brazos de Santiago the units of the Twenty-Fifth Army Corps, specifically the men of the 5th Massachusetts Cavalry, served out much of their time in Texas performing the arduous task of manual labor off-loading incoming transport ships and fortifying for any possible impending attack. Charles Waters, serving in Company A, for instance, was put on detached service providing his knowledge and skills as a farrier at the headquarters of the Twenty-fifth Army Corps.[33]

Brazos de Santiago is situated at the southern tip of Texas ten miles from the border of Mexico on the Gulf of Mexico and at the mouth of the Rio Grande River. It was first used by the United States military during the Mexican War as a base of supply. A road was built down Brazos Island, across Boca Chica Bay to the Rio Grande in 1846. To cross Boca Chica Bay, General Zachary Taylor built a floating bridge to transport military supplies across the inlet to White's Ranch. Throughout the campaign against Mexico, a young junior officer serving in the 4th United States Infantry by the name of Ulysses S. Grant and a staff engineer, Robert E. Lee, were known to have crossed the tract of land several times.[34] If Charles Frances Adams, Jr., had still commanded the 5th Cavalry, upon disembarking at Brazos de Santiago, his description of it would have been indistinguishable from his view of Point Lookout, Maryland. Again here was "a low, sandy, malarial, fever-smitten, wind-blown, God-forsaken tongue of land"; five feet above sea level. Tropical storms had destroyed the villages at the mouth of the Rio Grande in 1840 and all buildings at Brazos de Santiago in 1844.[35]

On May 12, 1865, two hundred fifty Federal soldiers under the command of Colonel Theodore H. Barrett marched down Brazos

Island, across Boca Chica Bay and joined fifty more troops at White's Ranch. The next day, May 13th, one hundred ninety Confederates met at Palmito Hill driving the Federal troops back to Boca Chica Bay. Since Robert E. Lee had surrendered at Appomattox, Virginia, on April 9, 1865, the battle of Palmito Ranch was to be the last significant land battle of the war. Due to the remote location, word did not reach either force until May 18, 1865, that the war had ended.[36]

On August 1st, Samuel Emory Chamberlain, having had prior service with the 1st Massachusetts Cavalry, became colonel of the 5th. Chamberlain had ties to Texas in several ways throughout his life. Although born November 11, 1829, in Center Harbor, New Hampshire, his parents would relocate to Boston where Chamberlain spent most of his childhood. In 1844, at the age of 15, he would make his way west to Illinois and in June 1846 join the Alton Guards of the 2nd Illinois Volunteer Regiment to fight in the Mexican War. Transferring almost immediately upon arrival in Texas into the 1st United States Dragoons he would claim for a time to have served a stint with the Texas Rangers fighting guerrillas' bands in Mexico.

Samuel Emory Chamberlain became colonel of the 5th Massachusetts Cavalry August 1, 1865, having prior service with the 1st Massachusetts Cavalry (James L. Bowen, *Massachusetts in the War 1861–1865*, p. 898).

Deserting from the 1st United States Dragoons on March 22, 1849, he would make his way back to Boston were he settled down in 1855, ultimately marrying and having three children.[37]

With the outbreak of the Civil War, Chamberlain left his profession as a policeman to join the 3rd Massachusetts Militia as first lieutenant of Company C on April 23, 1861. After his three-month term of service expired he enlisted as a private with the 1st Massachusetts Cavalry on September 6, 1861. However, by the end of November of the same year Chamberlain had risen through the ranks and was captain of Company B. Promotions came quickly for Chamberlain and by July 28, 1865, he would muster out of the 1st Massachusetts Cavalry holding the commissioned rank of colonel. His service with the 1st Massachusetts Cavalry shows an active record including wounds at both Malvern Hill and Poolesville, Virginia, where he was wounded and captured. Subsequently, after being exchanged, Chamberlain would again be wounded at Kelly's Ford, Brandy Station, St. Mary's Church and Ream's Station, Virginia.[38]

Although Colonel Chamberlain was knowledgeable about the geographical and meteorological conditions of Texas, the conditions for himself and the 5th Massachusetts Cavalry were unbearable. The men had to combat heat, inadequate drinking water, insects, reptiles and a lack of firewood. The physical labor was hard, the climate demanding, and admitting oneself to the hospital was a fact of life. In his book *We All Got History* (1996), Nick Salvatore notes that within Company D, Texas proved to be fatal: "Thirteen of the company's fourteen deaths were the result of disease; most occurred at Brazos de Santiago."[39]

Margaret Humphrey substantiates these horrendous conditions in her study *Intensely Human* (2008) which examines the health of the black soldier in the American Civil War. Humphrey details the hospitalization of men serving in the areas of Brazos de Santiago, Clarksville and Brownsville, Texas, who were admitted to the Brownsville Post Hospital. Examining existing hospital registers she states, "The hospital did not open until 14 July 1865. Over the next two weeks, 842 patients entered the hospital; 46 percent of them had scurvy as an admitting diagnosis. Another 563 men arrived in August; 54 percent had scurvy as an admitting diagnosis. There were only 32 deaths in July but over the next month 129 men died in the hospital." Humphrey concludes, "Combining these six weeks, 35 deaths were from scurvy and 77 from diarrhea or dysentery."[40]

With the prospect of trouble with Confederates migrating to the area having come to an end and threats from the country of Mexico having subsided, Major General Philip Sheridan was by order of the War Department on August 1, 1865, "to cause all volunteer white troops—cavalry, infantry, and artillery—serving in the Department of Texas, that you think can be dispensed with, to be mustered out of service."[41] Sheridan received further orders in early September directing that "all organizations of colored troops in your department, which were enlisted in the northern States, be mustered out of service, *immediately.*"[42] Along with the drawdown of other Federal military forces making final preparations to board the military transports home, the 5th Massachusetts Cavalry was mustered out of Federal service at

Clarksville, Texas, as of October 31, 1865. The regiment immediately started for Massachusetts, completing most of the trip by steamship, by way of New Orleans and New York City. Quartermaster Sergeant Thomas J. Laurel, when writing for the *Anglo-African* on October 21, 1865, expressed his joy in returning to the Bay State and seeing friends and family, exclaiming "our many near and dear friends will be overjoyed to receive us, most particularly those who have young wives and sweethearts."[43]

"The Latest News by Telegraph to the N. O. Times" read the headline on page three of the *New Orleans Tribune* dated October 29, 1865. Detailing the United States, world and domestic affairs during the last week of October, the article imparts, "*Washington*, Oct. 25—It is understood that the President will recommend to Congress the recognition of the Imperial Government of Mexico. It is rumored that Hon. Reverdy Johnson and Gen. Dix will soon be appointed to places in Cabinet. Senor Romero, the Mexican minister has received dispatches of the capture of Matamoros, and of the entire occupation of the State of Tamaulipas, by the liberal forces under Juarez." Further detailing Washington affairs the *New Orleans Tribune* continued: "It is positively known that Mr. Jefferson Davis's trial will soon take place. *Washington*, Oct. 27.—The Tunis Ambassadors were last evening received by the President." Additionally, reporting the news provided from the *Galveston Bulletin* of October 26th the *New Orleans Tribune* provided readers the latest reports from Matamoros and the movements of the 5th Massachusetts Cavalry: "The U.S. Transport *St. Mary* arrived here yesterday morning, from Brazos Santiago, having on board 1050 colored troops, consisting of the 5th Massachusetts, and 43rd Pensylvania [sic] Cavalry. Col. Weldon [Lt. Col. Horace N. Weld], of the 5th Massachusetts, informs us that just before he left Brazos, it was reported that Matamoros had been taken by the liberals, and that they were now fortifying Bagdad." Sailing to New York it arrived with Adjutant General William Schouler, Commonwealth of Massachusetts, waiting to greet the officers and men, as they spent only "a few hours" before they continued their final journey to Boston, "proceeding by steam-boat and railroad." Upon arrival in Boston Harbor, the regiment was landed at Galloup's Island where it remained until late in November when it was paid off and discharged.[44]

With the vision of returning to civilian life and back pay in hand, a final ceremony awaited the men of the 5th Massachusetts Cavalry. It was ordered May 15, 1865, that "volunteer regiments and batteries, on their return to their respective States, when mustered out and discharged, should deposit their colors with the chief United States mustering-officers, to be by them transferred to the governors of the States."[45] By December 13th, the state of Massachusetts issued orders calling "for the deposit of the flags" and fulfilling the wishes of officers expressing interest in participating in the ceremony, "appointed the 22nd of the month for a grand procession, over which the old banners would float, and be borne to the Capitol."[46]

Major General Darius Nash Couch assumed overall command of the procession. Brigadier General Edward W. Hinks (the same Hinks whose 3rd Division of Smith's 18th Corps the 5th Massachusetts had been assigned to when they saw the elephant at Baylor's Farm a year and a half earlier) was appointed chief of staff. Lieutenant Colonel Christopher Columbus Holmes was charged with commanding the escort of honor, this escort being composed of men from the independent corps of cadets.[47]

Although the weather was cold, throngs of citizens crowded the downtown streets on the day of the parade, December 22, 1865. The ground wore a slight covering of snow as the 5th Massachusetts Cavalry donned their uniforms to march through Boston's streets. The citizens were in high spirits and proudly "displayed the 'stars and stripes,' and the national flag floated proudly on the breeze from every flag staff and public building in the city." The procession took to forming on Park Street, Tremont Street, and Beacon Street malls. Accordingly, General Couch's headquarters tent was erected near the gate opening on the Park Street Mall and "the colors of the different regiments were delivered to the officers of the respective commands from his tent."[48]

The jubilant procession of regiments commenced at the appointed time of eleven o'clock. According to the adjutant generals report of the proceedings, the brigade of cavalry "consisted of a delegation of the First Frontier Cavalry, forty strong; the Fifth (Colored) Cavalry, under the command of Major Adams, fifty men; and the Third Massachusetts, Lieut.-Col. Muzzey, a hundred men and twenty officers." Thus the brigade of cavalry formed ranks with the 3rd having "the right of the brigade; then followed the 5th; and the representatives of the Frontier Cavalry were the last in the Cavalry line." They were joined by almost every regiment from the state of Massachusetts. The regiments proudly paraded and brandished their battle flags, each embroidered with the names of the engagements they had participated in. The parade culminated at the state capitol, passing in front of Governor John Andrew.[49]

In his work *We All Got History* (1996), author Nick Salvatore observes the special significance of the 5th presenting their colors to Major General Darius Nash Couch. Their flag, with the inscription "Baylor's Farm" painted upon the standard, was proof of their ability as fighting men. Couch was the same officer who in June 1863 had refused to accept black soldiers for the defense of Pennsylvania against the Confederate invasion by the Army of Northern Virginia. Salvatore concludes, "Given all that had transpired since the Fifth Massachusetts Cavalry had assembled at Readville, it was a fitting, if ironic, ending."[50]

General Couch addressed Governor Andrew and the throngs of onlookers as follows:

> May it please your Excellency,—We have come here to-day as the representatives of the army of volunteers furnished by Massachusetts for the suppression of the Rebellion, bringing these colors in order to return them to the State who intrusted them to our keeping. You must, however, pardon us if we give them up with profound regret; for these tattered shreds forcibly remind us of long and fatiguing marches, cold bivouacs, and many hard-fought battles. The rents in their folds, the battle-stains on their escutcheons, the blood of our comrades that has sanctified the soil of a hundred fields, attest the sacrifices that have been made, the courage and constancy shown, that the nation might live. It is, sir, a peculiar satisfaction and pleasure to us, that you who have been an honor to the state and nation from your marked patriotism and fidelity throughout the war, and have been identified with every organization before you, are now here to receive back, as the State custodian of her precious relics, these emblems of the devotion of her sons. May it please your Excellency, the colors of the Massachusetts volunteers are returned to the State.[51]

Governor Andrew replied with a brief eloquent address:

> General—This pageant, so full of pathos and of glory, forms the concluding seen in the long series of visible actions and events in which Massachusetts has borne apart for the overthrow of rebellion and the vindication of the Union.... General, I accept these relics in behalf of the people and the Government. They will be preserved and cherished, amid all the vicissitudes of the future, as mementoes of brave men and noble actions.[52]

The veterans themselves did not quietly fade away. Their service to their country has stood the test of time and exemplifies the best of American culture. A fitting summary of the record of performance of the USCT troops and that of the 5th Massachusetts Cavalry (Colored) came from trooper John O. Malone of Company F, who said, "The colored soldiers in this four years' struggle have proven themselves in every respect to be men."[53]

7

Forever Free: Life After War

"How you gonna keep 'em down on the farm after they've seen Paree?"

In the years after the disbanding of the 5th Massachusetts Cavalry, veterans of the regiment established post-war lives throughout various portions of our great nation. Many of the veterans, both enlistee and officer, sought political, entrepreneurial, agricultural, and civic occupations. These veterans began to build their lives, hoping to partake in the freedoms that they so dearly fought, and many of their comrades had died, to secure. During the closing months of the war and during the first half of the Reconstruction era, Federal legislation would be brought to a vote and ratified on the floor of Congress. This legislation, the Thirteenth, Fourteenth and Fifteenth amendments to the United States Constitution, including the Civil Rights Act of 1866, had a direct and powerful impact in providing further civil and protective rights to the post-war lives of the veterans of the 5th Massachusetts Cavalry and to all African Americans.

The Thirteenth Amendment ratified by the states on December 6, 1865, expressly declared, "Neither slavery nor involuntary servitude, except as a punishment for crime whereof the party shall have been duly convicted, shall exist within the United States, or any place subject to their jurisdiction." Along with the Civil Rights Act of 1866, which defined United States citizenship and equal protection under the law, the Fourteenth Amendment was ratified July 9, 1868. It stipulated that "all persons born or naturalized in the United States" were granted citizenship and states could not forbid that right. In so doing, the Fourteenth Amendment protected the person from being denied their rights to "life, liberty or property, without due process of law" or "equal protection of the laws."

In the granting the right to vote, the Fifteenth Amendment expressly stated that the "right of citizens of the United States to vote shall not be denied or abridged by the United States or by any State on account of race, color, or previous condition of servitude." Although the amendment would be ratified on February 3, 1870, the struggles African Americans faced would continue to be increased with Southern state legislatures enacting restrictive measures, so-called Jim Crow laws, which followed on the heels of Black Codes to intentionally deter the advancement of the African American race in their efforts to establish their full citizenship.

* * *

All soldiers, no matter the era, seem to have one thought on their minds while in the service; that thought is of home. The thought could be of loved ones or friends, the weather or food, but if that thought was of one thing from home then there just was nothing better on this Earth. Sadly, sometimes the boy who went innocently off to war is not the man who returns. It can be a very trying task for a soldier to return home to civilian life. After mustering out, Private Joseph Brunson returned home to Blairsville, Pennsylvania, to resume life as a civilian. As with many returning veterans from the Civil War he found life at home had changed and moved on in his absence. In Brunson's case, the grandparents who had helped raise him had passed away and the ties that bound him to Pennsylvania seemed to wane. In World War I, there was a popular song that went, "How you gonna keep 'em down on the farm after they've seen Paree?" Maybe the wanderlust that had sent Joseph Brunson off to join the Union army years before had returned to lure him to a new adventure. "After I was mustered out of services, I lived at Blairsville, Indiana County P.A. for six or seven year cannot say definitely," Joseph related in a later pension affidavit. "Then came to Kansas. I there lived two year at Hiawatha Brown County Kansas. Then went to Phillips County Kansas where I lived three year."[1]

Settlement of the prairie lands of Kansas did not begin until the 1850s, and then very slowly. Within years after the conclusion to the Civil War, pioneers rushed into the region by the tens of thousands. They were lured with the prospect of land being available to homestead. Under the terms of the Homestead Act of 1862, a man could stake a claim to a piece of unoccupied public land by living on it and cultivating it for five years, after which he could file for ownership. By its terms, for a fee of only ten dollars, any United States citizen or alien immigrant could claim 160 acres.[2] In the 1850s, while most Kansas prairie lay uninhabited, townships had been divided into a checkerboard pattern of square-mile plots by federal surveyors. Each square contained 640 acres and was known as a section. The sections were further divided up into quarters of 160 acres each, being the size allowed each settler under the Homestead Act.[3]

By the late 1870s when veterans applied for their land the choicest plots had been filled. These war veterans needed to spread westward into the prairie lands and did so using a later Homestead Act, the Soldiers' and Sailors' Homestead Act of June 8, 1872. This act is slightly different from the original of 1862 but still follows the same terms. An applicant was required to supply the Land Office with a copy of his discharge from the military, the exact location of the homestead and personal affidavits of proof of his claim. Joseph Brunson's application provides a fascinating glimpse into the veteran's life after the Civil War as a pioneer settler. The Soldiers' and Sailors' Homestead under act of June 8, 1872, affidavit reads:

> No. 12877 Land Office at Kirwin, Kansas October 16, 1879
>
> I, Joseph Brunson of Phillips Co. Kansas, do solemnly swear that I am a discharged soldier, of the age of (over) twenty-one years and a citizen of the United States; that I served for (at least) ninety days in Co. E Fifth Mass. Cavalry Regiment United States Volunteers; that I was mustered into the United States military service the 5th day of Feby, 1864, and was honorably discharged there from on the 31st day of Octr, 1865; that I have since borne true allegiance to the Government; and that I have made application No. 12877 to enter a tract of land under the provisions of the act of June 8, 1872, giving homesteads to honorable discharged Soldiers and sailors, their widows and orphan children; that I have made said application in good faith; and that I take said homestead for the purpose of actual settlement and cultivation, and for my own exclusive use and benefit, and for the use and benefit of no other person or persons whomsoever; and that I have not heretofore acquired a title to a tract of land under this, or the original homestead law, approved May 20, 1862, or the amendments thereto, or voluntarily relinquished, or abandoned, an entry heretofore made under said acts: So help me God.
>
> [signed] Joseph Brunson
>
> Sworn and subscribed to before me, Tho. M. Helm
>
> Register of the Land Office at Kirwin, Kansas, this 10th day of October 1879.
>
> [signed] T. M. Helm, Register.

Included in these records is a receipt for purchase that reads:

> Receiver's Receipts, No. 12877 Application No. 12877
>
> H O M E S T E A D
>
> Receiver's Office, [Notary Public stamped] Oct. 16, 1879
>
> Received of Joseph Brunson the sum of Fourteen dollars —— cents; being the amount of the Act of June 8, 1872 of fee and compensation of Register and

Commonwealth of Massachusetts.

ADJUTANT GENERAL'S OFFICE.

Boston, Mar" 6" 1891

The name of *Joseph Brunson* of *N° 9. Boston* aged *21*, occupation *Farmer*, is borne upon the Muster-out Roll of Co. *"E. 5"* Regt. Mass. Volunteer *Cavalry* Col. *Chamberlain*; enlisted on the *5* day of *Feby* *1864*, and mustered into service of United States on the *10* day of *Feby* *186d*, for *3* years *Mustered out* on the *31* day of *Oct* *1865*

Adjutant General.

Remarks. *Mustered out absent Sick*

Private Joseph Brunson's service certificate, proving his enlistment in the 5th Massachusetts Colored Cavalry. Brunson and other men of his regiment were often required to present similar documents when submitting pension claims (author's collection).

Receiver for the entry of SE4 of Section 18 in Township 5 of Range 18, under Section No. 2290, Revised Statues of the United States.
160 acres. [signed] L. J. Best, Receiver. $14.00[4]

Undoubtedly, having been born a free man from the North and having had the status of being a veteran strengthened Brunson's ideal of defending the social and political gains realized during the war.[5] However, for many other African Americans the amendment that forever prohibited slavery within the jurisdiction of the United States found a new awakening with the coming of the Exodus of 1879–1880.

On March 4, 1865, the United States Congress established the Bureau of Refugees, Freedmen, and Abandoned Lands; commonly referred to as the Freedmen's Bureau. This agency's main goal was to assist more than four million former slaves to have access to equal justice, fair labor practices, land, and education.[6] A desire for a home and a better chance at life was so strong to many black southerners that they overlooked warning signs given off by many of the unscrupulous con men. Swindlers were urging blacks to migrate to Kansas where they would obtain forty acres of land, a mule, and provisions to last a year, no strings attached. Inevitably, migration was heavy and circumstances were not what they professed to be in the exaggerated newspaper publications and reports by speculators.[7] Accordingly, on May 7, 1879, a convention of African Americans assembled in Nashville, Tennessee, to discuss the progress that the black citizens had made during the fifteen years since the Emancipation Proclamation. Delegates from Alabama, Arkansas, Georgia, Indiana, Illinois, Louisiana, Mississippi, Missouri, Nebraska, Ohio, Oregon, Pennsylvania, Tennessee, and South Carolina were in attendance. One of the main topics of discussion was the subject of migration to the new states west of the Mississippi River. The following resolution was adopted as a result of this meeting:

> Resolved, That it is the sense of this conference that the colored people should emigrate to those States and Territories where they can enjoy all the rights which are guaranteed by the laws and constitution of the United States, and enforced by the executive departments of such States and Territories; and we ask of the United States and appropriation of $500,000 to aid in the removal of our people from the South.[8]

The first wave of refugees reached Wyandotte, Kansas, in the beginning of April 1879. The Exodus was so enormous that by the first of August, over seven thousand had arrived in the state. It was so overwhelming that a relief society was formed and temporary barracks were erected in North Topeka for the shelter of those who poured into the city. An appeal went out to the public that addressed the situation in regards to the influx of refugees to the area:

TOPEKA, KAN., June 26th, 1879.
TO THE FRIENDS OF THE COLORED PEOPLE:
The directors of the Kansas Freedman's Relief Association, in view of the present

situation, deem it proper to make public this address, and ask the friends of the colored people to further aid in caring for the helpless and destitute refugees.

This is a matter not local to our State, but is one of national concern....

In organizing this association, we are moved by two controlling motives. The first was one of humanity. Many of them were old and decrepit, and many young and helpless, and with few exceptions were destitute....

Another incentive to meet this emergency was to maintain the honored traditions of our State which had its conception and birth in a struggle for freedom and equal rights for the colored man. She has shed too much blood for this cause to now turn back from her soil these defenseless people fleeing from the land of oppression....

We have made an effort to establish a colony about fifty miles west of this city in Wabaunsee County. Finding that good land could be bought for $2.65 per acre, we are locating about thirty families on forty acres each....

What we need is money with which to obtain shelter, medical assistance, and furnish transportation to such places as will give them employment. This we must have, or relinquish all further efforts at organized assistance to these refugees.

The good people who have already so generously contributed to the cause, have our sincere thanks.

All contributions should be sent to Gov. John P. St. John.[9]

Unrelentingly and after generous efforts employed by the relief association in North Topeka, the exodus continued unabated through the winter of 1879–1880 and increasing into the spring. During the winter and spring an estimated $25,000 was expended in relieving the black refugees and aiding them to find employment. In March alone some 250 to 300 African Americans established themselves in Topeka every week. There had already been between 20,000 to 25,000 black emigrants and in 1880 there would be upwards of 40,000. With the diminishing influx of migration by African Americans into the state, the Kansas Freedmen's Relief Association would finally be dissolved April 15, 1881.[10]

Although many African American veterans were not participants in the Great Exodus, their migration into the state of Kansas through the Soldier's and Sailor's Homestead Act provided another illustration as to how these veterans during this era contributed to the settlement of the majestic prairie lands of the west. Homage has to be given to these men who struggled against the odds of oppression to pave the way for a better life for themselves and for future generations.

Even into the turn of the 20th Century veterans of the 5th Massachusetts Cavalry, such as Irenas Johnson Palmer, were forthright opponents to the Southern Jim Crow laws and took an increased stand in being outspoken activists for the civil rights of African Americans. Palmer was born February 20, 1842, in Hinsdale, New York. In 1863 he made his way to Boston where he enlisted December 26th into Company A of the 5th Massachusetts Cavalry, being commissioned on February 1, 1864, as first sergeant. At the close of his service, in November 1865, Palmer made his way back to New York where he established himself as an architect and builder in Olean, New York. He wrote and published in 1902 *The Black Man's Burden; or, The Horrors of Southern Lynchings*, exposing the crimes committed by the South and the methods of those who took to lynching. He specifically detailed the lynching of Julius Gardner of Arkansas who was arrested by a southern lynch mob, lynched, and survived to tell the story.[11]

Among the ranks of the regimental veterans, one would hold the title of "King." At twenty-six years of age, escaped slave Samuel Ballton enlisted March 5, 1864, at West Roxbury and mustered into service as an enlisted private in Company H at Readville, Massachusetts. Having been promoted to the rank of corporal August 18, 1864, he held this rank upon mustering out and returning to civilian life. In the subsequent post-war era Ballton was able to effectively establish himself as a land owner and business entrepreneur. He established a profitable business venture in the growing, harvesting, and packaging of pickles in Greenlawn, New York. This was so profitable that in 1899 alone Ballton harvested 1.5 million cucumbers that were successively processed for pickling and packaged for distribution.[12] After that year, Samuel Ballton would forever be known as the "Pickle King" of Greenlawn, New York.

Not only could Ballton hold the title of "Pickle King," but he also rightfully could claim to have achieved the status of an entrepreneurial king. Besides instituting a successful pickling business, Ballton further achieved success with his endeavors into the real-estate and building trade, further increasing his personal income and making a mark on the community of Greenlawn. Indeed, Samuel Ballton's achievements are a lasting remembrance to a man who came up from the oppressive institution of slavery to fight for his own right to be free, and to establish a profitable and enduring life for him and his family.[13]

In the case of Robert Fitzgerald's service with the 5th Massachusetts Cavalry, his was short lived for in October 1864 he was discharged due to illness. After the war he relocated to Amelia County, Virginia, and established a school for freedmen. He attended Lincoln University in Pennsylvania for a short time and ultimately headed back south to Hillsborough, Orange County, North Carolina, where he again provided schooling for freedmen. In later life he operated a tannery and took up a partnership with his brother Richard, establishing a brick kiln in Durham, North Carolina; many buildings to this day stand as witnesses to the R. [Richard] B. Fitzgerald Brick Manufacturer Company.[14]

Several of the veterans of the regiment sought to establish their post-war lives in the regular army. A revealing look into one particular officer of the regiment can be found in the study of Second Lieutenant Francis S. Davidson. Davidson was born to an affluent and influential family with ties to the West Indies. He was appointed to the United States Military Academy at West Point, New York, in September 1861. His cadet career at West Point was marred by many academic shortcomings and marks upon his record. On January 31, 1865, he was discharged for "deficiencies in philosophy and conduct."[15] Still determined to pursue a military career, Davidson received a citizen appointment as second lieutenant in the 5th Massachusetts Cavalry on June 9, 1865. He joined the unit at Brazos de Santiago, Texas, and was mustered out with the regiment in October 1865.[16]

During the post-war years, Francis Davidson served in a lackluster manner with the 9th United States Cavalry. Having been arrested on several occasions he was dismissed from military service guilty of "breach of arrest, conduct unbecoming an officer and a gentlemen, and highly insubordinate conduct, all to the prejudice of good order and military discipline" on November 15, 1875.[17]

On February 23, 1903, then-president Theodore Roosevelt provided an objection to Senate Bill 1115 entitled "An Act for the relief of Francis S. Davidson, late first lieutenant, Ninth United States Cavalry." The act originated in the Senate and was enacted by both houses of Congress to authorize Roosevelt to "revoke General Court-Martial Orders Numbered Ninety-Three" which was handed down to Francis Davidson on November 15, 1875, and to "issue to him a certificate of discharge of that date, and to nominate and, by and with the advice and consent of the Senate" to appoint Davidson a first lieutenant in the mounted service of the United States Military. Furthermore, the act provided for the placement of Davidson on the retired list with the rank of first lieutenant providing that "no pay, compensation, or allowance shall be paid him from the date of his dismissal to the date of the passage of the Act."[18]

Roosevelt returned the bill to the Senate with a rebuttal outlining in detail the specific incidents which took place in regard to Francis Davidson having been court-martialed and dismissed from the service. He rejected to the bill by stating,

No act of special gallantry or conspicuous service marked the short period during which he [Davidson] was an officer of the Army. He is 56 years of age. This bill proposes to put him upon the retired list, where he would be supported for the remainder of his life at public expense without rendering any return. It does not appear that he is subject to any physical disability incurred in the line of duty or otherwise. The treatment thus proposed is denied by law to all the officers whose service has been continuous and faithful, for they are not entitled to the benefits of the retired list until after forty years' of service, or reaching the age of 64, or being physically disabled.[19]

Roosevelt tersely concluded that "an officer with this record should be rewarded is wholly without justification, and if that should be done it would involve a confusion between the treatment accorded to loyal and faithful service and that accorded to insubordination and unfaithful service, which could not fail to be most prejudicial to the morale and efficiency of the Army."[20]

Second Lt. Francis Snelling Davidson received a citizen appointment in the 5th Massachusetts Cavalry on June 9, 1865. He joined the unit at Brazos de Santiago, Texas, and was mustered out with the regiment in October 1865 (author's collection).

Barry I. Mickey in the November-December 1996 issue of *Military Images* magazine published a photograph of Lt. Francis S. Davidson while serving in the 5th Massachusetts Cavalry. Mickey relates that "Davidson may have been bi-racial, and thus among the first minorities to attend West Point."[21] Mickey further states:

The concept of race is cultural, and thus subjective, and has no biological significance; however, the photo portrays many of the features that our society has come to accept as typifying African Americans: wide nose, curly hair, and dark complexion. Davidson's grandfather, a native of New Hampshire, spent many years in Puerto Rico, where Davidson's father was born in 1822, and at least one uncle was a resident of Barbados. The origins of the maternal side of this tree are unknown.[22]

Although, we cannot say for certain if Lt. Francis Davidson was of African American descent what can be concluded is that Davidson is just one of the many enthralling characters to come out of the history of the 5th Massachusetts Cavalry.

* * *

"I feel greatly honored by your letter of June 29th. Nothing would give me greater pleasure than to accept office in your administration; but before I can give a definite answer I must ask for a short time to consider conditions," was the answer Robert Shaw Oliver had written from Albany, New York, July 1, 1903, to President Theodore Roosevelt regarding acceptance to the position of assistant secretary of war. Oliver's military service to his country was in stark contrast to that of Francis Davidson's. At age seventeen Oliver was the youngest to hold an officer's commission in the 5th Massachusetts Cavalry.[23]

While the 5th Massachusetts Cavalry was on duty at Point Lookout, Maryland, in 1864, Oliver reported to camp and was commissioned as second lieutenant in Company G on October 13, 1864. While serving with the regiment at Point Lookout, Maryland, Oliver requested a five day leave to report to Washington, D.C., where he specified that he was "an applicant for the U.S.M.A. at West Point. Hon. Charles Sumner Sen. has given me to understand that my presence is requested in Washington for the furtherance of obtaining an appointment thereto."[24] Although the record shows that Oliver was unsuccessful in obtaining the appointment, he did however, serve a brief stint as regimental adjutant and aide on the staff of the Twenty-fifth Army Corps along with being assistant adjutant general of the Third Division of the same corps while serving in Brazos de Santiago, Texas.

Upon mustering out, in November 1865, Oliver continued to pursue a career in the military. He served both as a lieutenant and captain with the 8th United States Cavalry along with a staff position as assistant inspector general of the District of Arizona. In 1880, he was appointed inspector general of the State of New York and was made general of the Third Brigade of New York's National Guard.[25] Now in 1903, Oliver telegrammed President Roosevelt, who was then staying at Oyster Bay, New York, avowing, "Would accept if possible to take office in September otherwise regret much that must decline for reasons given in my letter of ninth have written."[26] Having consulted the wishes of his wife along with being reassured that he was able to arrange his personal affairs, Oliver served in the capacity of assistant secretary of war under both Presidents Theodore Roosevelt and William Howard Taft, a service spanning ten years—1903–1913.

For both the officers and enlisted men political aspirations ran high during the post-war Reconstruction era. After mustering out with the regiment at the close of the war regimental adjutant Daniel Henry Chamberlain settled down in South Carolina in 1866. He established himself as a cotton planter on John's Island; however this proved to be unprofitable. On December 16, 1867, he returned north and wedded Alice Ingersoll. After his marriage he embarked on a career as attorney general of South Carolina. In 1874 he won the Republican nomination and election as governor of the state. In the 1876 election, anticipating re-nomination, he would be entangled in one of the most heated elections in South Carolina and Reconstruction history.[27]

Partnering with questionable fellow partisans and "adopting stern measures in connection with racial clashes," he lost support from many Democrats and the election ultimately went to ex–Confederate general Wade Hampton. The campaign was marked by vicious accusations and mud-slinging from both sides. Chamberlain and Hampton both claimed victory; Chamberlain was legitimately inaugurated on December 7th while Hampton, the Democratic nominee, was sworn in by the pseudo-government established by his own party. The issue was not settled until President Rutherford B. Hayes called a conference between the two factions and ultimately ordered federal troops surrounding the South Carolina statehouse to return to their barracks. Wade Hampton would in turn peacefully assume the office of governor.[28]

With no governing body to control and his political career all but ruined, Chamberlain returned north. He took a professorship at Cornell University, practiced law, traveled abroad in Europe, and returned in 1906 living his final year near Charlottesville, Virginia, passing away April 13, 1907.[29]

Likewise, First Lieutenant Curtis Hyde Whittemore was another officer of the regiment who sought out a political career in the Reconstruction-era South. In September 1862 he served as a private in the 44th Massachusetts Volunteer Militia mustering out in June 1863 with the rank of corporal. By January 1864 he took a commission as a second lieutenant and in due course mustered out with the rank of first lieutenant in the 5th Massachusetts Cavalry. After the war he relocated to the south, settling with his wife and family in Pulaski County, Arkansas, and served a stint in the Arkansas House of Representatives. He subsequently held a later career as Pulaski County,

Arkansas, Treasurer. He died in 1926 and is buried in Mount Holly Cemetery, Little Rock, Arkansas.[30]

It wasn't only the officers of the regiment who pursued and obtained political office during the post-war years. Enlisted men such as Private George Lawrence Mabson had their own aspirations. Mabson was the free mulatto son of a prominent white Wilmington, North Carolina, resident, George W. Mabson, and his African American wife, Eliza. Prior to the outbreak of the Civil War George Lawrence was sent north to obtain his education in Massachusetts. Once war was declared Mabson joined the United States Navy serving aboard the USS *Colorado*. At the close of his term of service, Mabson enlisted into the 5th Massachusetts Cavalry.[31]

Returning after the war to Wilmington, North Carolina, in 1868 Mabson was appointed to the command of the Twenty-Second Regiment North Carolina Militia by Republican governor William Woods Holden. Seeking a career as a lawyer, George Mabson, with the assistance of then-senator and former Civil War general Joseph C. Abbott, secured a policing position at the U.S. Capitol in Washington, D.C., and entered law school at Howard University. On June 16, 1871, with a law degree in hand, Mabson again returned to his native Wilmington, then a Republican majority held region, and successfully passed the state bar exam, becoming the first of his race to hold the title of lawyer in the state of North Carolina.[32]

Mabson was elected to serve as both a North Carolina State representative and senator between 1872 and 1874, but he was unsuccessful in obtaining a position in the United States Congress. However, he was the front runner in being chosen as inspector of customs in Wilmington. Senator George N. Hill in writing to then-president Ulysses S. Grant on December 6, 1873, declared, "I am candidly of the opinion that the appointment of Hon. George L. Mabson to the position of Collector of Customs, port of Wilmington N.C., will give entire satisfaction to the people most interested, and certainly to the party in this State favorable to the administration."[33] North Carolina representative Jacob T. Brown concluded in writing to President Grant, "Mr. Mabson, is the choice of the colored people, for the above position, and while they disclaim the least intention of raising the question of Color, they would regard his appointment as a very great compliment. For the past eight years, he has been constantly before the people of this state, as an orator in the interest of Republicanism."[34]

Although many of the veterans of the 5th Massachusetts Cavalry were able to establish seemingly successful careers in governmental positions, on the other hand, several former officers of the regiment came under investigation and criminal prosecution for their wrongdoings; such as Horace Weld and James Wheat. Under the column "Crimes and Criminals" the Monday, May 31, 1875, edition of the Chicago *Inter Ocean* announced, "ARREST OF A POSTOFFICE THIEF' Boston, May 30, —Horace N. Weld, for nine years employed in the Post office, was arrested on yesterday on a charge of stealing money from registered mail."[35] Horace Weld appeared before Henry L. Hallett, United States commissioner for the district of Massachusetts, and was held "in $300 for trial" according to the *Boston Daily Advertiser*.[36]

By the start of August 1875, Weld had appeared in court and pleaded guilty to the charges placed upon him. The *Boston Investigator* summed up the conviction in the August 4, 1875, edition reporting, "A Post Office Thief.—In the United States District Court recently, Horace N. Weld pleaded guilty of embezzling letters from the post office and was sentenced to Dedham jail for four years. Weld was a clerk in the registered letter department. His reputation had previously been excellent. He made a fine record in the war, enlisting as a private and being promoted to lieutenant-colonel."[37] For Weld, who had served an honorable career during the Civil War, having moved up through the junior officer ranks of the First Massachusetts Cavalry and then holding subsequent staff positions as major and lieutenant colonel with the 5th Massachusetts Cavalry, it was indeed an unworthy mark to his career.

October 1, 1890, found former captain of Company E James L. Wheat resigning from the position of postmaster of the United States House of Representatives for reasons of illegal government kickbacks. Prior to this Wheat, in the years after the Civil War, made his way west from Massachusetts and settled in Joliet, Illinois. He was for a time an instructor along with being in charge of the prison school at the Joliet, Illinois, Penitentiary. He served two terms as sergeant-at-arms of the Illinois State Senate, later relocating to Racine, Wisconsin, where he ran a successful business as a coal merchant. In 1889 he ran for the elected position of doorkeeper of the United States House of Representatives—a duty established in 1789 by the first Congress, whose responsibility it was to monitor the entry into the House chambers. Wheat lost the bid by a narrow margin; however, he was instead elected to the position of postmaster.[38]

During his bid for the position of doorkeeper the *Milwaukee Sentinel* wrote of Wheat, "A man of high character, exemplary habits, never having drank a drop of liquor in his life, a member of the Loyal Legion and active in G.A.R. matters of his locality, and highly esteemed by his friends and neighbors, Capt. Wheat possess, it would seem, all the qualities which go to make up an honorable, capable and worthy public officer."[39] Or so it had seemed, now James L. Wheat found himself embroiled in a full House investigation. The *Milwaukee Daily Journal* wrote, "Tares among the Wheat The House Postmaster Charged with Serious Offenses by His Employes ... a resolution will be introduced in the house in a day or two calling for an investigation of the office." The *Daily Journal* continues, "The formal charges against Mr. Wheat are signed by six employes [sic] of the house postoffice [sic]. These charges accuse the postmaster of being guilty of gross irregularities in conducting the business of the office. Among other offenses cited against him are the following: That his son, Walter R. Wheat, is receiving pay for two positions, while it is impossible for one man to do the work connected with these two positions, and in consequence the work falls upon other employees of the office." Furthermore, Wheat's son was thought guilty in "opening at least one sealed letter addressed to a member of the house" and that Wheat himself knew of the matter.[40]

The charges brought to the floor of the House were alleged by C. J. McCord (the son of Wisconsin congressman Myron H. McCord) and employees under James Wheat. Wheat contended that the charges were brought up because of resentment McCord had towards him. It seemed that the charges were eventually dropped. However, again in September new charges were leveled that Wheat was receiving monetary kickbacks. The *St. Paul Daily News* reported on September 25, 1890, that a resolution was presented and an investigation was moving forward in regards to Wheat having "gave a contact for carrying the mails of the House postoffice to one Culbertson, with the agreement that Culbertson would pay to him (Wheat) $150 per month out of the same, and that he did receive this amount at least five months."[41] With the 51st Congress soon coming to a close and the all but likely prospect that the Committee on Accounts would recommend Wheat's removal as postmaster, James L. Wheat formally submitted his resignation.[42]

* * *

When the smoke lifted from the battlefield, the war revealed different meanings to different individuals. For the men of the 5th Massachusetts Cavalry who had stepped forward with patriotic vigor when our nation was in peril, the toll of battle had its own significance and consequence. There were survivors who struggled through life with disabling wounds or suffered till the end of their days with such chronic complications as tuberculosis and dysentery. Within the regiment, some had paid the ultimate price of patriotism: seven enlisted men were killed and one-hundred sixteen men died from disease.[43] Those who did survive war wounds often struggled with the consequences of these debilitating injuries long after the close of the war unable to financially support themselves and provide for their families. Along these same lines, as the veterans' ages increased, so too would health complications begin to take a toll on their ability to physically take care of themselves. William Pencak states in his two volume work *Encyclopedia of the Veteran in America* (2009) that only 1 percent of black veterans established residency in soldiers homes for disabled veterans.[44] Thus, the hope of obtaining a government supported pension was all the more advantageous and coveted.

According to the Disability and Dependent Pension Act of June 27, 1890, it requires, in case of a soldier:

1. An honorable discharge.

2. A minimum service of ninety days.

3. A permanent disability not due to vicious habits. (It need not have originated in the service)

4. The rates under the Act are graded from $6 to $12, proportioned to the degree of inability to earn a support, and are not effected [sic] by the rank held.

5. A pensioner under prior laws may apply under this one, or a pensioner under this one may apply under the laws, but he cannot draw more than ONE pension for the same period.[45]

In the early 1890s, after substantiating his claim of a homestead, Private Joseph Brunson sold his farm due to his inability to physically work the land any longer. In an application form to the United States Pension Office, for a Declaration for an Invalid Pension, dated April 10, 1894, Brunson made a claim that he was unable to support himself by manual labor for reasons of "chronic diarrhea, dyspepsia of stomach, and varicose veins," claiming these illnesses resulted from his service in the Civil War.[46] Brunson further swore that the above stipulations were true to his knowledge. Furthermore, he stated that his physical disabilities included as follows: "Chronic diarrhea, stomach trouble with indigestion, muscular rheumatism, varicosity, or enlargement of veins, with kidney and liver trouble, also heart trouble. Eyes are weak."[47] His personal physician, H. B. [Harry Bowman] Felty, M. D., who with his brother J. W. Felty, had been practicing medicine for six years under the designation Felty Brothers Surgeons of Abilene, Kansas, furnished a handwritten affidavit that supported Joseph's claim:

> I have waited on and prescribed for Joseph Brunson repeatedly during a period of five years. Applicant is subject to attacks of indigestion and chronic dysentery of long standing. The attack of dysentery are always secondary to attacks of indigestion. This condition exists for many years and is incurable. Applicant also suffers from Varicose Veins in left extremity, extending from knee to ankle. This condition alone unfits him for manual labor. I have known Mr. Jos. Brunson for 5 yr. and during this time, I am in a position to know he has not been able to do a hard days work. I consider Mr. Brunson ¾ disabled. I consider a man in his condition entitled to a pension.[48]

After consideration of the pension claim submitted by Brunson, he was granted his invalid pension as of the date of March 16, 1898, from the Department of the Interior, Bureau of Pensions; Washington, D.C. This certificate, No. 957.008, for an original pension, was issued on the above date accompanied by a voucher which he had to return to the pension agent at Topeka, Kansas. In return a monthly check would be sent directly to Brunson's address which was simply stated as: "Joseph Brunson, Abilene, Kansas." The Bureau of Pensions deemed eight dollars to be the fitting monthly compensation for his degree of disability.

There were, unfortunately, veterans who struggled to obtain and were denied government pensions for varied reasons. Often these struggles stemmed from such deficiencies as knowing how to read and write; the fact that they could not obtain the needed legal assistance in filling out the applications due to limited income; or those who had no way to successfully substantiate that their disability was caused while in the service, or for that matter, that they had even served in the United States military. Author William Pencak found in his two volume study of military veterans that from a sampling of pension claimants, it was estimated that 92 percent of all white applicants were successful in obtaining a military pension compared to only 75 percent of all African American claimants.[49]

Fifth Massachusetts Cavalry veteran Henry Washington was one such veteran who ultimately failed to receive the needed medical disability pension. Not only had he applied for a disability pension three times throughout the course of his life, he was unanimously denied all three times. Authors William Dobak and Thomas Phillips bring to light Washington's plight in their study *The Black Regulars, 1866–1898* (2001). Washington's struggle is a heart-wrenching example of how

African American veterans struggled to obtain the needed disability pension only to be blocked by bureaucratic red tape.

After Henry Washington's service with the 5th Massachusetts Cavalry came to a close he continued his career as an army soldier. Having briefly served with the 40th Infantry in Boston he transferred to the 25th United States Infantry and ultimately, in 1875, obtained a transfer into the 9th United States Cavalry. Serving in that capacity until 1885, he again reenlisted into the 25th Infantry in Minnesota. During these succeeding years, Washington suffered from rheumatism which forced him to twice enter military hospitals. In 1904, after a service of over 20 years, Washington was then living at a soldiers' home in Minnesota. In 1912, he continued to suffer from what one doctor deemed to be "tubercular abscesses."[50] In filing for a disability pension, the Pension Bureau interviewed several of Washington's former comrades who indicated that he complained of soreness to his leg and hip. However, the Pension Bureau refused to grant Washington a disability pension because he was unable to successfully convince the bureau that his condition was incurred while in the service with the 9th Cavalry and 25th Infantry regiments.[51]

In 1912, Washington for a second time sought a pension, this time a Civil War pension for his service with the 5th Massachusetts Cavalry; again he was denied, this time because he could not establish definitively that he was a veteran of the 5th Massachusetts. Washington had lost his military discharge certificate, and several former veterans of the regiment when asked by the Pension Bureau if they could identify him as a comrade could not definitively say yes.[52]

If being denied twice was not enough, Washington continued to persevere and for a third time applied for an Indian Wars pension. However, he was again blocked from obtaining a pension for the mere fact that his regiment's company was not directly involved in a combat role during the Ute War and that the regiment's service in New Mexico was not covered under the pension act of 1917. On April 18, 1927, Henry Washington passed away having never received his needed disability pension. Dobak and Phillips, in telling Washington's history, present a sad conclusion to his ordeal. Just forty-six days after his passing, Congress formally set into law that a soldier who served in any capacity in the Indian Wars or in any campaigns associated with them between 1817 and 1898 was entitled to an Indian Wars pension.[53]

Indeed, there not only had been veterans of the regiment that legitimately worked through obtaining the myriad of affidavits and needed paperwork to substantiate their claims, there were also those who sought to work around the legal process and falsely claim veteran status in hopes of garnering a pension from the government. The *New York Times* ran a headline on January 21, 1900, "A Pension Fraud Exposed. Venerable Witnesses Come from the South to Washington to Unmask Negro Imposter." The imposter in question was a man by the name of William H. Taylor who claimed to have been a veteran of the 5th Massachusetts Cavalry and was receiving a government pension. The *Times* reported, "The investigations of the Pension Bureau into frauds on the Government frequently result in the trial of interesting cases. There was concluded recently in the criminal court a quaint, dramatic trial, which brought up a vanished phase of American life and history and filled the courtroom with figures from ante-bellum days."[54] According to the *Times*, the man in question was "distinctly a modern negro, one of the coarse, commonplace type so familiar in the slums of Northern cities." The *Times* continued, "He has secured a pension on account of a gunshot wound in the hand, received at Petersburg."[55]

The defendant had a long, irregular scar on his hand to prove his war wound. He claimed to have been a slave in Maryland and ran away to Boston where he enlisted into the cavalry regiment. When questioned by the prosecution as to the historical facts of his service, Taylor seemed self-assured in his replies. The *Times* reported, "He talked along confidently and answered every question promptly. Sometimes his answers betrayed monumental ignorance of the subject…. But his story about his army experience was as straight as a string, and he had a score of witnesses. Two of them swore that they served with him when he was shot." Everything about Taylor seemed to be falling into place until the prosecution brought forth two witnesses to counter the claims being presented by the defendant; these witnesses were the real veteran William H. Taylor and Jane Coakley, the defendant's own aunt.[56]

Standing eye to eye after the testimony by the real William H. Taylor, the *New York Times* reported that "as the two men faced each other it seemed like the contrasting of two periods of American history. The old negro spoke softly, gravely, in the deliberate speech and with the unconscious dignity on which Southern writers of plantation days delight to dwell. He still had something of a soldierly bearing, and looked venerable with his white mustache and beard. His mild, serene speech and mellow Southern dialect contrasted wonderfully with the aggressive modernity of the claimant."[57]

Then Jane Coakley came to the stand testifying that the man being brought up on charges of pension fraud was in actuality her nephew by the name of Matt. When the judge asked her if she could identify the individual in the courtroom, Coakley stood in front of the defendant and proclaimed, "Matt! Matt! My sister's boy! How could you do it, Matt? How could you lie and swear what's false and bring disgrace on folks that's good and true?"[58]

The defense, in hopes of countering these claims, brought to the stand the former slave owner of the defendant. However, it all came to a close in the courtroom when the former slave owner testified that the defendant was just a boy when the war broke out and he left the child to be cared for by the household while he was serving the Confederacy. This sealed the prosecution's claim of pension fraud.[59]

Unfortunately, with the passing of time, it seems that somehow there are always individuals who find the desire to falsely proclaim veteran status, the reasons of which we many never know. Whether or not it is for unscrupulous motives, such as in the case of William H. Taylor involving pension fraud, it is an everlasting blemish upon the true service, devotion and achievements that the veterans of the 5th Massachusetts Cavalry enacted on behalf of their country.

Regrettably, to be able to track and discover the histories of what became of all the veterans of the 5th Massachusetts Cavalry would be a daunting challenge and one which would encompass more space than is allotted to this study. However, by highlighting and taking into consideration several of these veterans' achievements, sacrifices, and struggles during the post-war era we garner an overall increased understanding of the veteran's contributions to society. These men, by not only adding positively and in many cases negatively to the political, economic, and social make-up of the country continue to augment and expand our collective understanding of their history. Their story is sewn into the fabric of our nation, and in so doing, evokes a greater appreciation in the overall historical narrative to which the colored soldiers enacted in their own march to being—forever free.

8

In Reunion and Remembrance

"Re-Unions of the colored soldiers and sailors are not merely to parade the services of those who were there during the struggle, but rather that the survivors may realize how, and to what extent, the loyal hearted people of the nation remember what they did for the race."
—George M. Arnold. Washington, D.C., Aug. 17, 1887

For many of the veterans, devotion to each other's service, brotherly comradeship and experiences would be extended with membership in post-war fraternal organizations such as the G.A.R. The Grand Army of the Republic, its official name, was organized in 1866 to benefit the Union veterans of the Civil War. In order to be eligible for membership, a soldier or sailor had to have an honorable discharge from the United States service, never borne arms against the Union, and have served sometime between April 19, 1861, and August 20, 1866. The prevailing view among historians of the G.A.R. has been that some black veterans were treated as second class members of the organization as it was in their military days, and many black veterans formed their own all-black posts. As Donald Shaffer contends in his book *After the Glory: The Struggle of Black Civil War Veterans* (2004), "Equality in the Grand Army of the Republic was more of an ideal than a reality, but it was one of the few organizations of the period that even bothered to pay lip service to the concept and actually offered tangible examples of equality in operation. They usually spent most of their time at separate posts, but white and black veterans did rub shoulders at the national and departmental encampments and in a number of integrated posts in the North."[1]

Recently, Barbara Gannon challenges this segregationist view of the G.A.R. in her book, *The Won Cause: Black and White Comradeship in the Grand Army of the Republic* (2011), stating, "One cannot exaggerate the importance of finding so many white Americans of this era willing to accept black veterans as their equals in their local social organizations. Black veterans were the political and social equals of white Americans in one of the most prestigious organizations in the United States." She further contends, "In an era in which race trumped virtually all other social identities, black and white veterans created an interracial organization at both the national and local levels."[2]

White comrades realized that black veterans had done their undeniable part in saving the Union and that they were owed a debt of gratitude. During the 1891 Detroit encampment this ideal of interracial comradeship was expressed: "A man who is good enough to stand between the flag and those who would destroy it when the fate of the nation was trembling in the balance," they stated, "is good enough to be a comrade in ... the Grand Army of the Republic."[3] One example can be found with 5th Massachusetts Cavalry veteran Stephen Jacob, who transferred from one post into the integrated Welch Post of Ann Arbor, Michigan, in 1886.[4] This grassroots concept of a band of brothers who fought and were faithful to the Union, in the end, superseded the color of their skin. Private Joseph Brunson of Company E, joined the Ellsworth, Kansas, Ellsworth G.A.R. Post No. 22 named for 2nd Lieutenant Allen Ellsworth, commander of a military fort established during the Civil War southeast of what would become the town of Ellsworth.[5] Indeed, Brunson may have been tolerated as a member of Post 22 because Ellsworth was a small community in the middle of rural Kansas where to maintain an active membership all honorably discharged veterans were accepted. Or, on the other hand, the post members may have had no decidedly racist leanings towards their membership whether white or black and welcomed Brunson unreservedly as a comrade in arms; there is no way of knowing which was the case. It is recorded for, instance, that in 1894, G.A.R. Posts in Kansas reported 40 percent of black membership within integrated posts.[6] Gannon argues that this acceptance of integrated posts in Kansas stemmed from prior prewar and wartime anti-slavery sentiment. She states, "The Kansans who fought slavery more than a decade before the war began may have been more willing to accept African Americans in their posts than the men who had grown up in a state that accepted race-based slavery."[7] However, as in Ellsworth Post 22, the membership's current residency didn't necessarily mirror their wartime locale.

In the twenty-two years since the disbanding of the 5th Massachusetts Colored Cavalry, a Grand Reunion of Colored Veterans would bring back members of the 54th and 55th infantries and the 5th Cavalry Regiments and sailors in Boston on August 1st and 2nd, 1887. This reunion of the surviving veterans was to commemorate the service of African Americans during the Civil War. It was an occasion to renew old acquaintances and revive a fraternal feeling among old comrades of the country. Their goal was to have the veterans appear in coat or blouse, hat or cap, or G.A.R. uniform. A program of music, prayer, and addresses were on the agenda. Members of the 5th Cavalry that served on the executive committee were Sergeants Amos Webber, Gustavus Booth, George T. Fisher, J. H. Bates, John Davis, Samual J. Patterson, and Benjamin W. Phoenix.[8]

"GRAND ARMY AT ST. LOUIS. THE RECEPTION AWAITING COLORED VETERANS," read the headlines in the August 20, 1887, *New York Freeman*. The editorial continued:

Objects Served by Re-unions of the Soldiers and Sailors of the Rebellion—What Their Achievements Did for the Race and the Union.

To the Editor of The New York Freeman:

In 1867 the citizens of Philadelphia made the survivors that had assembled in that city, during the month of January, welcome, thrice welcome, by tendering them a banquet, ovation and reception at National Hall. December 1884, a reception was tendered the colored soldiers and sailors at Memorial Chapel, Washington, D.C. April 27, 1887, a monster jubilee meeting, a reception and ovation was tendered them by the people of the last named city, at the Tabernacle on M street. August 1 and 2, 1887 the survivors of the 54th and 55th Infantry and 5th Massachusetts Cavalry and their friends, comrades and compatriots, from other portions of the country, had a big re-union and camp fire in Boston. Now for St. Louis in September. The National Encampment G.A.R. meets in St. Louis during the month of September, 1887, and while there the veterans of the various colored regiments, and colored sailors who will be present, are to be accorded a reception and camp fire by the citizens of that city. Inasmuch as no camp fire, re-union or reception has been tendered "our black boys in blue" "out West," it is gratifying to note the patriotic impulses that govern our friends in that city in this laudable work of showing the survivors of the war, of our race, that their deeds of heroism and valor, and great service to the race, hath an abiding place in the hearts of the people.

The ties next strongest to those that God has knit in our fibres, were forged when men stood arm to arm and knee to knee, as soldiers and sailors in the war for the Union. Make yourselves acquainted with this fact and you will readily understand how they feel toward those who honor and respect them for their past services and sacrifices for the cause of liberty. There is no way to gladden the veteran's heart or to soothe the evening of his life, better than by allowing him to see

African American G.A.R. members parading through New York City on May 30, 1912 (Library of Congress Prints and Photographs Division Washington, D.C. LC-USZ62-132913).

and know those who appreciate his services to the country. They stood sponsor to the downtrodden people of this land, in the war of the rebellion. Thirty thousand have gone to plead as only the dead can plead, for justice for the living.

> "The muffled drum's sad roll has beat
> At the soldiers' last tattoo:
> No more on life's parade shall meat [sic]
> That brave and daring few.
> On fame's eternal camping ground
> Their silent tents are spread,
> And glory guards with solemn round
> The bivouac of the dead."

Re-Unions of the colored soldiers and sailors are not merely to parade the services of those who were there during the struggle, but rather that the survivors may realize how, and to what extent, the loyal hearted people of the nation remember what they did for the race; furnish truthful history by actual participants, and give practical illustrations of scenes and incidents to those who have arrived upon the stage since 1865.

They figured in a time and during a struggle that drew largely upon the grit, courage and endurance of men. Their heroism was displayed to such an extent that men wondered the purpose of God in putting such manhood under dusky skins. They helped to save from dismemberment a union of States, a country that only recognized them as property, chattels, that would (not then) know them only as property in man. They served as soldiers and seaman, in the army and navy of a country that had accepted the fiat Negroes have no rights that white men need respect. Yet these same men, hated and despised as they were, in the days of the nation's vain glory, hypocrisy and haughtiness, poured out their blood in fields of battle and ships of war, thereby persuading the nation to believe them men, entitled to some rights that others need respect. They washed the blood scars of slavery out of the American flag, and painted freedom there; they snatched the black lies out of every false star upon its folds and set in their stead the diadem of liberty; they tore the Dred Scott decision from the statutes and wrote there "All men are equal before God." They fought for freedom and the union, and to the union and the nation they consecrated a heroism and pure loyalty that has never been surpassed by any race since the foundation of the present civilization. What have they done? They destroyed the auction block, spiked collar, branding iron and whipping post; put a stop to trading in human flesh, and the parting of man and wife, and children from their mother's breast; told the Negro trader stand from under those that God hath joined together let not man put asunder. By coolness, steadiness, bravery, courage and a God-inspired loyalty, the colored soldier and sailor made himself respected of men, and won plaudits of admiration from unwilling lips, and thereby lifted the race from the low state that cruel slavery had thrown it in, to the proud distinction of citizenship.

> George M. Arnold.
> Washington, D.C., Aug. 17[9]

The honoring of their friends, comrades and compatriots did not merely start with the post-war reunions and parades but rather during the Civil War itself. Citizens of Boston and those throughout the country who subscribed to William Lloyd Garrison's abolitionist newspaper *The Liberator* would open the latest issue on Friday, November 25, 1864, and read the following obituary and tribute to Sergeant William Henry Skeene of the 5th Massachusetts Cavalry:

> Died—At Point Lookout, Md., Nov. 5th, Sergeant William Henry Skeene, of the Massachusetts 5th Cavalry, aged 31. Funeral services were conducted at the Joy Street Church by the Pastor, Rev. H. H. White, and Rev. L. A. Grimes, on Sunday, the 13th, from whence the remains were conveyed to Cambridge Cemetery under military escort of the Shaw Guards, (Capt. Lewis Gaul,) of which company deceased was a member. The coffin was draped with the American flag, the pallbearers being members of the 5th Cavalry and Massachusetts 54th and 55th Volunteer Regiments. Salutes were fired over the grave. This was the first instance of a colored military funeral in Massachusetts.[10]

Sergeant Skeene was born in Boston. At the age of thirty he was working as a porter when he enlisted from Cambridge, Massachusetts, into Company B, 5th Massachusetts Cavalry, January 4, 1864. He was swiftly appointed corporal of Company B on January 6th and by May 2, 1864, was promoted to sergeant. Skeene was present with the 5th Cavalry throughout its engagement at Baylor's Farm, Virginia. Ultimately, Sergeant Skeene was taken by gastric fever, otherwise known as typhoid fever, sometime during the month of October into early November. Service records indicate that William Henry Skeene passed away on

Bronze relief sculpture in memory of Robert Gould Shaw by Augustus Saint-Gaudens in Boston. Veterans of the 54th, 55th, and 5th Massachusetts regiments were invited to attend its dedication on May 31, 1897 (Library of Congress Prints and Photographs Division Washington, D.C. LC-DIG-det-4a25021).

November 6, 1864, while in the regimental hospital at Point Lookout, Maryland. Besides being the recipient of the first instance of a colored military funeral in Massachusetts, Skeene exemplified the many African American soldiers who gave their lives for the cause of freedom not merely for their own race but for the country as a whole; his deeds and theirs are not forgotten.[11]

A bronze relief sculpture in memory of Robert Gould Shaw and the 54th Massachusetts Infantry is located at 24 Beacon Street in Boston. The sculpture depicts the 54th Massachusetts Regiment marching down Beacon Street on May 28, 1863. Augustus Saint-Gaudens took almost fourteen years to complete the high-relief bronze monument.[12] Veterans of the 54th and 55th Massachusetts Infantry and 5th Massachusetts Cavalry were invited to attend the dedication ceremony on May 31, 1897. On April 3, 1897, the *Springfield Republican* announced the invitation:

Survivors of the 54th and 55th Massachusetts infantry, and the 5th Massachusetts cavalry regiments, are invited by the committee in charge to participate in the ceremonies of the dedication of the memorial to Col Robert Gould Shaw at Boston on Memorial day, Monday, May 31. They are asked to report by letter at once to one of the committee. It is desired, but not essential, that comrades should wear either the uniform of a United States soldier, or the uniform of the Grand Army. Robert A. Bell Grand Army post 134, 46 Joy street, Boston, has placed its hall at the service of visiting veterans.

There will be a short parade. The battalion will form at 9 o'clock Monday morning on Arlington street, from which point it will be escorted by the 1st corps cadets and 7th New York regiment to the Memorial monument on the Common. Officers are requested to wear uniforms with belts and sashes, but not side-arms. All survivors, however, will be welcome, whether with or without uniforms. The committee are Lieut Charles L. Mitchell, customhouse, Boston; Lieut William H. Dupree, secretary, station A, Boston; Lieut John Ritchie, 10 Mt Vernon street, Boston; Col Henry S. Russell, Bristol street, Boston. The committee learns that 1000 members of the famous New York 7th regiment (of which Col Shaw was also a member during the war) have signified their intention to parade with their regiment, and that the regiment will be accompanied by its band of 90 pieces.[13]

With the increase in G.A.R. membership over the post-war years many regimental and national reunions would take place on the great battlefields of the Civil War. Veterans would dedicate regimental monuments in the locations on the field of battle where they participated and fought so gallantly. It was often found that while veterans tromped the battlefields with old comrades and family, telling of their feats in battle, they would come across lost and discarded war relics. The *Springfield Republican* of February 7, 1897, published a brief but intriguing notice:

The adjutant-general's office is in receipt of a letter from Judson Cunningham of Richmond, Va., stating that he picked up on the battle-field near that city a medalion [sic] bearing on one side a bust of George Washington, and the inscription, "George Washington, Born February 22, 1732."; on the other the inscription, "G. H. Truby, Co. H, 5th Mass. Cav. Alleghany Co., Pa. Mr. Cunningham desires to ascertain if possible, the present address of G. H. Truby, that he may have his property restored to him, or, if he is dead, to his heirs.[14]

Judson Cunningham served in Company A of the 4th Battalion Virginia Local Defense Troops—Naval Battalion. Organized on June 22, 1863, it was formed for the local defense and special service of Richmond, Virginia. Its six companies were made up of employees from the Naval Ordnance Works, the Navy Yard, Rockett's Navy yard, and the Richmond and Danville Railroad. Cunningham was approximately 14 when he was enlisted in the battalion. Census and city directory records indicate that he was working as a druggist by the 1890s in Richmond.[15]

George Trubey or Truby was born about 1843 in Allegany, Pennsylvania. He stated that he was twenty-one and working as a teamster when he mustered into Company H, 5th Massachusetts Cavalry. Trubey would go on to serve throughout his entire term of enlistment and mustered out with the regiment October 31, 1865.[16] Research did not indicate whether or not Judson Cunningham was successful in returning George Trubey's identification disc to him or his heirs. These relics of war are silent witnesses to the heroic deeds of so many soldiers during the war.

By the summer of 1938, approximately 10,000 veterans of the American Civil War were still living throughout the United States and abroad. Indeed, the ranks of the veterans of the Blue and Gray were slowly dwindling; soon their service to their country would be a passing memory and no longer would they share with future generations their recollections of acts of service to their country. The rolling hills and fields of Gettysburg, Pennsylvania, would again play host to the gathering of Union and Confederate veterans. The 75th Anniversary of the Battle of Gettysburg played host to nearly 2000 veterans; most were now in advanced age, the average being ninety-four. Ninety-two-year-old Thomas Walters had made the trip east from Los Angeles to attend the gathering of veterans at Gettysburg. He was one of only thirty-five African Americans to have served throughout the Civil War in a regiment of color and attend the festivities. Born in Jamesville, New York, at age 18 he enlisted and served with Company C, 5th Massachusetts Cavalry.[17]

The Saturday, July 9, evening edition of the Ogden, Utah, *Standard Examiner* gave fanfare to his momentous trip east. The *Standard Examiner*, announcing the arrival of seven veterans, stated, "Warriors Returning to Coast from Gettysburg.... Homeward Bound.... A few of the Civil War veterans who visited Ogden today on their way home after attending the blue and gray encampment at Gettysburg." Walters recalled his service with the regiment and their victorious entrance into Richmond and that Lincoln was there but he didn't have an opportunity to see the president. With another large scale war looming in Europe and the possibility of United States involvement, the *Standard Examiner* asked each veteran in the party what their thoughts and opinions were to this pending crises. "The veterans were divided over prospects of America entering another war," stated the *Examiner*. "Thomas Walters, 92-year-old Negro, who served two years with the Fifth Massachusetts Cavalry, said, 'There are other wars going on right now in Spain and China, and I think we'll have another. But I can't tell if there will be one in this country.'" Thomas Walters passed away on April 4, 1941, and is interred in the Los Angeles National Cemetery.[18]

Today we are reminded of the heroic deeds and service of the approximately 200,000 African Americans, including the men of the 5th Massachusetts Cavalry, who served their country and fought for their own freedoms during the American Civil War. The men's memoirs, letters, military records, along with the many battlefields and locations in which they served are our only reminders and connections to their achievements. What has come to pass of the locales that the 5th Massachusetts Cavalry encountered during their service in the war? The regiment's military enlistment and training site of Camp Meigs, Readville, Massachusetts, is presently referred to as Camp Meigs Park, engulfed within Boston proper. The 139-acre Camp Meigs, located south of the present-day Neponset Valley Parkway and bounded by Stanbro Street, Parkson Street, Clifford Street, and Hyde Park Avenue, has fallen to the encroachment of urban sprawl and development. A warehouse complex occupies a large portion of the historic site. Cutting across the area are railroad tracks used by the Massachusetts Bay Transportation Authority's commuter trains and Amtrak's Boston/New York Service. The only really true open green space on the Camp Meigs site is the park, which has a basketball court, a youth baseball field, tennis courts, and a playground. Unfortunately, even this island of green space is enveloped by a sea of residential housing. The only evidence that there was ever a military establishment in the vicinity is several historical markers, a small monument, and a replica of a Civil War cannon.

The small stone monument donated by the Boston Black Graduate Student Coalition in 1990 has the following inscriptions upon its sides: "54th Infantry 55th Infantry 5th Cavalry Dedicated to the African-American Troops who trained here and distinguished themselves in the Civil War—and to those who continue the fight for equal rights and equal justice." The reverse side reads and quotes Frederick Douglass, "Once let the black man get upon his person the brass letters US; let him get an eagle on his button and a musket on his shoulder and bullets in his pocket, and there is no power on earth which can deny that he has earned the right to citizenship in the United States."

However, a new birth might be in the near future for this extraordinarily important location to so much of Massachusetts Civil War history and that of the 5th Massachusetts Cavalry. A June 27, 2004, *Boston*

Globe news article headlined "Belatedly, Giving Glory Where It's Due Memorial to Black War Heroes Eyed," asserts that the City of Boston awarded a $15,000 grant to the Heritage Guild, Inc., to advance its plans for a memorial at Camp Meigs Park. The guild, an organization of African American women, has developed a design for $400,000 in landscaping and historic markers at the state owned park and playground. It further recounts that with winding brick stone walkways and 3-foot-high stone walls the history of Camp Meigs would be told in "engravings on the stone walls." Furthermore, "slate pieces on the paths would be engraved with the occupations of the men who trained at the camp; many would be marked 'ex-slave.' The chain-link outfield fence in the existing baseball field would be replaced with a wood and steel structure, the top of which would sway with the wind ... intending to illustrate the link between the Civil War and baseball, which was played at Civil War camps."[19]

The site at which the 5th Massachusetts Cavalry saw the elephant, that being the Baylor's Farm and portions of the Petersburg battlefield, has had the ill-fate to succumb to the encroachment of urban sprawl. Today it is a mixture of suburban residential housing and small commercial strip malls. The only testament as to the achievements of the 5th Massachusetts Cavalry and the other 18th Corps units engaged during the morning attack of June 15, 1864, on Baylor's Farm is a small wayside interpretive center and marker two and half miles east of the main Petersburg defenses near the modern intersection of I-295 and Route 36. Fortunately, remains of the many inner defensive redoubts and trench works established by the Confederates along the Petersburg front that were assaulted by units towards evening on the 15th of June have been meticulously preserved through the efforts of the National Park Service.

What has become of the Union prisoner of war camp at Point Lookout, Maryland? The lighthouse, which is owned by the U.S. Navy, is still at the tip of the Point. The earthworks of Fort Lincoln still exist on the river shore near Cornfield Harbor. The barracks and officer quarters of the fort and a portion of the prison pen have been recreated by members of the Friends of Point Lookout. Open graves from which the Confederate dead were removed a century ago are still discernible near the shore of the bay. Likewise, the cemetery to which the Confederate remains were taken for re-interment is located along Maryland Route 5 north of the park. A memorial to the dead has been erected by the State of Maryland and is administered by the federal government. Much of the original prison stockade has been engulfed by the bay waters, but portions of the perimeter walls have also been recreated by the Friends of Point Lookout.

Of course, out of the ruins and ashes of Richmond, Virginia, arose a new metropolitan city. After some one hundred fifty years the capital of the Confederacy remains the state capital of Virginia. Many of the landmarks and landscapes that the 5th Massachusetts Cavalry set their eyes on when entering Richmond in April 1865 have been preserved as historic interpretive sites, i.e., the White House of the Confederacy, the Richmond Iron Works, the land encompassing Belle Isle, and Robert E. Lee's home.

If one was to travel to Brazos de Santiago, Texas, today he would find a much different appearance from what the 5th Massachusetts Cavalry encountered. A storm reduced Clarksville, Texas, along the mouth of the Rio Grande, and Bagdad, Mexico, on October 2-3, 1867, and a more severe storm erased the final remnants of Clarksville in 1874.[20] No buildings survive today on Brazos or Boca Chica Island from the time. Because of numerous hurricanes that have flooded the area over the eras, no buildings or towns have been established within these vicinities. Today portions of the land have been set aside as a state wildlife sanctuary and historic park. However, just due north of the area of Brazos de Santiago is one of the most sought after college spring break havens of the world. The area has come under increased commercialized development encompassing hotel resorts and attractions considering its close proximity to South Padre Island. It is a far cry from the disease ridden, sandy strip of land that so affected the majority of troops upon disembarking there in 1865.[21]

Beyond the shores of Brazos de Santiago the 5th Massachusetts Cavalry carried forward the legacy of their wartime experiences and the gains achieved by their service to future generations. Sergeant Joshua Dunbar, age forty-two from Troy, Ohio, enlisted as a private in Company F, on January 9, 1864. Before enlisting Dunbar had escaped from slavery and previously served with the 55th Massachusetts Infantry. Dunbar was promoted from corporal to sergeant May 1, 1865, and was honorably discharged October 31, 1865.[22] Upon returning to civilian life, Dunbar settled with his wife, Matilda, also a former slave, in Ohio. Matilda gave birth in 1872 to a child who would become a renowned African American poet, Paul Laurence Dunbar. Their son gained notoriety for his many published works, as well as novels, short stories, and song lyrics, specifically his writings entitled *Our Martyred*

Soldiers (1888), *The Colored Soldiers* (1889), and *Poems of Cabin and Field* (1899). He received increased acclaim with his many writings covering issues of civil rights and the struggles African Americans encountered before and during his own lifetime.[23]

Just as Joshua Dunbar's life experience and legacy had influenced many of his descendants; so too had Robert G. Fitzgerald's. The marriage of Fitzgerald to Cornelia Smith of Chapel Hill, North Carolina, would in due course produce a granddaughter by the name of Anna Pauline "Pauli" Murray, a nationally recognized writer, lawyer, civil rights and women's rights activist, and in 1977 the first black woman ordained an Episcopal priest.

William S. McFeely, in the new introduction to Benjamin Quarles' reprinted book *The Negro in the Civil War* (1989), wrote that African Americans were "without equivocation" the active participants "in their own emancipation."[24] Their history, their military service, their accounts and struggles are forever a part of our collective history. The history of the 5th Massachusetts Cavalry is a chronicle that has truly never received the proper attention that it deserves. As we have learned, for a history that had never been published in depth, the account is intriguing and full of historically significant and enthralling complex characters that shaped the outcome of the American Civil War and the nation as a whole. At long last they could rightfully and definitively answer the question posed in the old plantation spiritual, "Do you think I'll make a soldier?" with a resounding yes!

Accordingly, every soldier who served with the 5th Massachusetts Cavalry played an integral part in President Abraham Lincoln's goal of a "new birth of freedom." The history and legacy of the regiment, including the men who served in its ranks, has had a lasting impact on our understanding of the African American experience during the American Civil War. Without these glimpses into their past we might lose an exceedingly essential piece of our nation's historical structure. As President Abraham Lincoln once stated:

> You say you will not fight to free negroes. Some of them seem willing to fight for you.... [When victory is won] there will be some black men who can remember that, with silent tongue, and clenched teeth, and steady eye and well-poised bayonet, they have helped mankind on to this great consummation.[25]

Chapter Notes

"The Colored Soldiers"

1. Paul Laurance Dunbar, *The Complete Poems of Paul Laurance Dunbar with the Introduction to "Lyrics of Lowly Life" by W.D. Howells* (New York: Dodd, Mead, 1922), 50–52.

Preface

1. Gary W. Gallagher, *Causes Won, Lost and Forgotten: How Hollywood and Popular Art Shape What We Know About the Civil War* (Chapel Hill: University of North Carolina Press, 2008) 9–10.
2. Gary W. Gallagher, *The Union War* (Cambridge, MA: Harvard University Press, 2011), 78.
3. Bruce Levine, *Half Slave and Half Free: The Roots of the Civil War* (New York: Hill and Wang, 1992), 257.

Introduction

1. Bruce Catton, *America Goes to War* (New York: MJF Books, 1997), 68.
2. This area of Virginia became West Virginia in 1863.
3. James McPherson, *Battle Cry of Freedom: The Civil War Era* (New York: Ballantine Books, 1988), 235.
4. *Ibid.*; Michael J. Varhola, *Everyday Life During The Civil War: A Guide For Writers, Students and Historians* (Cincinnati: Writer's Digest Books, 1999), 21–29. Ben Williams, *A Diary from Dixie* (Cambridge, MA: Harvard University Press, 1980), 20.
5. Lloyd Lewis, *Sherman: Fighting Prophet* (New York: Harcourt, Brace, 1932), 138.
6. *Chicago Tribune*, September 23, 1862.

7. James M. McPherson, *Marching Toward Freedom: Blacks in the Civil War, 1861–1865* (New York: Facts On File, 1991), 21–22.
8. Abraham Lincoln: "Final Emancipation Proclamation," January 1, 1863, in John G. Nicolay and John Hay, *Abraham Lincoln Complete Works: Comprising His Speeches, Letters, State Papers, and Miscellaneous Writings.* Vol. 2 (New York: Century, 1920), 287–288.
9. William F. Fox, *Regimental Losses in the American Civil War 1861–1865* (Albany, NY: Albany, 1889).
10. J. David Hacker, "A Census-Based Count of the Civil War Dead," *Civil War History* 57, no. 4 (December 2011): 307–348.
11. Nicholas Marshall, "The Great Exaggeration: Death and the Civil War," *The Journal of the Civil War Era* 4, no. 1 (March 2014): 13.
12. *Chicago Tribune*, July 23, 1862.
13. *New York Tribune*, May 1, 1863.
14. Speech given by Wendell Phillips entitled "State of the country." See: Wendell Phillips, *Speeches, Lectures and Letters* (Boston: Lee and Shepard, 1894), 553.
15. Frederic May Holland, *Frederick Douglass: The Colored Orator* (New York: Funk and Wagnalls, 1891), 300–301.
16. For a detailed account of African Americans in the Revolutionary War see Michael Lee Lanning, *Defenders of Liberty: African Americans in the Revolutionary War* (New York: Citadel Press, 2000). For a detailed study of African Americans serving in the United States Navy during the Civil War see also Steven J. Ramold, *Slaves, Sailors, Citizens: African Americans in the Union Navy* (DeKalb: University of Northern Illinois Press, 2001).

17. William A. Gladstone, *United States Colored Troops 1863–1867* (Gettysburg, PA: Thomas, 1990), 9. Ira Berlin, Joseph P. Reidy, and Leslie Rowland, *Freedom's Soldiers: The Black Military Experience in the Civil War* (New York: Cambridge University Press, 1998), 29.

18. William A. Gladstone, *United States Colored Troops 1863–1867*, 9; Ira Berlin, Joseph P. Reidy, & Leslie Rowland, *Freedom's Soldiers: The Black Military Experience in the Civil War*, 29; For the pay provisions of the Militia Act, see George P. Sanger, *Statutes at Large, Treaties, and Proclamations of the United States*, vol. 12 (Boston: Little, Brown, 1863), 599. For the pay allotted white soldiers of various ranks, see U.S. War Department, Revised United States Army Regulations (Washington: Government Printing Office, 1863), 358–63.

19. Varhola, *Everyday Life During the Civil War: A Guide for Writers, Students and Historians*, 37; McPherson, *Marching Toward Freedom*, 91–95; Sanger, *Statutes at Large, Treaties, and Proclamations of the United States*, vol. 13, pp. 126–30. For an examination of the Confiscation Acts see Silvana R. Siddali, *From Property to Person: Slavery and the Confiscation Acts 1861–1862* (Baton Rouge: Louisiana State University Press, 2005); See also Massachusetts Adjutant-General's Report, *Public Documents of Massachusetts: Being the Annual Reports of Various Public Officers and Institutions, for the Year 1864*, vol. 2, no. 7 (Boston: Wright & Potter, State Printers, 1865), 82–83.

20. Geoffrey C. Ward, Ric Burns, and Ken Burns, *The Civil War: An Illustrated History* (New York: Knopf, 1990); McPherson, *Marching Toward Freedom: Blacks in the Civil War 1861–1865*, 78.

21. Geoffrey C. Ward, R. Burns, K. Burns, *The Civil War: An Illustrated History* (New York: Knopf, 1990); Ira Berlin, Joseph P. Reidy, and Leslie Rowland, *Freedom's Soldiers: The Black Military Experience in the Civil War*, 20.

22. Joseph Glatthaar, *Forged in Battle: The Civil War Alliance of Black Soldiers and White Officers* (New York: The Free Press, 1990), 178.

23. Gladstone, *United States Colored Troops 1863–1867*, 9; Joseph Glatthaar, *Forged in Battle: The Civil War Alliance of Black Soldiers and White Officers*, 10; Dudley Taylor Cornish, *The Sable Arm: Black Troops in the Union Army, 1861–1865* (Lawrence: University Press of Kansas, 1987), 92–93. For a record of the 1st South

Carolina Infantry and the part taken by Thomas Wentworth Higginson see Thomas Wentworth Higginson, *Army Life in a Black Regiment* (Boston: Fields, Osgood, 1870).

24. Gladstone, *United States Colored Troops 1863–1867*, 9; Glatthaar, *Forged in Battle: The Civil War Alliance of Black Soldiers and White Officers*, 7–9; Cornish, *The Sable Arm: Black Troops in the Union Army, 1861–1865*, 65–68.

25. Henry Hopkins, *Official Military History of Kansas Regiments: During the War for the Suppression of the Great Rebellion* (Leavenworth, KS: Burke, 1870), 407–42; Glatthaar, *Forged in Battle: The Civil War Alliance of Black Soldiers and White Officers*, 7; Cornish, *The Sable Arm: Black Troops in the Union Army, 1861–1865*, 69–78.

26. Peter H. Clark, *Black Brigade of Cincinnati: Being a Report of Its Labor and Muster-Roll of Its Members; Together with Various Orders, Speeches, Etc. Relating to It.* (Cincinnati: Boyd, 1864), 5–6.

27. *Ibid.*, 15–16.

28. *Ibid.*, 16.

29. *Ibid.*, 3.

30. *Ibid.*, 28; Military Service Records: Powhatan Beaty, National Archives and Records Administration, Washington, D.C.; O.R., Ser. 1, Vol. 42, p. 168, Major General Benjamin Butler October 11, 1864.

31. Gladstone, *United States Colored Troops, 1863–1867*, 11, 101–107, 112–113; Catherine Clinton, *The African American Experience 1565–1877* (New York: Eastern National, 2004), 41–42; Massachusetts Historical Society, *We Fight for Freedom: Massachusetts, African-Americans, and the Civil War* (Boston: Massachusetts Historical Society Picture Book, 1993), 14; Joseph Glatthaar, *The Civil War's Black Soldiers*, Civil War Series (Eastern National Park and Monument Association, 1996), 53; William F. Fox, *Regimental Losses in the American Civil War, 1861–1865*. It should be noted that actual numbers in soldier enlistments and actual battles engaged vary from source to source, i.e., depending on whether or not the source is citing numbers related to all black soldiers or just those that served under the USCT-USCC designation not including state-designated units. For numbers related to navy enlistments see Joseph P. Reidy, "Black Men in Navy Blue During the Civil War," *Quarterly of the National Archives and Records Administration* 33, no. 3 (Fall 2001). For further information related to the percentages of military aged black men enlisting in Federal

units from Confederate states see Gallagher, *The Union War*, 146.

32. For further information about the Medal of Honor and those who have been awarded it, see Congressional Medal of Honor Society, www.cmohs.org.

33. P. C. Headley, *Massachusetts in the Rebellion* (Boston: Walker, Fuller, 1866), 450.

34. O.R., Ser. 3, Vol. 3, p. 215–16, General Orders No. 143, War Department, Adjutant Generals Office.

35. *Ibid.*

36. *Ibid.*

37. John Andrew to E.M. Stanton, Sept. 5, 1863, Andrew Papers, Massachusetts State Archives, Letters Official, vol. 36, p. 87, quoted in John D. Warner, Jr., "Crossed Sabres: The History of the 5th Massachusetts Volunteer Cavalry," Ph.D. diss., Boston College, 1997, p. 36.

38. *Ibid.*

39. Edwin Stanton to J. A. Andrew, Sept. 10, 1863, Andrew Papers, Massachusetts State Archives, Letters Official, Vol. 36, p. 358, quoted in Warner, "Crossed Sabres," p. 37; J. A. Andrew to J. M. Forbes, Nov. 20, 1863, Nov. 21, 1863, Andrew Papers, Massachusetts State Archives, Letters Official, Vol. 39, pp. 321–325, 443–446, quoted in Warner, "Crossed Sabres," p. 37.

40. O.R., Ser. 3, Vol. 3, pp. 1090–1091, Correspondence, Major C. W. Foster, War Department, Adjutant Generals Office to Governor John A. Andrew, November 23, 1863.

41. *Ibid.*

42. O.R., Ser. 3, Vol. 3, pp. 1095–1096, Correspondence, Governor John A. Andrew to Edwin M. Stanton, November 25, 1863.

43. O.R., Ser. 3, Vol. 3, p. 1108, Correspondence, Major C. W. Foster, War Department, Adjutant Generals Office to Governor John A. Andrew, December 2, 1863.

44. Oliver Wendell Holmes, *Speeches by Oliver Wendell Holmes, Jr.* (Boston: Little, Brown, 1891), 11

Chapter 1

1. Marshall William Taylor, *A Collection of Revival Hymns and Plantation Melodies* (Cincinnati: Taylor and Echols, 1882), pp. 253–54. See also Benjamin Quarles, *The Negro in the Civil War* (Boston: Little, Brown, 1969), 199.

2. The Holy Bible, New International Version (Grand Rapids, MI: Zondervan, 2006), 990.

3. *Ibid.*, 976.

4. W. A. Stokinger, A. K. Schroeder, and Capt. A. A. Swanson, *Civil War Camps at Readville: Camp Meigs Playground and Fowl Meadow Reservation* (Boston: Reservations and Historic Sites Metropolitan District Commission, 1990), 2.

5. Luis F. Emilio, *History of the Fifty-fourth Regiment of Massachusetts Volunteer Infantry, 1863–1865* (Boston: Boston Book, 1891), 19.

6. For a description of Camp Meigs see Massachusetts Metropolitan District Commission, *Camp Meigs and the Civil War* (Boston: Commonwealth of Massachusetts, Massachusetts District Commission, 1995); Massachusetts Metropolitan District Commission, *The Black Regiments of Camp Meigs* (Boston: Commonwealth of Massachusetts, Massachusetts District Commission, 1995); Luis F. Emilio, *History of the Fifty-fourth Regiment of Massachusetts Volunteer Infantry, 1863–1865* (Boston: Boston Book, 1891), 19.

7. *Massachusetts Soldiers, Sailors and Marines in the Civil War*, 492.

8. Thomas H. O'Conner, *Civil War Boston: Home Front and Battlefield* (Boston: Northeastern University Press, 1997), pp. 134–135; J. A. Andrew to E.M. Stanton, September 5, 1863, John Andrew Papers, Massachusetts State Archives, vol. 36, p. 87; Henry Greenleaf Pearson, *Life of John A. Andrew: Governor of Massachusetts, 1861–1865*, vol. 2 (Boston: Houghton, Mifflin, 1904), pp. 93–94.

9. Archibald H. Grimke, "Colonel Shaw and his Black Regiment," *The New England Magazine* (February 1890), 678; John H. Eicher and David J. Eicher, *Civil War High Commands* (Stanford, CA: Stanford University Press, 2001), 466; See also, Alonzo H. Quint, *The Record of the Second Massachusetts Infantry 1861–1865* (Boston: Walker, 1867), 489.

10. *The Harvard Graduates Magazine* 14 (1905–1906), pg. 36–37; Elizabeth Cabot Putnam, *Memoirs of the War of '61* (Boston: Ellis, 1920), 38.

11. Thomas Wentworth Higginson, *Harvard Memorial Biographies*, vol. 1 (Cambridge, MA: Sever and Francis, 1866), 349.

12. American Unitarian Association, *Sons of Puritans: A Group of Brief Sketches* (Boston: American Unitarian Association, 1908), 158;

13. *Ibid.*, 158; Putnam, *Memoirs of the War of '61*, pg. 39.

14. American Unitarian Association, *Sons of Puritans: A Group of Brief Sketches*, pg. 158.

15. For further information regarding the California 100 and Battalion see Larry Rogers and Keith Rogers, *Their Horses Climbed Trees: A Chronicle of the California 100 and Battalion in the Civil War; from San Francisco to Appomattox* (Atglen, PA: Schiffer Military History, 2001).

16. Massachusetts Adjutant General's Office, *Massachusetts Soldiers, Sailors and Marines in the Civil War*, 493–544.

17. Record First Michigan Cavalry Civil War, 1861–1865, vol. 31 (Kalamazoo, MI: Ihling Bros. and Everard, 1905); Record of Service of Michigan Volunteers in the Civil War, 1861–1865, p. 117; Michigan Historical Collections, *Collections of the Michigan Pioneer and Historical Society*, vol. 28 (Lansing, MI: Smith, 1900), p. 30.

18. Allen Johnson, *Dictionary of American Biography*, vol. 3 (New York: Charles Scribner's Sons, 1929), 595.

19. *Ibid.*

20. *The Harvard Magazine*, vol. 10 (Cambridge: MA: Sever and Francis, 1864), 220. In 2004 James D. Julia, Inc., Auction House sold George Fisher's sword with the Harvard presentation inscription, http://jamesdjulia.com/item/lot-1132-important-dbl-inscribed-civil-war-us-colored-troop-cavalry-officers-saber-5th-massachusetts-cavalry-53193/.

21. Allen Johnson, *Dictionary of American Biography*, vol. 2, 494, 496–497; Barnhart, *The New Century Cyclopedia of Names*, 606.

22. Johnson, vol. 2, 494; Barnhart, 606.

23. Johnson, vol. 2, 494.

24. Massachusetts Adjutant General's Office, *Massachusetts Soldiers, Sailors and Marines in the Civil War*, 493.

25. Charles P. Bowditch, "War Letters of Charles P. Bowditch," *Massachusetts Historical Society Proceedings* 57 (Oct. 1923—June 1924), 453–454.

26. *Ibid.*, pg. 459.

27. *Ibid.*; Barnhart, *The New Century Cyclopedia of Names*, 605; Johnson, *Dictionary of American Biography*, vol. 2, 492.

28. Johnson, Vol. 2, 492.

29. *Milwaukee Daily Sentinel*, December 5, 1863.

30. Several state newspapers published in full Governor Andrew's General Order No. 44 throughout the six months the 5th Massachusetts Cavalry trained at Camp Meigs; see, for example, *Cambridge Chronicle*, January 2, 1864–May 14, 1864.

31. *Ibid.*, Governor Andrew, General Order No. 44, December 1863.

32. *Ibid.*

33. *Ibid.*

34. Warner, "Crossed Sabres," pp. 45–50.

35. Tom Calarco, *Places on the Underground Railroad* (Santa Barbara, CA: Greenwood Press, 2011), 55–56; Christopher R. Reed, *Black Chicago's First Century*, Vol. 1, *1833–1900* (Columbia: University of Missouri Press, 2005), pp. 72, 98; John Jones to Governor Andrew, quoted in Warner, "Crossed Sabres," p. 47.

36. Warner, "Crossed Sabres," 47–48. Christopher Reed states in *Black Chicago's First Century*, Vol. 1, *1833–1900*, pp. 144–145, that John Jones' establishment served as a recruiting office for the 54th Massachusetts Infantry and "possibly then for the Fifth Massachusetts Cavalry and Fifty-Fifth Massachusetts Infantry Regiments, before it provided the same function for the Twenty-ninth Illinois."

37. For information related to Illinois state quota disputes related to raising United States Colored Regiments, see Edward A. Miller, Jr., *The Black Civil War Soldiers of Illinois: The Story of the Twenty-ninth U.S. Colored Infantry* (Columbia: University of South Carolina Press, 1998). See also, Richard Reid, *African Canadians in Blue: Volunteering for the Cause in the Civil War* (Vancouver: University of British Columbia Press, 2014), 87–89.

38. *Chicago Tribune*, December 23, 1863.

39. For information regarding the establishment of the Black Committee see Russell Duncan, *Where Death and Glory Meet: Colonel Robert Gould Shaw and the 54th Massachusetts Infantry* (Athens: University of Georgia Press, 1999), 59–63, along with Frank Preston Stearns, *The Life and Public Services of George Luther Stearns* (Philadelphia: Lippincott, 1907); Luis F. Emilio, *History of the Fifty-fourth Regiment of Massachusetts Volunteer Infantry, 1863–1865*, p. 11.

40. Donald Yacovone, *Freedom's Journey: African American Voices of the Civil War* (Chicago: Lawrence Hill Books, 2004), 202.

41. Massachusetts Adjutant General's Office, *Massachusetts Soldiers, Sailors and Marines in the Civil War*, 492.

42. *Ibid.*

43. *Ibid.*

44. Pauli Murray, *Proud Shoes: The Story of an American Family* (New York: Harper & Row, 1978).

45. *Ibid.*

46. Letter from John Andrew to Secretary of War Edwin Stanton, 14 March 1864,

GO1, Series 568X, vol. 42, pp. 387–389, Massachusetts State Archives.

47. Massachusetts Adjutant General's Office, *Massachusetts Soldiers, Sailors and Marines in the Civil War*, 516.

48. *Ibid.*

49. See Varhola, *Everyday Life During the Civil War*, 62–66. See also, McPherson, *Battle Cry of Freedom*, p. 608.

50. Joseph Brunson, Personal Affidavit, Department of Veteran Affairs, dated August 13, 1913, Ellsworth, KS.

51. Massachusetts Adjutant General's Office, *Massachusetts Soldiers, Sailors and Marines in the Civil War*, 492–544.

52. Daniel E. Sickles, *The Union Army: States and Regiments*, vol. 1 (Madison, WI: Federal, 1908), 215.

53. Ralph L. Rusk, ed., *The Letters of Ralph Waldo Emerson*, vol. 5 (New York: Columbia University Press, 1941), 349.

54. *Ibid.*

55. Warner, "Crossed Sabres," p. 193.

56. *Ibid.*; Military Service Records: Edward J. Bartlett, National Archives and Records Administration, Washington, D.C.; Frank Preston Stearns, *Life and Public Service of George L. Stearns* (Philadelphia: Lippincott, 1907), 312; Warner, "Crossed Sabres," pp. 368–369.

57. Massachusetts Adjutant General's Office, *Massachusetts Soldiers, Sailors and Marines in the Civil War*, 492; John David Smith, ed., *Black Soldiers in Blue: African American Troops in the Civil War Era* (Chapel Hill: University of North Carolina Press, 2002), 300; *Anglo-African*, May 7, 1864. Amos Webber would eventually go on to be promoted to sergeant.

58. Bowditch, "War Letters," pp. 472–473.

59. *Springfield Republican* published as *Springfield Weekly Republican*, January 30, 1864, p. 8.

60. Donald Yacovone, "The Fifty-Fourth Massachusetts Regiment, the Pay Crisis, and 'Lincoln Despotism,'" in *Hope and Glory: Essays on the Legacy of the Fifty-Fourth Massachusetts Regiment*, edited by Martin Blatt, Thomas J. Brown, and Donald Yacovone (Amherst: University of Massachusetts Press, 2001), 38.

61. Emilio, *History of the Fifty-fourth Regiment of Massachusetts Volunteer Infantry, 1863–1865*, p. 136.

62. *Ibid.*, 137.

63. Warner, "Crossed Sabres," pp. 182–183.

64. *Ibid.*, 193–194.

65. *Ibid.*, 194.

66. *Ibid.*

67. *Ibid.*, 204.

68. *Ibid.*, 212.

69. William Schouler, *A History of Massachusetts in the Civil War* (Boston: Dutton, 1868), 503–504; See also, *Private and Special Statutes of the Commonwealth of Massachusetts, 1863*, vol. 11 (Boston: Wright & Potter, 1869), 459.

70. Robert Fitzgerald Diary, Manuscripts Department, Library of the University of North Carolina at Chapel Hill, Southern Historical Collection #M-4177, Fitzgerald Family Papers, hereinafter noted as Fitzgerald Diary; Murray, *Proud Shoes: The Story of an American Family*, p. 140; For a detailed examination of the pay and bounty issue related to the 5th Massachusetts Cavalry see also Warner, "Crossed Sabres," pp. 182–183, 194, 204–205, 212.

Chapter 2

1. *The Liberator*, February 26, 1864.

2. *Ibid.*, May 13, 1864.

3. *Ibid.*

4. Massachusetts Adjutant General's Office, *Massachusetts Soldiers, Sailors and Marines in the Civil War*, 493–544; James Lorenzo Bowen, *Massachusetts in the War, 1861–1865* (Springfield, MA: Bryan, 1889), 781–783.

5. Massachusetts Adjutant General's Office, *Massachusetts Soldiers, Sailors and Marines in the Civil War*, 492; *Boston Daily Globe*, July 31, 1887. See also Sickles, *The Union Army: States and Regiments*, vol. 1 (Madison, WI: Federal, 1908), 215.

6. Abijah P. Marvin, *History of Worcester in the War of the Rebellion* (Worcester, MA: Marvin, 1870), 311.

7. Fitzgerald Diary; Murray, *Proud Shoes: The Story of an American Family*, pg. 141.

8. Bowditch, "War Letters," pp. 473–475.

9. James Moore, M.D., *History of the Cooper Shop Volunteer Refreshment Saloon* (Philadelphia: Rodgers, 1866), 210–211.

10. Bowditch, "War Letters," pp. 473–475.

11. Military Service Records: Erick Wulff, National Archives and Records Administration, Washington, D.C.

12. *Ibid.*; Robert Garth Scott, *Fallen Leaves: The Civil War Letters of Major Henry Livermore Abbott* (Kent, OH: Kent State University Press, 1991), 146–147; George Anson Bruce, *The Twentieth Regiment of*

Massachusetts Infantry, 1861–1865 (Boston: Houghton, Mifflin, 1906), 504.

13. Robert Garth Scott, *Fallen Leaves: The Civil War Letters of Major Henry Livermore Abbott*, 146–147.

14. Military Service Records: Erick Wulff, National Archives and Records Administration, Washington, D.C.; Emilio, *History of the Fifty-fourth Regiment of Massachusetts Volunteer Infantry, 1863–1865*, p. 334.

15. Military Service Records: Erick Wulff, National Archives and Records Administration, Washington, D.C.

16. C.R. Douglass to Frederick Douglass, May 31st, 1864, Douglass Papers, Manuscript Division, Library of Congress. See also Warner, "Crossed Sabres," pp. 233–234.

17. Military Service Records: Amos F. Jackson, National Archives and Records Administration, Washington, D.C.; Military Service Records: Albert White, National Archives and Records Administration, Washington, D.C.

18. Glennette Tilley Turner, *The Underground Railroad in Illinois* (Glen Ellyn, IL: Newman Educational, 2001), 26; Wagoner obituary, *Rocky Mountain News*, January 28, 1901.

19. Military Service Records: Albert White, National Archives and Records Administration, Washington, D.C.

20. *Ibid.*

21. Sworn witness affidavits, Military Service Records: Erick Wulff, National Archives and Records Administration, Washington, D.C.

22. *Ibid.*

23. Military Service Records: Albert White, National Archives and Records Administration, Washington, D.C.

24. Military Service Records: Erick Wulff, National Archives and Records Administration, Washington, D.C.

25. *Ibid.*

26. *Ibid.*

27. Fitzgerald Diary; Murray, *Proud Shoes: The Story of an American Family*, pg. 142

28. Bowditch, "War Letters," pp. 473–475.

29. *Ibid.*

30. *Ibid.*

31. Putnam, *Memoirs of the War of '61*, pg. 39; American Unitarian Association, *Sons of Puritans: A Group of Brief Sketches*, pg. 158–159; Headley, *Massachusetts in the Rebellion*, p. 497.

32. Bowditch, "War Letters," pp. 473–475.

33. *Ibid.*

34. Fitzgerald Diary. For a detailed study of the life of Paul Jennings see Elizabeth Dowling Taylor, *A Slave in the White House: Paul Jennings and the Madisons* (New York: Palgrave Macmillan, 2012).

35. *Ibid.*, 192–194.

36. *Ibid.*, 207–212.

37. Marvin, *History of Worcester in the War of the Rebellion*, 311; Massachusetts Adjutant General's Office, *Massachusetts Soldiers, Sailors and Marines in the Civil War*, 492; See also Warner, "Crossed Sabres," p. 240.

38. Massachusetts Adjutant General's Office, *Massachusetts Soldiers, Sailors and Marines in the Civil War*, 492; Fitzgerald Diary; Headley, *Massachusetts in the Rebellion*, 497.

39. *Boston Daily Advertiser* May 20, 1864.

40. O.R., Ser. 1, Vol. 36, Ch. 48, Pt. 2, p. 430, Major-General Benjamin F. Butler to Lieutenant-General Grant, May 5, 1864. See also Benjamin Franklin Butler, *Butler's Book* (Boston: Thayer, 1892), 1062.

41. O.R., Ser. 1, Vol. 36XXXVI, Ch. 48, Pt. 2, p. 517, Benjamin F. Butler to Secretary of War Edwin M. Stanton, May 7, 1864; Butler, *Butler's Book*, pp. 1063–1064.

42. O.R., Ser. 1, Vol. 36, Ch. 48, Pt. 2, p. 555, Secretary of War Edwin M. Stanton to Benjamin F. Butler, May 8, 1864.

43. O.R., Ser. 1, Vol. 36, Ch. 48, Pt. 2, p. 561, Lieutenant-General Ulysses S. Grant to Major-General Henry Halleck, May 9, 1864.

44. O.R., Ser. 1, Vol. 36, Ch. 48, Pt. 2, p. 688, Major-General Henry Halleck to Major-General Benjamin F. Butler, May 12, 1864.

45. Massachusetts Adjutant General's Office, *Massachusetts Soldiers, Sailors and Marines in the Civil War*, 492–493.

46. Bowditch, "War Letters." pp. 475–476.

47. Fitzgerald Diary.

48. *Ibid.*

49. *Ibid.*

50. *Ibid.*

51. *Ibid.*

52. Bowditch, "War Letters," pg. 476.

53. Fitzgerald Diary.

54. Bowditch, "War Letters," pp. 475–476.

55. Military Service Records: John Gambol, National Archives and Records Administration, Washington, D.C.

56. Fitzgerald Diary; Murray, *Proud Shoes: The Story of an American Family*, pp. 146–147.

57. Bowditch, "War Letters," p. 476.
58. *Ibid.*, 478–479.
59. *Ibid.*, 479.
60. Massachusetts Adjutant-General's Report, *Public Documents of Massachusetts: Being the Annual Reports of Various Public Officers and Institutions, for the Year 1864*, vol. 2, no. 7 (Boston: Wright & Potter, 1865), 984–985.
61. Bowditch, "War Letters," p. 476.
62. Thomas L. Livermore, *Days and Events, 1860–1866* (Boston: Houghton Mifflin, 1920), 343.
63. Bowditch, "War Letters," pp. 477–478.
64. Livermore, *Days and Events, 1860–1866*, p. 336.
65. *Ibid.*
66. Bowditch, "War Letters," pp. 477–478.
67. *Ibid.*
68. Livermore, *Days and Events, 1860–1866*, p. 336.

Chapter 3

1. Massachusetts Adjutant-General's Report, *Public Documents of Massachusetts: Being the Annual Reports of Various Public Officers and Institutions, for the Year 1864*, vol. 2, no. 7 (Boston: Wright & Potter, 1865), 984–985; Murray, *Proud Shoes: The Story of an American Family*, p. 147.
2. Thomas J. Howe, *The Petersburg Campaign: Wasted Valor, June 15–18, 1864* (Lynchburg, VA: Howard, 1988) 12.
3. Fitzgerald Diary; Murray, *Proud Shoes: The Story of an American Family*, p. 147.
4. O.R., Ser. 1, Vol. 26, Ch. 48, Pt. 2, pp. 287–289, Report by Maj. Gen. Quincy A. Gillmore to Maj. Gen. Benjamin F. Butler, June 10, 1864. See also Benjamin Franklin Butler and Mrs. Jessie Ames Marshall, *Private and Official Correspondence of Gen. Benjamin F. Butler During the Period of the Civil War*, vol. 4 (Norwood, MA: The Plimpton Press, 1917), 327–328.
5. Butler, *Private and Official Correspondence of Gen. Benjamin F. Butler*, 329–331; Howe, *The Petersburg Campaign: Wasted Valor, June 15–18, 1864*, 12; O.R., Ser. 1, Vol. 26, Ch. 47, Pt. 3, pp. 719–720, Reports by Maj. Gen. Quincy A. Gillmore to Maj. Gen. Benjamin F. Butler, June 9, 1864.
6. A. Wilson Greene, *Civil War Petersburg: Confederate City in the Crucible of War* (Charlottesville: University of Virginia Press, 2006), pp. 174–176.

7. A. M. Keiley, *In Vinculi: Or The Prisoner of War, Being the Experience of a Rebel in Two Federal Pens, Interspersed with Reminiscences of the Late War, Anecdotes of Southern Generals, Etc.* (New York: Blelock, 1866), pp. 14–15.
8. *Ibid.*; Howe, *Petersburg Campaign: Wasted Valor*, 12; John Horn, *The Petersburg Campaign, June 1864–April 1865* (Conshohocken, PA: Combined Books, 2000), 44–45; Alfred Roman, *The Military Operations of General Beauregard*, vol. 2 (New York: Harper & Brothers, 1884), 222–228.
9. Greene, *Civil War Petersburg: Confederate City in the Crucible of War*, 176; R. E. Colston, "Repelling the First Assault on Petersburg," in Robert Underwood Johnson and Clarence Clough Buel, *Battles and Leaders of the Civil War*, vol. 4 (New York: Century, 1887–1888), pp. 535–536.
10. R. E. Colston, "Repelling the First Assault on Petersburg," in Johnson and Buel, *Battles and Leaders of the Civil War*, p. 535.
11. Barton Haxall Wise, *The Life of Henry A. Wise of Virginia, 1806–1876* (New York: Macmillan, 1899), 344.
12. Howe, *Petersburg Campaign: Wasted Valor*, 12; Horn, *The Petersburg Campaign, June 1864–April 1865*, 44–45; Wise, *The Life of Henry A. Wise of Virginia, 1806–1876*, 344. For further study of the fighting on June 9, see William Glenn Robertson, *Petersburg Campaign: The Battle of Old Men and Young Boys, June 9, 1864* (Lynchburg, VA: Howard, 1989).
13. Howe, *Petersburg Campaign: Wasted Valor*, 12; Roman, *The Military Operations of General Beauregard*, vol. 2, p. 228; P.G.T. Beauregard, "Four Days of Battle at Petersburg," in Johnson and Buel, *Battles and Leaders of the Civil War*, vol. 4, p. 541.
14. Butler and Marshall, *Private and Official Correspondence of Gen. Benjamin F. Butler During the Period of the Civil War*, vol. 4, 366–367.
15. Fitzgerald Diary.
16. *Ibid.*; Murray, *Proud Shoes: The Story of an American Family*, p. 148.
17. Bowditch, "War Letters," pp. 479–481.
18. Wise, *The Life of Henry A. Wise of Virginia, 1806–1876*, 344–346; P.G.T. Beauregard, "Four Days of Battle at Petersburg," in Johnson and Buel, *Battles and Leaders of the Civil War*, vol. 4, pp. 540–541; Greene, *Civil War Petersburg: Confederate City in the Crucible of War*, 176. See

also Howe, *Wasted Valor*, June 15–18, 1864, 167n25.

19. Joy Case, "Arlington National Cemetery," *Let's Take a Look at Virginia*, 2006, 1–2.

20. O.R., Ser. 1, Vol. 51, Ch. 63, Pt. 1, pp. 265–269, Report filed by Col. Samuel A. Duncan, June 25, 1864; pp. 263–265 Report filed by Col. John H. Holman, June 20, 1864.

21. O.R., Ser. 1, Vol. 40, Ch. 52, Pt. 1, pp. 728–730, Report filed by Brig. Gen. August V. Kautz, June 20, 1864; Wise, *The Life of Henry A. Wise of Virginia, 1806–1876*, 344–346.

22. Livermore, *Days and Events, 1860–1866*, p. 356.

23. Edward G. Longacre, *Army of Amateurs: General Benjamin F. Butler and the Army of the James, 1863–1865* (Mechanicsburg, PA: Stockpole Books, 1997), 144. See also Neil Hunter Raiford, *The 4th North Carolina Cavalry in the Civil War: A History and Roster* (Jefferson, NC: McFarland, 2003) 66–74.

24. Livermore, *Days and Events, 1860–1866*, p. 356.

25. Bowditch, "War Letters," pp. 479–481.

26. O.R., Ser. 1, Vol. 51, Ch. 63, Pt. 1, pp. 265–269, Report filed by Col. Samuel A. Duncan, June 25, 1864. See also Noah Andre Trudeau, *Like Men of War: Black Troops in the Civil War 1862–1865* (Boston: Little, Brown, 1998), 221.

27. *Lowell Daily Citizen and News*, June 27, 1864, letter from Charles Douglass to his father, Frederick Douglass, describing the events which took place at Baylor's Farm, VA.

28. *Ibid.*

29. Fitzgerald Diary.

30. Bowditch, "War Letters," pp. 479–481.

31. Charles Douglass, *Lowell Daily Citizen and News*, June 27, 1864.

32. O.R., Ser. 1, Vol. 51, Ch. 63, Pt. 1, pp. 263–265, Report filed by Col. John H. Holman, June 20, 1864.

33. Charles Douglass, *Lowell Daily Citizen and News*, June 27, 1864.

34. *Ibid.*

35. Bowditch, "War Letters," pp. 479–481.

36. Raiford, *The 4th North Carolina Cavalry in the Civil War: A History and Roster*, 66–74; O.R., Ser. 1, Vol. 51, Ch. 63, Pt. 1, p. 263–265, Report filed by Col. John H. Holman, June 20, 1864.

37. O.R., Ser. 1, Vol. 51, Ch. 63, Pt. 1, pp.

265–269, Report filed by Col. Samuel A. Duncan, June 25, 1864. Duncan provides a detailed report regarding the capture of the Confederate works. For further reading of the Confederate perspective see Raiford, *The 4th North Carolina Cavalry in the Civil War* and Robert H. Moore II, *Graham's Petersburg, Jackson's Kanawha, and Lurty's Roanoke Horse Artillery* (Virginia Regimental Histories Series: Howard, 1996), also Wise, *The Life of Henry A. Wise of Virginia, 1806–1876*.

38. Longacre, *Army of Amateurs: General Benjamin F. Butler and the Army of the James, 1863–1865*, 145.

39. *Ibid.*; O.R., Ser. 1, Vol. 51, Ch. 63, Pt. 1, pp. 265–269, Report filed by Col. Samuel A. Duncan, June 25, 1864.

40. Bowditch, "War Letters," pp. 479–481.

41. Livermore, *Days and Events, 1860–1866*, pp. 357–358.

42. Bowditch, "War Letters," pp. 479–481.

43. Edwin S. Redkey, *A Grand Army of Black Men: Letters from African-American Soldiers in the Union Army, 1861–1865.* (Massachusetts: Cambridge University Press, 1992), 98–99

44. Fleetwood quoted in, Noah Andre Trudeau, *Like Men of War*, 222.

45. O.R., Ser. 1, Vol. 40, Ch. 52, Pt. 1, pp. 720–723, Report of Brig. Gen. Edward W. Hinks, June 20, 1864.

46. O.R., Series 1, Vol. 40, Ch. 52 , Pt. 2, pp. 489–491, Report of Brig. Gen. Edward W. Hinks to Maj. Gen. William F. Smith, June 27, 1864.

47. Bowditch, "War Letters," pp. 479–481.

48. *Ibid.*

49. *Lowell Daily Citizen and News*, June 27, 1864.

50. William Farrar Smith, *From Chattanooga to Petersburg Under Generals Grant and Butler* (Boston: Houghton, Mifflin, 1893), pp. 24–25.

51. P.G.T. Beauregard, "Four Days of Battle at Petersburg," in Johnson and Buel, *Battles and Leaders of the Civil War*, vol. 4, p. 541.

52. Fox, *Regimental Losses in the American Civil War* (1861–1865); Massachusetts Adjutant General's Office, *Massachusetts Soldiers, Sailors and Marines in the Civil War*, 492–493; Marvin, *History of Worcester in the War of the Rebellion*, 311; Massachusetts Adjutant-General's Report, *Public Documents of Massachusetts: Being the Annual Reports of Various Public Officers*

and Institutions, for the Year 1865 (Boston: Wright & Potter, 1866), 123.

53. *Lowell Daily Citizen and News,* June 27, 1864.

54. Fitzgerald Diary.

55. Quarles, *The Negro in the Civil War,* 299.

Chapter 4

1. Bowditch, "War Letters," p. 479.

2. *Ibid.,* 481–482.

3. *Ibid.*

4. *Ibid.,* 482–483.

5. *Ibid.*

6. *Ibid.,* 481–482.

7. *Ibid.,* 482–483.

8. *Ibid.*

9. 1860 U.S. census, population schedule, NARA microfilm publication M653, 1,438 rolls (Washington, D.C.: National Archives and Records Administration, n.d.); Slave Schedule, United States of America, Bureau of the Census, *Eighth Census of the United States, 1860* (Washington, D.C.: National Archives and Records Administration, 1860), M653, 1,438 rolls; Find A Grave.com, digital images (http://www.findagrave.com, accessed March 1, 2015), Rushmore Family, Blanford Cemetery, Petersburg, VA, Memorial #29819298, 29819291, 29819243; S. Millett Thompson, *Thirteenth Regiment of New Hampshire Volunteer Infantry in the War of the Rebellion, 1861–1865: A Diary Covering Three Years and a Day* (Boston: Houghton, Mifflin, 1888), 394–395.

10. Bowditch, "War Letters," pp. 481–482; Thompson, *Thirteenth Regiment of New Hampshire Volunteer Infantry in the War of the Rebellion, 1861–1865,* pp. 394–395.

11. Bowditch, "War Letters," pp. 481–482.

12. Military Service Records: Joseph Jackson, National Archives and Records Administration, Washington, D.C.

13. Massachusetts Adjutant-General's Report, *Public Documents of Massachusetts: Being the Annual Reports of Various Public Officers and Institutions, for the Year 1864,* p. 985.

14. Bowditch, "War Letters," pp. 481–482.

15. Horn, *The Petersburg Campaign June 1864–April 1865,* pp. 75–95.

16. Bowditch, "War Letters," pp. 483–484.

17. *Ibid.*

18. *Ibid.,* 484.

19. Edward W. Beitzell, *Point Lookout Prison Camp for Confederates,* 76, excerpt from the Diary of Bartlett Yancey Malone Co. H, 6th N. C. Infantry C.S.A.

20. O.R. Ser. 1, Vol. 40, Chapter 52, Pt. 2, p. 582, Colonel Alonzo Draper to Secretary of War Edwin Stanton, Point Lookout, Maryland July 1, 1864.

21. *Ibid.,* p. 582, Major-General C.C. Augur to Colonel Alonzo Draper, Headquarters Department of Washington, 22nd Army Corps, July 1, 1864.

22. *Vain Efforts to Avoid Prison by B. T. Holliday, Winchester, Va.* (Reprint from the *Confederate Veteran* 28, no. 10).

23. *Ibid.*

24. William C. Davis, *The Fighting Men of the Civil War* (London: Salamander Books, 1999), 170–71.

25. Gerald J. Sword, "Another Look at the Point Lookout Prison Camp for Confederates," *Chronicles of St. Mary's* 28, no. 3.

26. Point Lookout, MD, State Park. Information obtained through the state park archives and interpretive center. See also National Park Service U.S. Department of the Interior Point Lookout Confederate Cemetery, www.nps.gov/.../Maryland/Point_Lookout_Confederate_Cemetery.html, retrieved January 19, 2014; Descendants of Point Lookout POW Organization, http://www.plpow.com/Prison History.htm, retrieved January 19, 2014.

27. Point Lookout, Maryland State Park. Information obtained through the state park archives and interpretive center; See also National Park Service U.S. Department of the Interior Point Lookout Confederate Cemetery www.nps.gov/.../Maryland/Point_Lookout_Confederate_Cemetery.html retrieved January 19, 2014; Edwin W. Beitzell, *Point Lookout Prison Camp for Confederates* (Baltimore: Abell, 1972); Lonnie R. Speer, *Portals to Hell: Military Prisons of the Civil War* (Mechanicsburg, PA: Stackpole Books, 1997), 151–154.

28. Edwin W. Beitzell, *Point Lookout Prison Camp for Confederates* (Baltimore, MD: Abell, 1972); Lonnie R. Speer, *Portals to Hell: Military Prisons of the Civil War* (Mechanicsburg, PA: Stackpole Books, 1997) 151–154.

29. Edwin W. Beitzell, *Point Lookout Prison Camp for Confederates* (Baltimore, MD: Abell, 1972); Lonnie R. Speer, *Portals to Hell: Military Prisons of the Civil War,* 151–154.

30. Sword, "Another Look at the Point Lookout Prison Camp for Confederates."

31. Francis Lord, *Collectors Encyclopedia of the Civil War* (Secaucus, NJ: Castle Books, 1979), 279–280; Sword, "Another Look at the Point Lookout Prison Camp for Confederates." See also James S. Hutchins, "An 1860 Pamphlet on the Sibley Tent," *The Company of Military Historians* 57, no. 2 (Summer 2005).

32. Sword, "Another Look at the Point Lookout Prison Camp for Confederates."

33. Bowditch, "War Letters," pp. 485–486.

34. *Ibid.*, pp. 490–491.

35. For information related to the transfer of 36th USCT and Butler's plan to reorganize his regiments in the Army of the James see James K. Bryant II. *The 36th United States Colored Troops in the Civil War: A History and Roster* (Jefferson, NC: McFarland, 2012), 102–103.

36. *Ibid.*, pp. 484–485.

37. Keiley, *In Vinculis: Or The Prisoner of War, Being the Experience of a Rebel in Two Federal Pens, Interspersed with Reminiscences of the Late War, Anecdotes of Southern Generals, Etc.* (New York: Blelock, 1866), p. 100; See also Nick Salvatore, *We All Got History: The Memory Books of Amos Weber* (New York: Times Books, 1996), 132–133; Smith, ed., *Black Soldiers in Blue: African American Troops in the Civil War Era*, 299.

38. Bowditch, "War Letters," p. 485.

39. *Ibid.*, p. 485–488.

40. Point Lookout, MD, State Park. Information obtained through the state park archives and interpretive center; B. Franklin Cooling, *Monocacy: The Battle That Saved Washington* (Shippensburg, PA: White Mane, 2000), 26, 86.

41. *Chronicles of St. Mary's* 31, no. 10 (October 1983); *Vain Efforts to Avoid Prison by B. T. Holliday, Winchester, Va.*

42. Bowditch, "War Letters," p. 487.

43. *Ibid.*, 488.

44. William Whatley Pierson, ed., *The Diary of Bartlett Yancey Malone* (Chapel Hill: University of North Carolina, 1919), 52.

45. Bowditch, "War Letters," p. 490.

46. *The Daily Age*, August 4, 1864.

47. *Republican Farmer*, August 12, 1864.

48. Salvatore, *We All Got History: The Memory Books of Amos Weber*, 137–138.

49. Pierson, ed., *The Diary of Bartlett Yancey Malone*, 52.

50. Bowditch, "War Letters," p. 491.

51. Pierson, ed., *The Diary of Bartlett Yancey Malone*, 52.

52. Bowditch, "War Letters," p. 492.

53. Salvatore, *We All Got History: The Memory Books of Amos Weber*, 138.

54. *Ibid.*, 139.

55. *Ibid.*, 139–140.

56. Thomas Lowery, *Sexual Misbehavior in the Civil War* (Bloomington, IN: Xlibris, 2006), 173; Military Service Records, William A. Underhill, National Archives and Records Administration, Washington, D.C.; Military Service Records, George Butler, National Archives and Records Administration, Washington, D.C.; Court-Martial Case Files, Records of the Office of the Judge Advocate General (Army), RG 153, NARA. See also Salvatore, *We All Got History: The Memory Books of Amos Weber*, 138.

57. Bowditch, "War Letters," p. 488; Massachusetts Advocate General's Office, *Massachusetts Soldiers, Sailors and Marines in the Civil War*, 493.

58. Johnson, *Dictionary of American Biography*, vol. I, 48.

59. Johnson, *Dictionary of American Biography*, vol. I, 49; John H. Eicher and David J. Eicher, *Civil War High Commands* (Stanford, CA: Stanford University Press, 2001), 98.

60. Johnson, *Dictionary of American Biography*, 48.

61. Worthington Chauncey Ford, *A Cycle of Adams Letters 1861–1865* (New York: Kraus Reprint, 1969), 175.

62. *Ibid.*, 186, 189.

63. *Ibid.*, 194–195.

64. *Ibid.*, 199.

65. Military Service Records, James M. Cutting, National Archives and Records Administration, Washington, D.C.; Military Service Records, Edward Jarvis Bartlett, National Archives and Records Administration, Washington, D.C.; Military Service Records, George A. Fisher, National Archives and Records Administration, Washington, D.C. See also Massachusetts Advocate General's Office, *Massachusetts Soldiers, Sailors and Marines in the Civil War*, 493, 511–512.

66. Military Service Records, Charles Waters, National Archives and Records Administration, Washington, D.C. See also John C. Leffel, *History of Posey County, Indiana* (Chicago: Standard Publishing, 1913), 98–105.

67. Abraham Lincoln, "Proclamation 116—Calling for 500,000 Volunteers," July 18, 1864, in John G. Nicolay and John Hay, *Abraham Lincoln Complete Works: Comprising His Speeches, Letters, State Papers,*

and *Miscellaneous Writings*, vol. 2 (New York: Century, 1920), 550–551.

68. Military Service Records, Charles Waters, National Archives and Records Administration, Washington, D.C; Massachusetts Advocate General's Office, *Massachusetts Soldiers, Sailors and Marines in the Civil War*, 498.

69. Point Lookout, MD, State Park. Information obtained through the state park archives and interpretive center.

70. Ford, *A Cycle of Adams Letters, 1861–1865*, 212–215.

71. William S. McFeely, *Fredrick Douglass* (New York: Norton, 1991), 230.

72. *Ibid.*, 230.

73. Massachusetts Advocate General's Office, *Massachusetts Soldiers, Sailors and Marines in the Civil War*, 528.

74. See Redkey, *A Grand Army of Black Men*, 119–121. Redkey provides a published account of the Thanksgiving celebration published in the December 17, 1864, weekly *Anglo-African* newspaper. His general feeling is that Sergeant Amos Webber was the soldier who wrote the account.

75. Lloyd Lewis, *Sherman Fighting Prophet*, 470.

76. *Ibid.*

77. Katherine Murphy, *The Civil War and "Colored" Regiments from Massachusetts: Amos F. Jackson Writes Home.* College of the Holy Cross, Worcester, MA. Retrieved online 1/6/2014, http://college.holycross.edu/projects/worcester/afrcamerican/civilwar.htm; *Massachusetts Soldiers, Sailors and Marines in the Civil War* lists Alfred, Company E; James, Company I; Lorenzo, Company A; and William Hazzard, Company B, all serving the 5th Massachusetts Cavalry. James would be discharged for disability on May 20, 1865.

78. *The Liberator*, February 24, 1865, page 31.

79. Eicher and Eicher, *Civil War High Commands*, 466.

80. O.R., Ser. 1, Vol.46, Chapter 58, Pt. 3, pp. 58, 70.

81. *Ibid.*, 70–71.

82. *Ibid.*, 83.

Chapter 5

1. Richard Wayne Lykes, *Petersburg National Military Park, Virginia*, series no. 13 (Washington, D.C.: National Park Service Historical Handbook, 1961).

2. Godfrey Weitzel, *Richmond Occupied: Entry of the United States Forces into Richmond, Virginia, April 3, 1865,* edited by Louis Manarin (Richmond, VA: Richmond Civil War Centennial Committee), 45.

3. *Ibid.*, 45–46.

4. David D. Ryan, *Four Days in 1865: The Fall of Richmond* (Richmond, VA: Cadmus Marketing, 1993), 5; A. A. Hoehling and Mary Hoehling, *The Day Richmond Died* (San Diego, CA: Barnes, 1981), 111–112; Burke Davis, *The Long Surrender* (New York: Random House, 1985), 21–22.

5. *Richmond Dispatch*, May 7, 1862, p. 3.

6. *Richmond Whig*, April 4, 1865.

7. Weitzel, *Entry of the United States Forces Into Richmond, Virginia, April 3, 1865*, 54.

8. Trudeau, *Like Men of War*, 420.

9. Ford, *A Cycle of Adams Letters 1861–1865*, 261.

10. *Richmond Whig*, April 27, 1865.

11. See Nelson Lankford, *Richmond Burning* (New York: Viking 2002), 130–131; James McPherson, *The Negro's Civil War* (New York: Ballantine Books, 1991), 241.

12. O.R. Ser. 1, Vol. 46, Chapter 58, Pt. 1, p. 1227–1228, Report No. 248 of Maj. Gen. Godfrey Weitzel April 17, 1865, detailing the operations of the 25th Army Corps.

13. *Ibid.*

14. *Richmond Whig*, April 4, 1865.

15. Weitzel, *Entry of the United States Forces into Richmond, Virginia, April 3, 1865*, p. 53.

16. *Ibid.*

17. *Ibid.*

18. Trudeau, *Like Men of War*, 423; Smith, *Black Soldiers in Blue: African American Troops in the Civil War Era*, 300; *Anglo-African*, April 22, 1865.

19. Trudeau, *Like Men of War*, 423.

20. Sallie A. Brock, *Richmond During the War: Four Years of Personal Observation* (New York: Carleton, 1867), 367. See also Hoehling and Hoehling, *The Day Richmond Died*, 205.

21. Nellie Grey was a pseudonym for a woman in Richmond used by author Myrta Lockett Avary in *A Virginia Girl in the Civil War, 1861–1865: Being a Record of the Actual Experiences of the Wife of a Confederate Officer* (New York: Appleton, 1903), 362–363; Hoehling and Hoehling, *The Day Richmond Died*, 207.

22. Quarles, *The Negro in the Civil War*, 331.

23. Redkey, *A Grand Army of Black Men*, 177–178; Ronald S. Coddington, *African*

American Faces of the Civil War: An Album (Baltimore: The Johns Hopkins University Press, 2012), 211.

24. Cornish, *The Sable Arm: Black Troops in the Union Army, 1861–1865*, 282.

25. Letter from Charles Francis Adams to Governor John Andrew, 5 April 1865, GO1, Series 567X, v. W81, p. 20½, Massachusetts State Archives.

26. *Chicago Tribune*, April 6, 1865.

27. Many historians of the fall of Richmond story have referred to the Mary Custis Lee account; see Burke Davis, *The Long Surrender*, 39–41.

28. *New York Herald*, April 13, 1865.

29. Weitzel, *Entry of the United States Forces into Richmond, Virginia, April 3, 1865*, p. 64; Lankford, *Richmond Burning*, 142; Jay Winik, *April 1865* (New York: HarperCollins, 2001), 120.

30. Brock, *Richmond During the War: Four Years of Personal Observation*, 372; Hoehling and Hoehling, *The Day Richmond Died*, 240–41.

31. Hoehling and Hoehling, *The Day Richmond Died*, 240–41.

32. *Richmond Whig*, April 5, 1865, and reprinted in the *New York Tribune*, April 8, 1865, p. 12.

33. Isaiah King's recollections were published in an article entitled "Our Heroes of '61: A Series of Tabloid Reviews of the Dramatic Civil War Experiences of the Last Survivors of the New Bedford Post, G.A.R.," by J. H. Newton, published in the *New Bedford Evening Standard*, May 26, 1932.

Chapter 6

1. Ford, *A Cycle of Adams Letters, 1861–1865*. 262.

2. Burke Davis, *Appomattox: Nine April Days, 1865* (New York: Reinhart, 1959), 241.

3. *Ibid.*, 303.

4. Military Service Records, Charles Francis Adams, Jr., National Archives and Records Administration, Washington, D.C.

5. Ford, *A Cycle of Adams Letters, 1861–1865*, 267.

6. Chris M. Calkins, *The Final Bivouac: The Surrender Parade at Appomattox and the Disbanding of the Armies April 10–May 20, 1865* (Lynchburg, VA: Howard, 1988), 127.

7. *Ibid.*, 77.

8. Major R. C. Eden, *The Sword and Gun: A History of the 37th Wis. Volunteer Infantry* (Madison, WI: Atwood & Rubles, 1865), 56.

9. *Ibid.*, 56–57; Chris M. Calkins, *The Final Bivouac*, 127.

10. O.R., Ser. 1, Vol. 46, Chapter 58, Pt. 3, pp. 909–910.

11. J. L. Smith, *History of the 118th Pennsylvania Volunteers* (Philadelphia: Smith, 1905), 599–600.

12. *Ibid.*

13. Military Service Records, Charles Francis Adams, Jr., National Archives and Records Administration, Washington, D.C.

14. Charles Bracelen Flood, *Grant and Sherman: The Friendship That Won the Civil War* (New York: Farrar, Straus, and Giroux, 2005), 342–343.

15. O.R., Ser. 1, Vol.46, Chapter 58, Pt. 3, p. 144.

16. *Ibid.*, p. 1062.

17. *Ibid.*, p. 1068.

18. *Ibid.*, p. 1168.

19. *Ibid.*, 1168–1169.

20. Ford, *A Cycle of Adams Letters, 1861–1865*, 270; Francis Heitman, *Historical Register and Dictionary of the United States Army, 1789–1903* (Washington, D.C.: Government Printing Office, 1903); James Grant Wilson and John Fiske, *Appleton's Cyclopedia of American Biography* (New York: Appleton, 1887–1889); Eicher and Eicher, *Civil War High Commands*, 98.

21. *United States Army and Navy Journal*, vol. 2 (June 3, 1865), 649,. See also Salvatore, *We All Got History: The Memory Books of Amos Weber*, 146.

22. Donald R. Shaffer, *After the Glory: The Struggle of Black Civil War Veterans* (Lawrence: University Press of Kansas, 2004), 23–24, 26; Ulysses S. Grant, *Personal Memoirs of U.S. Grant*, vol. 2 (New York: Webster, 1886), 545–546. See also Gallagher, *The Union War*, pp. 8–31, for information related to the absence of U.S.C.T. units in the Grand Review and being sent to Texas.

23. O.R., Ser. 1, Vol. 48, Chapter 60, Pt. 2, p. 476.

24. Flood, *Grant and Sherman: The Friendship That Won The Civil War*, 360.

25. R.J.M. Blackett, ed., *Thomas Morris Chester, Black Civil War Correspondent: His Dispatches form the Virginia Front* (New York: De Capo Press, 1989), 353.

26. Company Muster-Rolls, 5th Mass. Cav., NARA; "FROM FORTRESS MONROE." *New York Times*, June 16, 1865, p. 1.

27. *New York Times*, June 16, 1865, p.1; Correspondent of the *Philadelphia Inquirer*, "Reported Mutiny among the Colored Troops—the Cavalry Refuse to Go South—they Quietly Submit to Being Disarmed."

New York Times, June 16, 1865, p. 1. The paper falsely listed the 5th United USCC as being a part of the cavalry brigade when in actuality they most likely were referring to the 5th Massachusetts Cavalry which was then assigned to the brigade.

28. *Ibid.* For further details regarding the role of the 1st USCC in the mutiny incident see Frederick W. Browne, "My Service in the U.S. Colored Cavalry," paper read before Ohio Comandery, Military Order of the Loyal Legion of the United States, March 4, 1908, in *Sketches of the War History, 1861–1865* (Cincinnati: Clark, 1908). See also Salvatore, *We All Got History*, 146.

29. Alexander H. Newton, *Out of the Briars: An Autobiography and Sketch of the Twenty-ninth Regiment Connecticut Volunteers* (Philadelphia: A.M.E. Book Concern, 1910), 69–70; See also Margaret Humphreys, *Intensely Human: The Health of the Black Soldier in the American Civil War* (Baltimore: The Johns Hopkins University Press, 2008), p. 122.

30. *Boston Daily Advertiser*, Tuesday, July 11, 1865, Issue 8.

31. O.R., Ser. 1, Vol. 46, Chapter 58, Pt. 3, p. 144.

32. This and subsequent references to Clarksville, Texas, relate not to the modern day Clarksville located in Red River County, Texas, in the Piney Woods region of Northeast Texas. Rather, reference to the Federal army's occupation of Clarksville refers to the location along the mouth of the Rio Grande River and is often referred to as one of the "Lost Cities of the Rio Grande." See Steve Hathcock, "Clarksville, The Lost City of the Rio Grande," South Padre Island Texas Information, South Padre TV Blog, October 28, 2011, http://southpadretv.tv/clarksville-the-lost-city-of-the-rio-grande-825/.

33. Military Service Records, Charles Waters, National Archives and Records Administration, Washington, D.C.

34. Betty Dooley-Awbrey and Stuart Awbrey, *Why Stop?: A Guide to Texas Roadside Historical Markers* (Lanham, MD: Taylor Trade, 2013), 64–65. See also Humphreys, *Intensely Human: The Health of the Black Soldier in the American Civil War.* Also, William A. Dobak, *Freedom by the Sword: The U.S. Colored Troops, 1862–1867* (Washington, D.C.: Center of Military History, 2011).

35. David Roth, "Texas Hurricane History," Camp Springs, MD: National Weather Service (www.wpc.ncep.noaa.gov/research/txhur.pdf) accessed January 16, 2014, pp. 15–16.

36. Dobak, *Freedom by the Sword: The U.S. Colored Troops, 1862–1867*, pp. 431–434.

37. William G. Goetzmann, "Chamberlain, Samuel Emery," Handbook of Texas Online, http://www.tshaonline.org/handbook/online/article/fchah, accessed January 16, 2014, published by the Texas State Historical Association; Massachusetts Adjutant General's Office, *Massachusetts Soldiers, Sailors and Marines in the Civil War*, 493; Bowen, *Massachusetts in the War, 1861–1865*, pp. 898–899.

38. Bowen, *Massachusetts in the War, 1861–1865*, 898–899. See also Military Service Records, Samuel Emory Chamberlain, National Archives and Records Administration, Washington, D.C. See also Eicher and Eicher, *Civil War High Commands*, p. 169.

39. Shaffer, *After the Glory: The Struggle of Black Civil War Veterans*, 27; Salvatore, *We All Got History*, 147; Massachusetts Adjutant-General's Report, *Public Documents of Massachusetts: Being the Annual Reports of Various Public Officers and Institutions, for the Year 1865* (Boston: Wright & Potter, 1866), pp. 668–669. For a study of the health of U.S.C.T. troops in Texas see also Humphreys, *Intensely Human: The Health of the Black Soldier in the American Civil War.*

40. Humphreys, *Intensely Human: The Health of the Black Soldier in the American Civil War*, p. 126.

41. O.R., Ser. 3, Vol. 5, p. 96.

42. *Ibid.*, 77.

43. Massachuetts Adjutant General's Office, *Massachusetts Soldiers, Sailors and Marines in the Civil War*, 492; Massachusetts Adjutant-General's Report, *Public Documents of Massachusetts: Being the Annual Reports of Various Public Officers and Institutions, for the Year 1865* (Boston: Wright & Potter, 1866), 48; Headley, *Massachusetts in the Rebellion*, 498; *Salem Register*, Nov. 23, 1865; Smith, *Black Soldiers in Blue: African American Troops in the Civil War Era*, 300; *Anglo-African*, October 21, 1865.

44. *New Orleans Tribune*, Oct. 29, 1865; Massachusetts Adjutant-General's Report, *Public Documents of Massachusetts: Being the Annual Reports of Various Public Officers and Institutions, for the Year 1865*, 668–669.

45. Headley, *Massachusetts in the Rebellion*, 654.

46. *Ibid.*

47. *Ibid.*
48. *Ibid.*, 655.
49. *Ibid.*, 655–656.
50. Salvatore, *We All Got History*, 150.
51. Headley, *Massachusetts in the Rebellion*, 656.
52. *Ibid.*, 656–657.
53. Trudeau, *Like Men of War*, 467; Smith, *Black Soldiers in Blue: African American Troops in the Civil War Era*, 300; *Anglo-African*, June 17, 1865.

Chapter 7

1. Joseph Brunson, Personal Affidavit, Department of Veterans Affairs dated October 18th, 1897, Dickinson County, KS.
2. Huston Horn, *The Pioneers* (New York: Time-Life Books, 1976), 191.
3. *Ibid.*, 199.
4. Joseph Brunson, Personal Affidavit, Department of Veterans Affairs.
5. For further information see Shaffer, *After the Glory: The Struggle of Black Civil War Veterans*, 80.
6. Civil War Society, *The Civil War Society's Encyclopedia of the Civil War* (Princeton, NJ: The Philip Lief Group, 1997), 135–137.
7. Clinton, *The African American Experience, 1565–1877*, 52.
8. Cutler, *History of the State of Kansas.*
9. *Ibid.*
10. *Ibid.* Also for further reading refer to Henry King, "A Year of the Exodus in Kansas," *Scribners Monthly, An Illustrated Magazine for the People* 20, no. 2, 211–218.
11. Military Service Records, Irenas J. Palmer, National Archives and Records Administration, Washington, D.C; Irenas J. Palmer, *The Black Man's Burden; or, The Horrors of Southern Lynchings* (Olean, NY: Olean Evening Herald Print, 1902); Obituary for Irenas J. Palmer, *Times Herald* (Olean, New York), Sunday, June, 7, 1919, pg. 5.
12. For a detailed account of Samuel Ballton's life see Betty DeRamus, *Forbidden Fruit: Love Stories from the Underground Railroad* (New York: Atria Books, 2005), pp. 189–205.
13. *Ibid.*
14. For further study of the Fitzgerald family in Durham, North Carolina, see also; W.E.B. Du Bois, "The Upbuilding of Black Durham," *World's Work* 23 (January 1912), 334–338; Jean Bradley Anderson, *Durham County: A History of Durham*

County, North Carolina (Durham, NC: Duke University Press, 2010), 133–134.
15. Barry I. Mickey, "Lt. Francis S. Davidson, 5th Massachusetts Cavalry," *Military Images* 28, no. 3 (November-December 1996), 24–25.
16. *Ibid.*, 24.
17. *Ibid.*, 25.
18. 57th Congress, 2nd Session, Senate Document No. 166. February 23, 1903, Francis S. Davidson, Message from the President of the United States, Returning with his objections, the bill (S. 1115) Entitled "An Act For the relief of Francis S. Davidson, late first lieutenant, Ninth United States Cavalry."
19. *Ibid.*
20. *Ibid.*
21. Mickey, "Lt. Francis S. Davidson, 5th Massachusetts Cavalry," p. 25.
22. *Ibid.*
23. Letter from Robert Shaw Oliver to Theodore Roosevelt, July 1, 1903, Theodore Roosevelt Papers, Manuscripts division. Library of Congress, http://www.theodorerooseveltcenter.org/Research/Digital-Library/Record.aspx?libID=o41099, Theodore Roosevelt Digital Library, Dickinson State University. Accessed November 28, 2014.
24. Military Service Records, Robert Shaw Oliver, National Archives and Records Administration, Washington, D.C., request to Brvt. Col. E. W. Smith A.A.G. Dept. of the James.
25. Albert Rathbone, *Samuel Rathbone and Lydia Sparhawk, his wife: A Record of Their Descendants and Notes Regarding Their Ancestors* (N.p.: n.p., 1937), 25–26.
26. Telegram from Robert Shaw Oliver to Theodore Roosevelt, July 11, 1903, Theodore Roosevelt Papers, Manuscripts division. Library of Congress, http://www.theodorerooseveltcenter.org/Research/Digital-Library/Record.aspx?libID=o41258. Theodore Roosevelt Digital Library, Dickinson State University. Accessed November 28, 2014.
27. Allen Johnson, *Dictionary of American Biography*, vol. 3 (New York: Charles Scribner's Sons, 1929), p. 595.
28. *Ibid.* See also Eric Foner, *Reconstruction: America's Unfinished Revolution, 1863–1877* (New York: Harper & Row, 1988), pp. 570–575, 582.
29. Johnson, *Dictionary of American Biography*, 595; Clarence Barnhart, *The New Century Cyclopedia of Names* (New York: Appelton-Century-Crofts, 1954), p. 887.
30. For resources related political offices

held by Curtis Whittemore see Congressional Series of United States Public Documents, vol. 1550, *Reports of Committees of the Senate of the United States for the Thirds Session of the Forty Second Congress, 1872–1873* (Washington, D.C.: Government Printing Office, 1872), pp. 317–318; For a record of Pulaski County treasurer see *Arkansas Biennial Report of the Secretary of State for the Years 1905–1906* (Little Rock, AR: Tunnah and Pittard, 1906), 280. See also Weston Arthur Goodspeed, LL.B., editor, *The Province and the States: Biography* (Madison, WI: Western Historical Association, 1904), 139; Charlie Daniels, *The Historical Report of the Arkansas Secretary of State* (Little Rock: University of Arkansas Press, 2008), 519.

31. William Benjamin Gould, *Diary of a Contraband: The Civil War Passage of a Black Sailor* (Standford, CA: Standford University Press, 2002), 30.

32. J. Clay Smith, Jr., *Emancipation: The Making of the Black Lawyer, 1844–1944* (Philadelphia: University of Pennslyvania Press, 1993), 201–202; William McKee Evans, *Ballots and Fence Rails: Reconstruction on the Lower Cape Fear* (Athens: University of Georgia Press, 1995), 139.

33. John Y. Simon, ed. *The Papers of Ulysses S. Grant,* vol. 24, 1973 (Carbondale: Southern Illinois University Press, 2000), 488.

34. *Ibid.,* 488.

35. *Inter Ocean,* Monday, May 31, 1875, p. 5.

36. *Boston Daily Advertiser,* Tuesday, June 1, 1875.

37. *Boston Investigator,* Wednesday, August 4, 1875, p. 6.

38. *The Milwaukee Sentinel,* Monday, November 4, 1889.

39. *Ibid.*

40. *Milwaukee Daily Journal,* Monday, April 28, 1890.

41. *St. Paul Daily News,* Thursday, September 25, 1890.

42. "The Resignation of House Postmaster James L. Wheat," History, Art & Archives United States House of Representatives, accessed November 28, 2014, http://history.house.gov/HistoricalHighlight/Detail/35849?ret=True.

43. Frederick H. Dyer, *A Compendium of the War of the Rebellion,* vol. 2 (Dayton, OH: Morningside Press Reprint, 1994), 1240.

44. William A. Pencak, ed., *Encyclopedia of the Veteran in America* (Santa Barbara, CA: ABC-CLIO, 2009), 10.

45. William Henry Glasson, *Federal Military Pensions in the United States,* edited by David Kinley (New York: Oxford University Press, 1918), 204–274; Henry Strong McCall, *The clerk's assistant: containing a large variety of legal forms and instruments, adapted not only to county and town officers, but to the wants of professional and business men throughout the United States,* ed. H.B. Bradbury (New York: The Banks Law Publishing Co., 1902), 993.

46. United States Pension Office, Declaration for Invalid Pension, dated April 10, 1894.

47. *Ibid.,* Invalid Pension dated June 26, 1897.

48. *Ibid.,* Physician's Affidavit dated September 27, 1897; *Journal of the Kansas Medical Society,* vol. 3 (Topeka: Kansas Medical Society, 1901–1984), 32.

49. Pencak, *Encyclopedia of the Veteran in America,* 96.

50. William A. Dobak and Thomas D. Phillips, *The Black Regulars, 1866–1898* (Norman: University of Oklahoma Press, 2001), 276.

51. *Ibid.,* 274–276.

52. *Ibid.,* 276.

53. *Ibid.,* 276–277.

54. *The New York Times,* January 21, 1900.

55. *Ibid.*

56. *Ibid.*

57. *Ibid.*

58. *Ibid.*

59. *Ibid.*

Chapter 8

1. Shaffer, *After the Glory: The Struggle of Black Civil War Veterans,* 158–159.

2. Barbara A. Gannon, *The Won Cause: Black and White Comradeship in the Grand Army of the Republic* (Chapel Hill: University of North Carolina Press, 2011), 6.

3. Shaffer, *After the Glory: The Struggle of Black Civil War Veterans,* 149.

4. Gannon, *The Won Cause,* 98.

5. *Ellsworth Reporter,* December 25, 1913.

6. Gannon, *The Won Cause,* 88.

7. *Ibid.,* 88–89.

8. Donald Yacovone, *We Fight For Freedom: Massachusetts, African-Americans, and the Civil War* (Boston: Massachusetts Historical Society Picture Book, 1993), 30.

9. *New York Freeman,* August 20, 1887.

10. *The Liberator,* November 25, 1864.

11. Military Service Records, William

Henry Skeene, National Archives and Records Administration, Washington, D.C.

12. Robert Gould Shaw and the 54th Regiment—Boston African American National Historic Site, National Park Service U.S. Department of the Interior.

13. *Springfield Republican*, April 3, 1897.

14. *Ibid.*, February 7, 1897.

15. Lee A. Wallace, *A Guide to Virginia Organizations, 1861–1865*; Joseph E. Crute, *Units of the Confederate States Army*; Federal Census, 1860, Hampton, Elizabeth City, Virginia; *Chataigne's Richmond City Directory, 1889–1890* (Richmond, VA: Chataigne, 1890); *Chataigne's Manchester Directory, 1889* (Richmond, VA: Chataigne, 1890).

16. Military Service Records, George H. Tubey, National Archives and Records Administration, Washington, D.C.

17. James M. Paradis, *African Americans and the Gettysburg Campaign* (Lanham, MD: Scarecrow Press, 2013), 114; Military Service Records, Thomas Walters, National Archives and Records Administration, Washington, D.C.

18. *Standard Examiner*, July 9, 1938; The National Cemetery Administration, *Los Angeles National Cemetery, Burial Ledger, 1921–1944*, National Archives and Records Administration, Washington, D.C.; *Applications for Headstones for U.S. Mili-*

tary Veterans, 1925–1941, National Archives Microfilm Publication: A1, 2110-C; RG 92.

19. *Boston Globe*, June 27, 2004, Third Edition, Section: City Weekly, p. 3.

20. See David Roth, "Texas Hurricane History," Camp Springs, MD: National Weather Service, www.hpc.ncep.noaa.gov/research/txhur.pdf. pp. 15–16. Accessed January 16, 2014.

21. For further information about the current locations and historic sites related to Brazos de Santiago see Dooley-Awbrey and Awbrey, *Why Stop?: A Guide to Texas Roadside Historical Markers.*

22. Massachusetts Adjutant General's Office, *Massachusetts Soldiers, Sailors and Marines in the Civil War*, 516.

23. Dunbar House State Historic Site, Home of Paul Laurence Dunbar, Dayton, Ohio. His home has been restored to appear as it did when he lived there. On display are Dunbar's bicycle built by his neighbors Orville and Wilbur Wright and a ceremonial sword presented to Dunbar by President Theodore Roosevelt.

24. Benjamin Quarles, *The Negro in the Civil War* (Cambridge, MA: Da Capo Press, 1989), vii.

25. McPherson, *Marching Toward Freedom: Blacks in the Civil War, 1861–1865*, 80.

Bibliography

Manuscripts

Fitzgerald Family Papers, Robert G. Fitzgerald Diaries, 1864 and 1867–1871, University of North Carolina, Chapel Hill.
Miscellaneous McGuire Family Papers, owned by Steven LaBarre.
Miscellaneous Smith Family Papers, owned by Steven LaBarre.

Newspaper Articles

Anglo-African (New York), May 7th, 1864.
Boston Daily Advertiser (Boston), May 20th, 1864; July 11th, 1865; June 1st, 1875.
Boston Globe (Boston), July 31st, 1887; June 27th, 2004.
Boston Investigator (Boston), August 4th, 1875.
Cambridge Chronicle (Cambridge, MA) January 1864–May 1864.
Chicago Tribune (Chicago), July 23rd, 1862; September 23rd, 1862; December 23rd, 1863; April 6th, 1865.
Daily Age (Philadelphia), August 4th, 1864.
Ellsworth Reporter (Ellsworth, KS), December 25th, 1913.
Inter Ocean (Chicago), May 31st, 1875, pg. 5, Issue 58, col E.
Liberator (Boston), February 26th, 1864; May 13th, 1864; November 25th, 1864; February 24th, 1865.
Lowell Daily Citizen and News (Lowell, MA), June 27th, 1864.
Milwaukee Daily Journal (Milwaukee), April 28th, 1890.
Milwaukee Sentinel (Milwaukee), December 5th, 1863; November 4th, 1889.
New Bedford Evening Standard (New Bedford, MA), May 26th, 1932.
New Orleans Tribune (New Orleans), October 29th, 1865.
New York Freeman (New York), August 20th, 1887.
New York Herald (New York), April 13th, 1865.
New York Times (New York), June 16th, 1865; January 21st, 1900.
New York Tribune (New York), May 1st, 1863; April 8th, 1865.
Republican Farmer (Bridgeport, CT), August 12th, 1864.
Richmond Dispatch (Richmond, VA), May 7th, 1865.
Richmond Whig (Richmond, VA), April 4th and 27th, 1865.
Rocky Mountain News (Denver), January 28th, 1901.
St. Paul Daily News (St. Paul, MN), September 25th, 1890.
Salem Register (Salem, MA), November 23rd, 1865.
Springfield Republican (Springfield, MA), January 30th, 1865; February 7th, 1897; April 3rd, 1897.

Standard Examiner (Ogden, UT), July 9th, 1938.
Times Herald (Olean, NY), June 7th, 1919.

City Directories

Chataigne's Manchester Directory, 1889. Richmond, VA: Chataigne, 1890.
Chataigne's Richmond City Directory, 1889–1890. Richmond, VA: Chataigne, 1890.

Archives

Abilene, Dickinson County, KS, Historical Society.
College of the Holy Cross, Worcester, MA. Murphy, Katherine. *The Civil War and "Colored" Regiments from Massachusetts: Amos F. Jackson Writes Home.*
Dunbar House State Historic Site Home of Paul Laurence Dunbar, Dayton, OH.
Ellsworth County, KS, Cemetery, Cemetery Records.
Ellsworth County, KS, Historical Society.
Fifty-Seventh Congress. Washington, D.C.: Government Printing Office, 1903.Kansas State Historical Society.
Historical and Genealogical Society of Indiana County, PA.
Historical Society of the Blairsville, Pennsylvania, Area.
Journal of the Kansas Medical Society (Topeka: Kansas Medical Society, 1901–1984), v. 31, p. 32.
Journal of the Senate of the United States of America, Being the Second Session of the Massachusetts State Archives.
National Archives. Consolidated Lists of Civil War Draft Registration Records (*Provost Marshal General's Bureau; Consolidated Enrollment Lists, 1863–1865*); National Archives, RG 110.
_____. Pension Records, National Archives, RG 15.
_____. Records of the Bureau of Land Management, National Archives, RG 49.
_____. Service Records, National Archives, RG 94.
Pennsylvania Historical and Museum Commission, Harrisburg, PA,
Pennsylvania Veterans Burial Cards, 1777–1999.
Point Lookout, MD, State Park Archives.
Texas Parks and Wildlife, Handbook of Texas Online.
U.S. Bureau of the Census: Allegheny County, PA, 1820; Dickinson County, KS, 1900; Ellsworth County, KS, 1910; Hampton City, Elizabeth City, VA, 1860; Indiana County, PA, 1850, 1860, 1870; Lee County, IA, 1860, 1870.
U.S. War Department. *Revised United States Army Regulations of 1861, with an Appendix Containing the Changes and Laws Affecting Army Regulations and Articles of War to June 25, 1863.* Washington: Government Printing Office, 1863.
_____. *The War of the Rebellion: A Compilation of the Official Records of the Union and Confederate Armies.* Washington: Government Printing Office, 1880–1901.

Periodical Articles

Bowditch, Charles P. "War Letters of Charles P. Bowditch." *Massachusetts Historical Society Proceedings* 57 (Oct. 1923–June 1924).
Case, Joy. "Arlington National Cemetery." *Let's Take a Look at Virginia* (2006): 1–2.
Du Bois, W.E.B. "The Upbuilding of Black Durham." *World's Work* 23 (January, 1912).
Grimke, Archibald H. "Colonel Shaw and his Black Regiment." *The New England Magazine* 7, no. 6 (February 1890): 678.
Hacker, J. David. "A Census-Based Count of the Civil War Dead." *Civil War History* 57, no. 4 (December 2011): 307–348.

Holliday, B. T. "Vain Efforts to Avoid Prison." *Chronicles of St. Mary's* 31, no. 10 (October 1983). Reprint from the *Confederate Veteran* 28, no. 10.

Hutchins, James S. "An 1860 Pamphlet on the Sibley Tent." *The Company of Military Historians* 57, no. 2 (Summer 2005).

King, Henry. "A Year of the Exodus in Kansas." *Scribners Monthly, An Illustrated Magazine for the People* 20, no. 2 (June 1880): 211–218.

Marshall, Nicholas. "The Great Exaggeration: Death and the Civil War." *The Journal of the Civil War Era* 4, no. 1 (March 2014): 13.

Massachusetts Metropolitan District Commission. *The Black Regiments of Camp Meigs*. Boston: Commonwealth of Massachusetts, Massachusetts District Commission, 1995.

Massachusetts Metropolitan District Commission. *Camp Meigs and the Civil War*. Boston: Commonwealth of Massachusetts, Massachusetts District Commission, 1995.

Mickey, Barry I. "Lt. Francis S. Davidson 5th Massachusetts Cavalry." *Military Images* 28, no. 3 (November-December 1996): 24–25.

Reidy, Joseph P. "Black Men in Navy Blue During the Civil War." *Quarterly of the National Archives and Records Administration* 33, no. 3 (Fall 2001).

Sword, Gerald J. "Another Look at the Point Lookout Prison Camp for Confederates." *Chronicles of St. Mary's* 28, no. 3 (1980).

United States Army and Navy Journal 2 (June 3, 1865).

Web Sources

Congressional Medal of Honor Society, www.cmohs.org.

Goetzmann, William G., "Chamberlain, Samuel Emery." Handbook of Texas Online, http://www.tshaonline.org/handbook/online/article/fchah, accessed January 16, 2014. Published by the Texas State Historical Association.

Hathcock, Steve. "Clarksville, The Lost City of the Rio Grande." South Padre Island Texas Information, South Padre TV Blog, October 28, 2011, http://southpadretv.tv/clarksville-the-lost-city-of-the-rio-grande-825/.

Julia, James D., Inc. http://jamesdjulia.com/item/lot-1132-import-dbl-inscribed-civil-war-us-colored-troop-cavalry-officers-saber-5th-massachusetts-cavalry53193/.

Letter from Robert Shaw Oliver to Theodore Roosevelt. July 1, 1903. Theodore Roosevelt Papers, Manuscripts division. Library of Congress, http://theodore rooseveltcenter.org/Research/Digital-Library/Record.aspx?libID=o41099. Theodore Roosevelt Digital Library Dickenson State University.

"The Resignation of House Postmaster James L. Wheat." History, Art & Archives United States House of Representatives, http://history.house.gov/Historical Highlight/Detail/35849?ret=True.

Roth, David. "Texas Hurricane History." Camp Springs, MD: National Weather Service, www.hpc.ncep.noaa.gov/research/txhur.pdf, accessed January 16, 2014.

Telegram from Robert Shaw Oliver to Theodore Roosevelt. July 11, 1903. Theodore Roosevelt Papers, Manuscripts division. Library of Congress, http://theodore rooseveltcenter.org/Research/Digital-Library/Record.aspx?libID=o41258. Theodore Roosevelt Digital Library Dickenson State University.

Books

American Unitarian Association. *Sons of Puritans: A Group of Brief Sketches*. Boston: American Unitarian Association, 1908.

Anderson, Jean Bradley. *Durham County: A History of Durham County, North Carolina*. Durham, NC: Duke University Press, 2010.

Arkansas Biennial Report of the Secretary of State for the Years 1905–1906. Little Rock, AR: Tunnah and Pittard, 1906.

Avary, Myrta Lockett. *A Virginia Girl in the Civil War, 1861–1865: Being a Record of the Actual Experiences of the Wife of a Confederate Officer.* New York: Appleton, 1903.

Barnhart, Clarence L. *The New Century Cyclopedia of Names.* New York: Appleton-Century-Crofts, 1954.

Beitzell, Edwin W. *Point Lookout Prison Camp for Confederates.* Baltimore: Abell, 1972.

Berlin, Ira; Joseph P. Reidy, and Leslie S. Rowland. *Freedom's Soldiers: The Black Military Experience in the Civil War.* New York: Cambridge University Press, 1998.

Blackett, R.J.M., ed. *Thomas Morris Chester, Black Civil War Correspondent: His Dispatches from the Virginia Front.* New York: Da Capo Press, 1989.

Bowen, James Lorenzo. *Massachusetts in the War, 1861–1865.* Springfield, MA: Bryan, 1889.

Brock, Sallie A. *Richmond During the War: Four Years of Personal Observation.* New York: Carleton, 1867.

Browne, Frederick W. *My Service in the U.S. Colored Cavalry.* Sketches of War History, 1861–1865. Cincinnati: Clark, 1908.

Bruce, George Anson. *The Twentieth Regiment of Massachusetts Infantry, 1861–1865.* Boston: Houghton, Mifflin, 1906.

Bryant, James K. II. *The 36th United States Colored Troops in the Civil War: A History and Roster.* Jefferson, NC: McFarland, 2012.

Butler, Benjamin Franklin. *Butler's Book.* Boston: Thayer, 1892.

_____, and Mrs. Jessie Ames Marshall. *Private and Official Correspondence of Gen. Benjamin F. Butler During the Period of the Civil War.* Vol. 4. Norwood, MA: The Plimpton Press, 1917.

Calarco, Tom. *Places on the Underground Railroad.* Santa Barbara: CA: Greenwood Press, 2011.

Calkins, Chris M. *The Final Bivouac: The Surrender Parade at Appomattox and the Disbanding of the Armies April 10–May 20, 1865.* Lynchburg, VA: Howard, 1988.

Catton, Bruce. *America Goes to War.* New York: MJF Books, 1997.

Civil War Society. *The Civil War Society's Encyclopedia of the Civil War.* Princeton, NJ: The Philip Lief Group, 1997.

Clark, Peter H. *Black Brigade of Cincinnati: Being a Report of Its Labor and Muster-Roll of Its Members; Together with Various Orders, Speeches, Etc. Relating to It.* Cincinnati: Boyd, 1864.

Clinton, Catherine. *The African American Experience 1565–1877.* American History Series. New York: Eastern National, 2004.

Coddington, Ronald S. *African American Faces of the Civil War: An Album.* Baltimore: Johns Hopkins University Press, 2012.

Cooling, B. Franklin. *Monocacy: The Battle That Saved Washington.* Shippensburg, PA: White Mane, 2000.

Congressional Series of United States Public Documents, Volume 1550, *Reports of Committees of the Senate of the United States for the Third Session of the Forty-Second Congress, 1872–1873.* Washington, D.C.: Government Printing Office, 1872.

Cornish, Dudley Taylor. *The Sable Arm: Black Troops in the Union Army, 1861–1865.* Lawrence: University Press of Kansas, 1987.

Crute, Joseph E. *Units of the Confederate States Army.* Midlothian, VA: Derwent Books, 1987.

Cutler, William G. *History of the State of Kansas.* Chicago: Andreas, 1883.

Daniels, Charlie. *The Historical Report of the Arkansas Secretary of State.* Little Rock: University of Arkansas Press, 2008.

Davis, Burke. *Appomattox: Nine April Days, 1865.* New York: Reinhart, 1959.

_____. *The Long Surrender*. New York: Random House, 1985.

Davis, William C. *The Fighting Men of the Civil War*. London: Salamander Books, 1999.

DeRamus, Betty. *Forbidden Fruit: Love Stories from the Underground Railroad*. New York: Atria Books, 2005.

Dobak, William A. *Freedom by the Sword: The U.S. Colored Troops 1862–1867*. Washington, D.C.: Center of Military History, 2011.

_____, and Thomas D. Phillips. *The Black Regulars, 1866–1898*. Norman: University of Oklahoma Press, 2001.

Dooley-Awbrey, Betty, and Stuart Awbrey. *Why Stop?: A Guide to Texas Roadside Historical Markers*. Lanham, MD: Taylor Trade Publishing, 2013.

Dunbar, Paul Laurance. *The Complete Poems of Paul Laurance Dunbar with the Introduction to "Lyrics of Lowly Life" by W.D. Howells*. New York: Dodd, Mead, 1922.

Duncan, Russell. *Where Death and Glory Meet: Colonel Robert Gould Shaw and the 54th Massachusetts Infantry*. Athens: University of Georgia Press, 1999.

Dyer, Frederick H. *A Compendium of the War of the Rebellion*. Dayton, OH: Morningside Press Reprint, 1994.

Eden, Major R. C. *The Sword and Gun: A History of the 37th Wis. Volunteer Infantry*. Madison: Atwood & Rubles, 1865.

Eicher, John H., and David J. Eicher. *Civil War High Commands*. Stanford, CA: Stanford University Press, 2001.

Emilio, Luis F. *History of the Fifty-fourth regiment of Massachusetts Volunteer Infantry, 1863–1865*, Boston: Boston Book, 1891.

Evans, William McKee. *Ballots and Fence Rails: Reconstruction on the Lower Cape Fear*. Athens: University of Georgia Press, 1995.

Flood, Charles Bracelen. *Grant and Sherman: The Friendship That Won the Civil War*. New York: Farrar, Straus and Giroux, 2005.

Foner, Eric. *Reconstruction: America's Unfinished Revolution, 1863–1877*. New York: Harper and Row, 1988.

Ford, Worthington Chauncey. *A Cycle of Adams Letters 1861–1865*. New York: Kraus Reprint, 1969.

Fox, William F. *Regimental Losses in the American Civil War, 1861–1865*. Albany, NY: Albany, 1889.

Gallagher, Gary W. *Causes Won, Lost and Forgotten: How Hollywood and Popular Art Shape What We Know About the Civil War*. Chapel Hill: University of North Carolina Press, 2008.

_____. *The Union War*. Cambridge, MA: Harvard University Press, 2011.

Gannon, Barbara A. *The Won Cause: Black and White Comradeship in the Grand Army of the Republic*. Chapel Hill: University of North Carolina Press, 2011.

Gladstone, William A. *United States Colored Troops 1863–1867*. Gettysburg, PA: Thomas, 1990.

Glasson, William Henry. *Federal Military Pensions in the United States*. Edited by David Kinley. New York: Oxford University Press, 1918.

Glatthaar, Joseph. *The Civil War's Black Soldiers*. Civil War Series. New York: Eastern National Park and Monument Association, 1996.

_____. *Forged in Battle: The Civil War Alliance of Black Soldiers and White Officers*. New York: Free Press, 1990.

Goodspeed, Weston Arthur, LL.B., ed. *The Province and the States: Biography*. Madison, WI: Western Historical Association, 1904.

Gould, William Benjamin. *Diary of a Contraband: The Civil War Passage of a Black Sailor*. Stanford, CA: Stanford University Press, 2002.

Grant, Ulysses S. *Personal Memoirs of U.S. Grant*. Vol. 2. New York: Webster, 1886.

Greene, A. Wilson. *Civil War Petersburg: Confederate City in the Crucible of War*. Charlottesville: University of Virginia Press, 2006.

The Harvard Magazine. Vol. 10. Cambridge: MA: Sever and Francis, 1864.

_____. Vol. 14. Boston: The Harvard Graduates' Magazine Association, 1905–1906.

Headley, P. C. *Massachusetts in the Rebellion*. Boston: Walker, Fuller, 1866.

Heitman, Francis. *Historical Register and Dictionary of the United States Army 1789–1903*. Washington, D.C.: U.S. Government Printing Office, 1903.

Higginson, Thomas Wentworth. *Army Life in a Black Regiment*. Boston: Fields, Osgood, 1870.

_____. *Harvard Memorial Biographies*. Vol. 1, Cambridge, MA: Sever and Francis, 1866.

History of Lee County, Iowa. Chicago: Western Historical, 1879.

Hoehling, A. A., and Mary Hoehling. *The Day Richmond Died*. San Diego: Barnes, 1981.

Holland, Frederic May. *Frederick Douglass: The Colored Orator*. New York: Funk and Wagnalls, 1891.

Holmes, Oliver Wendell. *Speeches by Oliver Wendell Holmes, Jr.* Boston: Little, Brown, 1891.

The Holy Bible, New International Version. Grand Rapids, MI: Zondervan, 2006.

Hopkins, Henry, *Official Military History of Kansas Regiments: During the War for the Suppression of the Great Rebellion*. Leavenworth, KS: Burke, 1870.

Horn, John. *The Petersburg Campaign June 1864–April 1865*. Conshohocken, PA: Combined Books, 2000.

Horn, Huston. *The Pioneers.* . New York: Time-Life Books, 1976.

Howe, Thomas J. *The Petersburg Campaign: Wasted Valor, June 15–18, 1864*. Lynchburg, VA: Howard, 1988.

Humphreys, Margaret. *Intensely Human: The Health of the Black Soldier in the American Civil War*. Baltimore: Johns Hopkins University Press, 2008.

Johnson, Allen. *Dictionary of American Biography*. New York: Charles Scribner's Sons, 1929.

Johnson, Robert U., and Clarence C. Buel, eds. *Battles and Leaders of the Civil War*. Vol. 4. P.G.T. Beauregard, *Four Days of Battle at Petersburg*. New York: Century, 1887–1888.

Keiley, A. M. *In Vinculis: Or The Prisoner of War, Being the Experience of a Rebel in Two Federal Pens, Interspersed with Reminiscences of the Late War, Anecdotes of Southern Generals, Etc.* New York: Blelock, 1866.

Lankford, Nelson. *Richmond Burning: The Last Days of the Confederate Capital*. New York: Viking, 2002.

Lanning, Michael Lee. *Defenders of Liberty: African Americans in the Revolutionary War*. New York: Citadel Press, 2000.

Leffel, John C. *History of Posey County, Indiana*. Chicago: Standard, 1913.

Levine, Bruce. *Half Slave and Half Free: The Roots of the Civil War*. New York: Hill and Wang, 1992.

Lewis, Lloyd. *Sherman: Fighting Prophet*. New York: Harcourt, Brace and Company, 1932.

Livermore, Thomas L. *Days and Events, 1860–1866*. Boston: Houghton Mifflin, 1920.

Longacre, Edward G. *Army of Amateurs: General Benjamin F. Butler and the Army of the James, 1863–1865*. Mechanicsburg, PA: Stackpole Books, 1997.

Lord, Francis A. *Collectors Encyclopedia of the Civil War*. Secaucus, NJ: Castle Books, 1979.

Lowery, Thomas. *Sexual Misbehavior in the Civil War*. Bloomington, IN: Xlibris, 2006.

Lykes, Richard Wayne. *Petersburg National Military Park, Virginia*. Washington, D.C.: National Park Service Handbook, 1961.

Marvin, Abijah P. *History of Worcester in the War of the Rebellion*. Worcester, MA: Marvin, 1870.

Massachusetts Adjutant-General's Office. *Massachusetts Soldiers, Sailors and Marines in the Civil War*. Norwood: The Norwood Press, 1932.

Massachusetts Adjutant-General's Report. *Public Documents of Massachusetts: Being the Annual Reports of Various Public Officers and Institutions, for the Year 1864*. Vol II, no 7. Boston: Wright & Potter, State Printers, 1865.

_____. *Public Documents of Massachusetts: Being the Annual Reports of Various Public Officers and Institutions, for the Year 1865*. Boston: Wright & Potter, State Printers, 1866.

Massachusetts Historical Society. *We Fight for Freedom: Massachusetts, African-Americans, and the Civil War*. Boston: Massachusetts Historical Society Picture Book, 1993.

McCall, Henry Strong. *The clerk's assistant: containing a large variety of legal forms and instruments, adapted not only to county and town officers, but to the wants of professional and business men throughout the United States*. Edited by H.B. Bradbury. New York: The Banks Law Publishing Co., 1902.

McFeely, William S. *Frederick Douglass*. New York: Norton, 1991.

McPherson, James. *Battle Cry of Freedom*. New York: Oxford University Press, 1988.

_____. *Marching Toward Freedom: Blacks in the Civil War 1861–1865*. New York: Facts On File, 1991.

_____. *The Negro's Civil War: How American Blacks Felt and Acted During the War for the Union*. New York: Ballantine Books, 1991.

Michigan Historical Collections. *Collections of the Michigan Pioneer and Historical Society*. Vol. 28 Lansing, MI: Smith, 1900.

Miller, Edward A. Jr. *The Black Civil War Soldiers of Illinois: The Story of the Twenty-ninth U.S. Colored Infantry*. Columbia: University of South Carolina Press, 1998.

Moore, James M.D. *History of the Cooper Shop Volunteer Refreshment Saloon*. Philadelphia: Rodgers, 1866.

Moore, Robert H. *Graham's Petersburg, Jackson's Kanawha, and Lurty's Roanoke Horse Artillery*. Virginia Regimental Histories Series. Lynchburg, VA: Howard, 1996.

Murray, Pauli. *Proud Shoes: The Story of an American Family*. New York: Harper & Row, 1978.

Newton, Alexander H. *Out of the Briars: An Autobiography and Sketch of the Twenty-ninth Regiment Connecticut Volunteers*. Philadelphia: A.M.E. Book Concern, 1910.

Nicolay, John G., and John Hay. *Abraham Lincoln, Complete Works: Comprising His Speeches, Letters, State Papers, and Miscellaneous Writings*. Vol. 2. New York: Century, 1920.

O'Conner, Thomas H. *Civil War Boston: Home Front & Battlefield*. Boston: Northeastern University Press, 1997.

Palmer, Irenas J. *The Black Man's Burden; Or, The Horrors of Southern Lynchings*. Olean, NY: Oleana Evening Herald Print, 1902.

Paradis, James M. *African Americans and the Gettysburg Campaign*. Lanham, MD: Scarecrow Press, 2013.

Pearson, Henry Greenleaf. *Life of John A. Andrew: Governor of Massachusetts, 1861–1865*. Vol. 2. Boston: Houghton, Mifflin, 1904.

Pencak, William A., ed. *Encyclopedia of the Veteran in America*. Santa Barbara, CA: ABC-CLIO, 2009.

Phillips, Wendell. *Speeches, Lectures and Letters*. Boston: Lee and Shepard, 1894.

Pierson, William Whatley, ed., *The Diary of Bartlett Yancey Malone*. Chapel Hill: University of North Carolina, 1919.

Private and Special Statutes of the Commonwealth of Massachusetts, 1863. Vol. 11. Boston: Wright & Potter, 1869.

Putnam, Elizabeth Cabot. *Memoirs of the War of '61*. Boston: Ellis, 1920.

Quarles, Benjamin. *The Negro in the Civil War*. Boston: Little, Brown, 1969.

_____. *The Negro in the Civil War*. Cambridge, MA: Da Capo Press, 1989.

Quint, Alonzo H. *The Record of the Second Massachusetts Infantry, 1861–1865*. Boston: Walker, 1867.

Raiford, Neil Hunter. *The 4th North Carolina Cavalry in the Civil War*. Jefferson, NC: McFarland, 2003.

Ramold, Steven J. *Slaves, Sailors, Citizens: African Americans in the Union Navy*. DeKalb: University of Northern Illinois Press, 2001.

Rathbone, Albert. *Samuel Rathbone and Lydia Sparhawk, His Wife: A Record of Their Descendants and Notes Regarding Their Ancestors*. N.p: n.p., 1937.

Record First Michigan Cavalry Civil War, 1861–1865. Vol. 31. Kalamazoo: MI: Ihling Bros. & Everard, 1905.

Redkey, Edwin S. *A Grand Army of Black Men: Letters from African-American Soldiers in the Union Army, 1861–1865*. Cambridge, MA: Cambridge University Press, 1992.

Reed, Christopher R. *Black Chicago's First Century*, Vol. 1, *1833–1900*. Columbia: University of Missouri Press, 2005.

Reid, Richard. *African Canadians in Blue: Volunteering for the Cause in the Civil War*. Vancouver: University of British Columbia Press, 2014.

Robertson, William Glenn. *Petersburg Campaign: The Battle of Old Men and Young Boys, June 9, 1864*. Lynchburg, VA: Howard, 1989.

Rogers, Larry, and Keith Rogers. *Their Horses Climbed Trees: A Chronicle of the California 100 and Battalion in the Civil War; from San Francisco to Appomattox*. Atglen, PA: Schiffer Military History, 2001.

Roman, Alfred. *The Military Operations of General Beauregard*. Vol. 2. New York: Harper & Brothers, 1884.

Rusk, Ralph L., ed. *The Letters of Ralph Waldo Emerson*. Vol. 5. New York: Columbia University Press, 1941.

Ryan, David D. *Four Days in 1865: The Fall of Richmond*. Richmond, VA: Cadmus Marketing, 1993.

Salvatore, Nick. *We All Got History: The Memory Books of Amos Weber*. New York: Times Books, 1996.

Sanger, George P. *The Statutes at Large, Treaties, and Proclamations, of the United States of America: From December 5, 1859, to March 3, 1863*. Vols. 12–13. Boston: Little, Brown, 1863.

Schouler, William. *A History of Massachusetts in the Civil War*. Boston: Dutton, 1868.

Scott, Robert Garth. *Fallen Leaves: The Civil War Letters of Major Henry Livermore Abbott*. Kent, OH: Kent State University Press, 1991.

Shaffer, Donald R. *After the Glory: The Struggles of Black Civil War Veterans*. Lawrence: University Press of Kansas, 2004.

Sickles, Daniel E. *The Union Army: States and Regiments*. Vol. 1. Madison, WI: Federal, 1908.

Siddali, Silvana R. *From Property to Person: Slavery and the Confiscation Acts 1861–1862*. Baton Rouge: Louisiana State University Press, 2005.

Simon, John Y., ed. *The Papers of Ulysses S. Grant*. Vol. 24. 1973. Carbondale: Southern Illinois University Press, 2000.

Smith, J. Clay, Jr. *Emancipation: The Making of the Black Lawyer, 1844–1944*. Philadelphia: University of Pennsylvania Press, 1993.

Smith, J. L. *History of the 118th Pennsylvania Volunteers*. Philadelphia: Smith, 1905.

Smith, John David, ed. *Black Soldiers in Blue: African American Troops in the Civil War Era*. Chapel Hill: University of North Carolina Press, 2002.

Smith, W. Wayne. *The Price of Patriotism: Indiana County, Pennsylvania, and the Civil War*. Shippensburg, PA: Burd Street Press, 1998.

Smith, William Farrar. *From Chattanooga To Petersburg Under Generals Grant and Butler*. Boston: Houghton, Mifflin, 1893.

Speer, Lonnie R. *Portals to Hell: Military Prisons of the Civil War.* Mechanicsburg, PA: Stackpole Books, 1997.

Stearns, Frank Preston. *The Life and Public Services of George Luther Stearns.* Philadelphia: Lippincott, 1907.

Stokinger, W. A., A. K. Schroeder, and Capt. A. A. Swanson. *Civil War Camps at Readville: Camp Meigs Playground and Fowl Meadow Reservation.* Boston: Reservations and Historic Sites Metropolitan District Commission, 1990.

Taylor, Elizabeth Dowling. *A Slave in the White House: Paul Jennings and the Madisons* New York: Palgrave Macmillan, 2012.

Taylor, Marshall William. *A Collection of Revival Hymns and Plantation Melodies.* Cincinnati Taylor and Echols, 1882.

Thompson, S. Millett. *Thirteenth Regiment of New Hampshire Volunteer Infantry in the War of the Rebellion, 1861–1865: A Diary Covering Three Years and A Day.* Boston: Houghton, Mifflin, 1888.

Trudeau, Noah Andre. *Like Men of War: Black Troops in the Civil War, 1862–1865.* Boston: Little, Brown, 1998.

Turner, Glennette Tilley. *The Underground Railroad in Illinois.* Glen Ellyn, IL: Newman, 2001.

Varhola, Michael J. *Everyday Life During the Civil War: A Guide For Writers, Students and Historians.* Cincinnati: Writer's Digest Books, 1999.

Wallace, Lee A. *A Guide to Virginia Military Organizations 1861–1865.* Lynchburg, VA: Howard, 1986.

Ward, Geoffrey C., Ric Burns and Ken Burns. *The Civil War: An Illustrated History.* New York: Knopf, 1990.

Warner, John D., Jr. "Crossed Sabres: The History of the 5th Massachusetts Volunteer Cavalry." Ph.D. diss., Boston College, 1997.

Weitzel, Godfrey. *Richmond Occupied: Entry of the United States Forces into Richmond, Va., April 3, 1865.* Edited by Louis Manarin. Richmond, VA: Richmond Civil War Centennial Committee, 1965.

Williams, Ben. *A Diary from Dixie.* Cambridge, MA: Harvard University Press, 1980.

Wilson, James Grant, and John Fiske. *Appleton's Cyclopedia of American Biography.* New York: Appleton, 1887–1889.

Winik, Jay. *April 1865: The Month That Saved America.* New York: HarpersCollins, 2001.

Wise, Barton Haxall. *The Life of Henry A. Wise of Virginia, 1806–1876* New York: Macmillan, 1899.

Yacovone, Donald. "The Fifty-Fourth Massachusetts Regiment, the Pay Crisis, and 'Lincoln Despotism.'" *Hope and Glory: Essays on the Legacy of the Fifty-Fourth Massachusetts Regiment.* Edited by Martin Blatt, Thomas J. Brown, and Donald Yacovone. Amherst: University of Massachusetts Press, 2001.

_____. *Freedom's Journey: African American Voices of the Civil War.* Chicago: Lawrence Hill Books, 2004.

_____. *We Fight For Freedom: Massachusetts, African-Americans, and the Civil War.* Boston: Massachusetts Historical Society Picture Book, 1993.

Index

Numbers in *bold italics* indicate pages with photographs